LEARNING, SOCIAL INTERACTION AND DIVERSITY – EXPLORING IDENTITIES IN
SCHOOL PRACTICES

Learning, Social Interaction and Diversity – Exploring Identities in School Practices

Edited by

Eva Hjörne
University of Gothenburg, Sweden

Geerdina van der Aalsvoort
University of Applied Sciences Saxion, The Netherlands

and

Guida de Abreu
Oxford Brookes University, UK

SENSE PUBLISHERS
ROTTERDAM / BOSTON / TAIPEI

A C.I.P. record for this book is available from the Library of Congress.

ISBN 978-94-6091-801-8 (paperback)
ISBN 978-94-6091-802-5 (hardback)
ISBN 978-94-6091-803-2 (e-book)

Published by: Sense Publishers,
P.O. Box 21858, 3001 AW Rotterdam, The Netherlands
http://www.sensepublishers.com

Printed on acid-free paper

TABLE OF CONTENTS

CONTRIBUTORS

Sangeeta Bagga-Gupta is Professor Chair at Örebro University, and CRR, University Hospital, Örebro in Sweden. She has a multidisciplinary background and has conducted/lead large scale ethnographical research in settings where a range of languages including Swedish, English, Swedish Sign Language, Finnish, Italian Hindi and minority/immigrant languages are used. Her current research interests lie at the intersections of the fields of (i) languages (including literacies, multilingualism), (ii) diversity (including ethnicity, gender and functional disabilities), (iii) culture and (iv) learning. She currently leads the national research school LIMCUL, Literacies, Multilingualism and Cultural Practices in present day societies.

Tony Cline is Co-Director of the part-time professional doctorate programme for experienced educational psychologists at University College London and Visiting Professor of Educational Psychology at the University of Bedfordshire. Tony initially worked in inner city and suburban areas around London as a teacher in primary and secondary schools and as an educationnal psychologist. His current interests include learning difficulties of bilingual pupils, selective mutism in childhood, young people's representations of child development and the analysis of the concept of school ethos.

Marcela Costanzi is Professor of Didactic of mathematics at the Universitat Ramón Llull in Barcelona, Spain. She is interested in teachers social representations' particularly linked to the teaching of mathematics to immigrant students.

Sarah Crafter, Senior Lecturer in Psychology and Research Fellow with the Centre for Children and Youth at the University of Northampton, UK. Sarah's main interests include home and school mathematics learning in culturally diverse settings, cultural identities of learners, child workers, young carers and language brokering.

Guida de Abreu is a Professor in Cultural Psychology at Oxford Brookes University, UK. Her main interests focus on theoretical and empirical work in cultural-developmental psychology. Using qualitative methodologies she investigates learning and identity development in culturally diverse settings, including the perspectives of children, young people, parents and teachers.

Annemieke Ensing, PhD in Developmental Psychology at the Rijksuniversiteit of Groningen, the Netherlands. Her main interest lies in the patterns of interaction as they arise between five year olds and their teacher during instruction on curriculum related tasks, and how these patterns are fundamental to the learning potential the child expresses during the interaction.

Ann-Carita Evaldsson is Professor at the Department of Education, Uppsala University, Sweden. Her research combines ethnography with conversation analysis and membership categorization analysis. Her work has mainly focused on preadolescent children's peer language practices, addressing topics such as play and games, moral ordering, identity-work (gender, class and ethnicity) and multilingualism.

Rinat Fellah, MA Student at Bar-Ilan University, Israel.

Núria Gorgorió is Full Professor in Mathematics Education at the Universitat Autònoma de Barcelona, Spain. She is interested in the processes of learning of mathematics of immigrant students, and how this processes are influenced by social representations hold by their teachers.

Michèle Grossen, Professor of Social Psychology at the University of Lausanne, Switzerland. Drawing on socio-historical psychology and a dialogical approach to language and cognition, her research interests include the study of social interactions and communication in learning situations as well as in therapeutic interviews.

Eva Hjörne, Associate Professor in Education at University of Gothenburg, Sweden. Her main interests are in the analysis of learning and social interaction, processes of marginalization and mediated action with special focus on categorizing and identity formation of pupils in school.

Gabrielle Ivinson is a Senior Lecturer at Cardiff School of Social Science, Cardiff University, Wales, UK. Her main research interests are curriculum and pedagogy, gender and schooling, young people, affect and poverty which she studies using Vygotskian sociocultural theory and Basil Bernstein's sociology of pedagogy.

Wen-Chuan Lin is an Assistant Professor in English Department, Wenzao Ursuline College of Languages, Taiwan. His main research interests are TESOL, EFL-related issues and computer mediated English writing instruction with the perspectives of Vygotskian Sociocultural Theory.

Yvonne Karlsson, PhD and a Senior Lecturer in Education at University of Gothenburg, Sweden. Her main interests are in the analysis of children's participation, agency space and identity work in school, and processes of marginalization and categorizations in school activities.

Kristiina Kumpulainen, PhD and the Director of the Information and Evaluation Services at the Finnish National Board of Education. She also holds adjunct professorships at the University of Helsinki and at the University of Turku. Dr. Kumpulainen specializes in sociocultural research on learning and education, learning environments, innovative pedagogies, and teacher professional development. In her publications, she has taken a particular interest in the methodological questions surrounding research on social interactions and learning processes.

Pernilla Larsson is a MA Student at University of Gothenburg, Sweden.

Montserrat Prat is a Post-doctoral Research Fellow at the Universitat Autònoma de Barcelona, Spain. She is interested in the processes of mathematics learning of immigrant students as transition processes where they reconstruct their identities and develop ways of understanding their own learning processes.

Evangelia Prokopiou, PhD and a Cultural Psychologist and she works as a social researcher, community worker and associate lecturer. She was trained in family and groups dynamics at the Athenian Institute of Anthropos (AIA), Greece. Her PhD thesis investigated the development of cultural identities of ethnic minority adolescents attending community schools in the UK. Her research interests focused on exploring changing sociocultural contexts and the development of identities of young people and their families in the islands of Cyclades, of unaccompanied asylum seekers in a reception centre in the island of Lesvos and of Children and Adolescents Mental Health Service's patients in the UK.

Jenny Ros is a PhD Student and Research Assistant at the Department of Psychology, University of Lausanne, Switzerland. Her doctoral dissertation concerns multidisciplinary team collaboration in psychiatry.

Merja Saalasti (M.Ed) is an English Teacher in a comprehensive school and a researcher in the Centre for Sociocultural Studies of Learning and Instruction, the University of Oulu. Her special interest is the role of digital video case material and social reflection. In current projects, Merja Saalasti's work focuses on understanding the social nature of pre service teachers' learning, and developing the methods enhancing dialogical culture in teachers' working communities.

Adina Shamir, PhD and a Senior Lecturer and Head of the Special Education Track at the School of Education, Bar-Ilan University, Israel. She has been serving as the coordinator of the SIG on Children with Special Needs of the European Association for Learning and Instruction (EARLI) since 2007. Her scientific research and publications lie in the area of cognitive and metacognitive development, involving research in Computer-Assisted Learning, Cognitive Modifiability and Learning Skills of students with Special Needs.

Roger Säljö, Professor of Education and Educational Psychology at the Department of Education, Communication and Learning at the University of Gothenburg, Sweden. His main research interests are within the areas of learning, development and communication in a sociocultural perspective. Prominent topics of interest concern the development and circulation of knowledge in society including how our modes of learning and appropriation of collective experiences of our society are shaped by sociocultural conditions, which include material and intellectual technologies linked to literacy, numeracy and other generic human skills.

Auli Toom, PhD, Adjunct Professor, and a senior lecturer in higher education at Faculty of Behavioural Sciences, University of Helsinki, Finland. Her major research interests are teacher's tacit pedagogical knowing, teacher knowledge, teacher reflection and teacher education. Recently her research work has focused on the learning processes during doctoral education and PhD research process as well as the development of expertise during university studies. Auli Toom has also strong theoretical and practical expertise on the video observation methodology.

Geerdina van der Aalsvoort is a Professor at Saxion University of Applied Sciences Deventer, The Netherlands. Based upon a transactional model of development she studies social interaction processes in relationship to learning potential assessment, play and school readiness. She applies both quantitative and qualitative methodologies to investigate how patterns in interaction patterns between teachers and students allow developmental progress with young children growing up at risk.

Paul van Geert, Professor of Developmental Psychology at University of Groningen, The Netherlands.

Eveline Wuttke, Professor in Business Education at Goethe University in Frankfurt, Germany. Her main research interests are the analysis of classroom talk, learning from errors and professional error competence of teachers, and economic literacy of young adults.

Tania Zittoun, Professor at the Institute of Psychology and Education of the University of Neuchâtel, Switzerland. She is interested in the relationships between informal and formal learning. Her work focuses on transitions in learning and developmental trajectories, and on the specific role of fiction and other symbolic resources in thinking.

EVA HJÖRNE, GEERDINA VAN DER AALSVOORT AND
GUIDA DE ABREU

1. EXPLORING PRACTICES AND THE CONSTRUCTION OF IDENTITIES IN SCHOOL

An Introduction

Learning is to a large extent an ongoing social process as both students and their teachers learn by being part of shared social practices through social interactions that facilitate learning gains. Learning gains are facilitated by different factors. Sociocultural research shows that the organization of schooling promotes or restricts learning, and is a crucial factor to understand how children from a diversity of backgrounds profit from instruction. This is a first urgent issue to be considered by teachers and teacher education in our socio and culturally diverse society. A second issue is the on-going debate about learning as a process that involves the construction of identities in schools and classrooms, and in the transitions between school and home practices. Last but not least, since school practices can be addressed from the perspective of diversity and special educational needs an on-going discussion about optimizing pedagogical approaches is of main importance to allow maximum educational effectiveness. Roger Säljö is in the introductory chapter elaborating more on these issues including a brief historical view of learning and schooling.

The book presents results of empirical research examining school practices as part of educational systems. The main theoretical framework is sociocultural theory. Therefore, the connection to social and cultural elements that shape school and classroom practices is described and discussed in every contribution of the book to offer increased knowledge within the field of instruction and learning. The book includes findings from classrooms based upon teachers' approaches and students' viewpoints within classrooms as well as the role of parents in education, and the role of school as an institution in society. Three types of identities that are constructed through participation in school practices are examined: cultural identities, student identities and teacher identities. Thus the book aims at contributing to a broader understanding of practices in school by presenting research findings that were retrieved from classroom settings and related social practices, such as the transitions between home and school practices.

E. Hjörne et al. (eds.), Learning, Social Interaction and Diversity – Exploring Identities in School Practices, 1–7.

A MEETING OF SPECIAL INTEREST GROUPS IN 2008

The book is a result of research presented during the EARLI in-between meeting in Gothenburg, May 2008, organised by three SIGs: Social Interaction in Learning and Instruction, Learning and Teaching in Culturally Diverse Settings, and Special Educational Needs. The small scale conference allowed the SIG members to exchange and discuss research activities related to their special interest groups. The book is a result of this meeting since several papers presented at the meeting are included in this publication. This is not the first book that came out after a SIG meeting. Looking back on former publications the book 'Social Interaction in Learning and Instruction. The Meaning of Discourse for the Construction of Knowledge' edited by Helen Cowie and Geerdina van der Aalsvoort was published in 2000. The book contained the papers that had been presented at the meeting in Leiden 1998 of SIG Social Interaction in Learning and Instruction. In 2009 two publications came out. Both books resulted from meetings of SIG members especially the one in Lisbon in 2004 that gathered members of SIG Social Interaction in Learning and Instruction, and SIG Special Educational needs. 'Investigating classroom interaction. Methodologies in action' was edited by Kristiina Kumpulainen, Cindy Hmelo-Silver and Margarida Cesar. In this book diverse approaches to investigate classroom practice are discussed. Main themes are encompassing different timescales and emphasis on learning as a process that develops over time. The second book edited by Margarida Cesar and Kristiina Kumpulainen called 'Social Interactions in Multicultural Settings' offers the results of studies that embrace the fact that most of the classrooms are multilingual and multicultural.

Motivated by the challenges the former book editors encountered we stress that the theme of social interaction in learning and instruction from a multicultural perspective including special educational needs deserves another book that represents the contributions of active, devoted and highly skilled EARLI members.

EXPLORING PRACTICES AND THE CONSTRUCTION OF IDENTITIES IN SCHOOL IN THREE THEMES

One common theme that emerges in the empirical analysis of the various chapters is the link between school practices and the development of identities. Various facets of the way in which learners' identities are constructed in their participation in school learning practices are examined. Three particular identities are stressed in the studies presented: cultural identities, student identities and teacher identities. The studies illustrate complex relationships between identities as constructed at a social level, such as "student identities" as embedded in the practices of schools as institutions, and in the practices of key relevant others such as parents and teachers, and identities as constructed by learners (by the person as a participant in the social practice of schooling).

Part 1: Constructing cultural identities

Michele Grossen, Tania Zittoun and Jenny Ros examine how secondary school students make sense of cultural elements taught in three different disciplines: philosophy, literature and general knowledge. Drawing upon socio-cultural and dialogical approaches the chapter addresses two complementary questions: Do students make sense of a cultural element taught in class by referring to cultural elements they know from other contexts? Conversely, do they make sense of personal or social phenomena occurring outside the school by referring to cultural elements taught at school? Starting with the assumption that cultural elements at school have some connection with cultural elements in other contexts the chapter presents a theoretical and empirical analysis of *"boundary crossing events"*. These are events where either the teacher or a student attempts to make connections between a cultural element that is part of the lesson, and other elements that belong to the outside world. The analysis illustrates how the teacher and the students manage the tensions between activities, identities and bodies of knowledge linked to school practices, and those that are connected with outside school. The chapter offers a unique contribution suggesting that identity connections can sometimes facilitate the opening of potential appropriation space for school learning, and at other times prevent the creation of such a space.

Evangelia Prokopiou, Tony Cline and Guida de Abreu illustrate the complexity of the socio-cultural macrosystem in pluralistic societies and its impact on the development of identities of young people from minority ethnic backgrounds. They theorise the influence of multiple heterogeneous contexts by revisiting and elaborating on Bonfenbrenner's model, dialogical self theory and cultural developmental theory to understand the cultural and dialogical nature of the processes through which ethnic minority young people develop their identities in community schools. In their contribution they explore how second and third generation British-born young people of Pakistani and Greek-Cypriot origin perceive themselves as ethnic minority pupils in both community and mainstream education as well as in their role as members of the wider society. They illustrate how dialogical negotiation of aspects of differences/ similarities resulted in multivoiced cultural identities which emerged through a constant positioning and re-positioning within communities and school contexts.

Sarah Crafter elaborates the role of parents in supporting their children's school learning. Drawing on the notions of cultural models and cultural settings her chapter examines the kinds of resources parents use to make sense of their child's mathematics homework. Two parental resources for making sense of mathematics homework are scrutinized: (a) the child, and (b) cultural models of child development. The way the parents make sense of their experiences of supporting their children's school mathematical learning at home both draws on their own cultural identities and on the cultural identities underlying school practices. This is examined in terms of the cultural models about child development held by the parents often at odds with those held by the school institution. These different models between home and school are deeply rooted on cultural representations of what is optimal child development, and what practices contribute to its achievement.

Wen Chuan Lin and Gabriella Ivinson examine the impact of ethnic cultural legacies in learning English as a foreign language. Taking a socio-cultural perspective they intend to broaden theories of learning a second language by recognizing that students' learning has to be situated within broader frames of analysis including the political, institutional, local and ethnic cultural contexts in which individuals encounter English. Their analysis draws on empirical research conducted in Taiwan. Two substantive issues are explored in their research; (1) differences between ethnic groups' situated experiences of, and access to, English, (2) the relationship between ethnic group cultures in four groups (Hokkien, Chinese Mainlander, Hakka and indigenous people) and experiences of American and Anglo culture. Their findings illustrate a complex intersection of ethnic cultural identities and the way students from each group learn English. Historical cultural legacies interacted with what kinds of resources became locally available in relation to English learning, and students from some groups come to school already better equipped to access Anglo-American English than other groups. Similarly to what has been highlighted by Crafter to understand how students access school learning resources it is necessary to search beyond academic cultures. In particular both studies show that the students' home cultures intersect in complex ways with their school cultures shaping trajectories of learning.

Sangeeta Bagga-Gupta offers critical reflections on the meanings of cultural diversity and human identities in complex Northern European settings through the socio-historical analysis of demographic data and national educational policies and through the analysis of mundane interactions in different types of language profile schools in present day Sweden. Current discourses of multilingualism and multiculturalism in Sweden are problematic in that they appear to be based upon a-historical assumptions about migration and diversity and upon monolingual perspectives that "normalize" a particular view of human communication. Issues related to language-contact, language-switching and language-chaining are exemplified as well as issues related to the situated nature of human identity in classroom interaction. Bagga-Gupta calls attention for the intersections between languages, human identity and cultural identities, arguing that "it is not human characteristics like ethnicity or deafness or age that are significant, but rather issues of human difference in relation to *languages and literacies in use* that are significant".

Part 2: Constructing student identities

Eveline Wuttke states that classrooms are environments that are highly dependent on communication. By talking with each other teachers and students give, accept, and exchange information. Mostly this is done with the intention to help students to acquire knowledge. Other important functions of communication are the circulation of interaction rules and the organization of social relationships. Mostly, communication follows quite standardized patterns and is structured by socially accepted ways in which knowledge is presented. She looks closely at patterns of classroom talk to answer three research questions: In case students are given the chance to actively participate in classroom talk: To what extent do they seize their chance? Of which quality is their talk? What are the effects of students talk?

Ann-Carita Evaldsson and Yvonne Karlsson present their findings about how a group of preadolescent boys are ascribed a more permanent (and deviant) identity as 'boys with externalizing behaviours' in talk-in-interaction within a routinely organized remedial activity in a special educational needs unit. In such activity, the boys' emotional, social and behavioural deficiencies are made a daily topic of inquiry and talked into being in order to remedy the referred to problem behaviours.

Eva Hjörne and Pernilla Larsson focus on different strategies for disciplining boys in the remedial class during the 1960s. In which ways are boys made accountable for disruptive school behaviour during regular learning- and teaching practices? What strategies are used by the teachers and why? The research is based on a historical material of video-recorded classroom interaction from 1968. The issues explored in their study concern the activity of regulating or disciplining boys during a specific lesson called "ABC in conduct", and how different strategies and accounts or categories invoked by teachers, determine the nature of the daily schooling experiences and, in a long-term perspective, the educational career and identities of the children.

Adina Shamir and Rinat Fellah describe the findings when using electronic books with children to enhance their emergent literacy. The large population of children with learning disabilities (LD) in Israeli schools and worldwide has increased the priority of finding new interventions and learning tools for these children very early in their schooling. One dominant difficulty faced by this community is the acquisition of reading and writing skills, for which the foundations are laid in preschool. However, the growing entry of computer programs such as electronic books (e-books) into the learning environment of kindergartens and schools now provides ample opportunities for computer use in the support of children's language and literacy development. In their study they investigated the effects of activity with an educational e-book developed by the authors on the emergent literacy of 5- to 7-year-old kindergarteners who had been diagnosed at risk of learning disabilities.

Part 3: Constructing teacher identities

Kristiina Kumpulainen, Auli Toom and Merja Saalasti explore the ways in which the collaborative investigation of video cases of authentic classroom teaching and learning situations can afford opportunities for student teachers' agency work and support their professional identity formation in teacher education. In particular, the potential of digital video telling cases has been recognized in their power to create social and discursive spaces for pre-service and in-service teachers to investigate and reflect upon teaching and learning practices in local and distant classrooms. The study aims to gain an understanding of students teachers' identity building processes by examining: What kinds of discursive identities and positions do student teachers construct into being in their written essays over their pedagogy course focusing on teaching and learning of mathematics?, and Which topics and issues dominate students' reflection processes as they describe their professional learning processes over the course?

Annemieke Ensing, Geerdina van der Aalsvoort and Paul van Geert bring to attention how for a long time the potential to learn was related to specific ways to assess children by ways of dynamic assessment (DA). DA is a generic term for procedures that embed intervention within the ongoing assessment, and that usually include a pretest-training posttest format that directly links assessment to intervention. As the child engages in the assessment task, the assessor can observe the child's strengths and weaknesses. By looking at the learning processes during the course of problemsolving, the examiner can discover how the child learns and how the child can best be instructed. The authors present learning potential as a dynamic system that allows insight in the actual emergence of learning processes. The processes that are responsible for learning potential to be revealed are still unclear. The study aims at answering the questions: What patterns during the instruction elicits response to instruction emerge? Is it verbal instruction that evokes a child's response or are non-verbal behaviors responsible for it?

Marcela Constanzi, Nuria Gorgorió and Montserrat Prat draw to attention that a mathematics classroom attended by immigrant students may be considered a culturally diverse setting because, most probably, the students and teacher that are interacting in it have been socialized within communities having different cultural frames of reference. The different understandings of the processes and facts related to the teaching and learning of mathematics, of the ways of teaching and learning, or the different values attached to mathematical knowledge, are linked to cultural understandings, and shape the way people act and interact within the mathematics classroom. Details are presented of ongoing research on student teachers' representations on the learning of mathematics of their immigrant students. Their analysis illustrates how teachers' social representations mediate practices in the mathematics classroom, conditioning the possibilities of student participation, legitimating certain ways of learning, and favouring the development of certain mathematical identities.

REFERENCES

Cowie, H., & van der Aalsvoort, G. (Eds.) (2000). *Social interaction in learning and instruction. The meaning of discourse for the construction of knowledge*. Amsterdam: Pergamon Press.

Kumpulainen, M., Hmelo-Silver, C. E., & César, M. (Eds.) (2009). *Investigating classroom interaction. Methodologies in action*. Rotterdam: Sense Publishers.

César, M., & Kumpulainen, M. (Eds.) (2009). *Social interactions in multicultural settings*. Rotterdam: Sense Publishers.

Eva Hjörne
Department of Education and Special Education
University of Gothenburg

Geerdina van der Aalsvoort
School of Education
Saxion University of Applied Science Deventer

Guida de Abreu
Psychology Department
Oxford Brookes University

ROGER SÄLJÖ

2. SCHOOLING AND SPACES FOR LEARNING

Cultural Dynamics and Student Participation and Agency

INTRODUCTION

All over the world education is expanding as a social activity. In what is commonly referred to as the information or knowledge society, politicians, business leaders, scholars, high-profile representatives of international organizations and large proportions of the public seem to agree that learning is a key to success and to survival for societies in a time characterized by global competition. According to this dogma, the so-called knowledge economy, fuelled by digital technologies and new forms of global collaboration (Castells, 1996), requires citizens with advanced information skills keen to engage in life-long learning starting already in preschool and continuing throughout working life.

This identification of knowledge as a key element in social development and competition has resulted in an increased political emphasis on monitoring the performance of educational systems. High-stakes international tests, such as PISA,[1] TIMSS[2] and others, are used as bench marking systems and the hope is that they will provide insights into the relationships between investments and outcomes in education. The ambition is that eventually politicians will be able to act on such performance indicators by making educational systems more efficient and competitive.

While comparing achievements, and learning from other countries, is commendable, the problems of such comparisons are not that they are carried out, but, rather, that they rely on traditional and narrow perspectives of what going to school and learning are all about. The tests are all paper-and-pencil exercises where students sit alone and answer questions during an hour or two, and they do this without access to technologies they rely on in their everyday lives, generally without collaborating with peers and their activities are not embedded in any other activity than taking a test for its own sake. Thus, competences aimed for a digital and globalized society are assessed on the basis of indicators that precede the

---

[1] Programme for International Student Assessment.
[2] Trends in International Mathematics and Science Study.

E. Hjörne et al. (eds.), Learning, Social Interaction and Diversity – Exploring Identities in School Practices, 9–14.

digital revolution, and which reflect a narrow, product-oriented view of what it means to know something.

Such views on the role of education and educational effectiveness are consequential. The abstract nature of the public debate that follows from heavy reliance on these kinds of accountability systems tends to view schooling mainly as a means-to-an-end activity. Schooling and learning are meaningful to the extent that they provide skills for a distant future, for adulthood and for the labour market of the future (about which we know very little). The perspective on education, teaching and learning that many of the modern accountability systems imply is antithetical to the view that John Dewey tried to communicate, when he argued that education "is a process of living and not a preparation for future living" (1897, p. 78).

If we follow this Deweyan principle of attending to schooling as "a process of living", the explorations take us into the daily lives of teachers, students and others as they engage in joint activities, and it opens up for a more differentiated view of what education contributes, for society as well as for the individual. As the chapters in this book illustrate, schooling in contemporary society is a complex and diverse phenomenon. Increasing social complexity, demographic changes, continuous development of new technologies and new production systems, rising expectations of literacy and other skills in the population are examples of factors that change the conditions of life in classrooms, and large-scale benchmarking systems give little, if any, guidance about how to adapt to such new circumstances.

TEACHING AND LEARNING AS INTERACTIONAL PRACTICES IN CONTEMPORARY SOCIETY

The assumption that education can be considered mainly as a means-to-an-end practice, which is legitimate to the extent that it cultivates the human capital in line with market expectations, threatens the integrity of teaching and learning as human activities, as significant elements of people's lives and as objects of inquiry for research. As an antidote to such trends, it is important to analyse what educational practices are all about in contemporary society, and what challenges and options students and teachers face. This is in large part an empirical problem of having access to in-depth and situated descriptions and analyses of how such practices unfold, of understanding the logic of the contributions that the parties make, and of scrutinizing the role that the activities have for the development of learners.

In order to succeed with such analytical enterprises of showing the significance of education in the lives of people, there is an obvious need for broadening the conceptual lenses through which schooling and learning are studied. We need to include, and consider seriously, issues of how children's opportunities for participating and contributing to activities are organized, and what the implications of their involvement are in terms of their future life. What arenas for learning and engagement are created in schools and classrooms, what is the continuity (Dewey, 1963) between in-school and out-of-school experiences, and how are children's identities shaped during their course of participation in institutional practices?

These are some of the issues that deserve attention and that should be brought to public attention as backgrounds for discussing and evaluating education.

Our concept of schooling – one classroom, one teacher, one class and one subject at a time – has a long history. In fact, it goes back to the first schools established in Mesopotamia over five thousand years ago (Kramer, 1981). In the so-called *edduba*, the tablet house, boys from the elite of society learned to read and write in order to prepare for their future careers as scribes (Burns, 1989). In these schools, the mysteries of cuneiform reading and writing were taught under what seems to have been a hard regime with frequent use of corporeal punishment as a method of making students comply with whatever rules the authority deemed relevant (Falkenstein, 1948). Also, the idea of conceiving of learning as essentially reproducing what the teacher presented was born in these particular circumstances, where students were trained to copy signs and texts produced by others; the closer to the original the copy made by the student was, the better the result.

When schools were opened up for the children of all social backgrounds, which in European countries did not happen until the 19th century in the wake of industrialization (Sandin, 1986), the institutional practices were largely modeled on established traditions: teachers taught and students reproduced, and the asymmetrical communication patterns of the classroom survived. Religious indoctrination and moral disciplining were often important goals, and there were generally quite low expectations that what you learned in school would be important in other spheres of life, except, possibly, for mastering basic reading and writing. But by opening up schools to children with all backgrounds, we see how diversity challenges institutional practices, and since then the problem of how to productively deal with individual differences and issues of diversity has been part of the public debate.

For a long time many of the problems of adaptation to schooling experienced by marginal groups (children from lower social classes, from minority groups, children with disabilities and so on) were solved through the classical method in education: they simply dropped out of the system at the earliest possible opportunity. Low-paying jobs appeared for many as a more attractive alternative. In the American context, for instance, leaving school was not considered a social problem until relatively recently, and as late as in the 1940s "less than half of individuals age 25-29 completed high school" (Shannon & Bylsma, 2003, p. 2). By marginalizing children who did not fit in, the traditional format of schooling, by and large, could be maintained even as the social circumstances were changing.

The explanations offered for school disengagement are interesting, and they tell us a lot about the wider social and political climate under which schools have operated during the past 150 years or so (Deschenes, Cuban, & Tyack, 2001; Hjörne & Säljö, 2004, 2008). An initial focus on the inferior moral fiber of the lower classes as the preferred explanation of school failure was later replaced by the intellectual deficit paradigm, which has continued to serve as a strong explanatory framework well into our time. In the postwar period, we have seen other types of explanations emerge such as poor family conditions, ethnic

11

background, and in recent years we have seen a proliferation of learning disabilities all the way from MBD (Minimal Brain Damage/Dysfunction) via dyslexia (which has a longer history, cf. Zetterqvist Nelson & Sandin, 2005) to ADHD and a range of similar neuropsychological diagnoses. To match these categorization practices, the political debate about how to solve the problems has swayed back and forth between strategies of integration and mainstreaming of pupils with special needs to inventing dedicated pedagogical practices for various categories of learning disabled.

Today, however, the dropout option is not so attractive or politically viable. Even if it would make the lives of teachers and school administrators simpler, the demands of modern society are such that politicians, parents and many other stakeholders worry about early school leavers, and they worry a lot. Current EU ambitions, for instance, are to reduce the proportion of early school leavers (defined as students who only finish lower secondary education) from the present 14.4 per cent to under 10 per cent by 2020 (European Union, 2011). High unemployment rates and other social problems throughout the life-span are overrepresented in these groups, and the ambition is therefore to keep students in school as long as possible. Over the years, a range of politically motivated counter strategies have been launched: early intervention programs, supplemental programs, individualized education, alternative schools and alternative pedagogies are among the initiatives tested (Shannon & Bylsma, 2003, p. 59ff).

Research has an important role to play when it comes to providing tools and analyses for understanding the dynamics of education in complex societies. One such strategic function is to give access to the daily practices of schooling as they unfold *in situ*. Any productive discussion about schooling, and about the possibilities for developing teaching and learning practices, must be grounded in concrete analyses of the nature of the varied and diverse activities that go on in classrooms and other educational settings. Classroom activities should not be black-boxed but rather unpacked in their details and functional patterns. Important tasks to attend to include understanding the trajectories of participation and learning, and how children (or adults, for that matter) stay involved or risk becoming disengaged by specific educational practices.

In such analyses, understanding the identity development of children throughout schooling is one important task, and this includes attending to what happens to their institutional identities as well (Gee, 2000). How are the difficulties learners encounter interpreted by institutional representatives, and how can pedagogical practices be organized in manners that allow for children to continue seeing themselves as committed learners within the frames offered by schooling? From the research point of view this implies aiming for "thick descriptions" (Geertz, 1973) and accounts of learning that focus on issues of participation and involvement as an alternative to resting content with thin descriptions in terms of abstract outcome measures of products of learning.

Analysing the agency of children and adults as learners in educational settings implies paying attention to how their ambitions, as expressed by their trajectories of participation, may stay aligned with the normative expectations of educational institutions (Edwards & Mackenzie, 2005). Showing the contingencies between instructional practices and student engagement both generally, and with respect to particular kinds of activities, may help increasing institutional and political sensitivity in response to current transformations of social life, where diversity is an important issue. The chapters in this volume thematize some of the dimensions of this diversity which emanates from so many sources. The authors scrutinize features of schooling such as classroom practices and their connectedness to children's cultural experiences in various areas, the assumptions underlying remedial teaching, changes in literacy practices and expectations related to the digital technology and other significant issues. In a concrete sense, they illustrate some of the challenges the institution, and all its participants and stake-holders, currently face. An important tension emerges from these analyses: what should schooling and instruction be like in contemporary society, and what are the relevant criteria for judging success, not only of children but also of the manners in which educational practices manage to adapt to diversity.

REFERENCES

Burns, A. (1989). *The power of the written word. The role of literacy in the history of western civilization.* New York, NY: Peter Lang.

Castells, M. (1996). *The information age: Economy, society and culture (Vol. 1).* Oxford, England: Blackwell Publishers.

Deschenes, S., Cuban, L., & Tyack, D. (2001). Mismatch: Historical perspectives on schools and students who don't fit them. *Teachers College Record, 103*(4), 525-547.

Dewey, J. (1897). My pedagogic creed. *School Journal, 54*, 77-80.

Dewey, J. (1963). *Experience and education.* New York, NY: Collier Macmillan.

Edwards, A., & Mackenzie, L. (2005). Steps towards participation: The social support of learning trajectories. *International Journal of Lifelong Education, 24*(4), 287-302.

European Union (2011). European Commission launches action plan to reduce early school leaving. Downloaded February 27, 2011, from http://youth-partnership-eu.coe.int/youth-partnership/news/news_261.html.

Falkenstein, A. (1948). Der "Sohn des Tafelhauses" [The "son of the tablet house"]. *Die Welt des Orients, 2*, 172-186.

Gee, J. P. (2000). Identity as an analytic lens for research in education. *Review of Research in Education, 25*, 99-125. doi: 10.3102/0091732X025001099

Geertz, C. (1973). *The interpretation of cultures.* New York, NY: Basic Books.

Hjörne, E., & Säljö, R. (2004). The pupil welfare team as a discourse community: Accounting for school problems. *Linguistics and Education, 15*, 321-338.

Hjörne, E., & Säljö, R. (2008). *Att platsa i en skola för alla. Elevhälsa och förhandling om normalitet i den svenska skolan* [To fit into a school for all. Pupil health and negotiating normality in the Swedish school]. Stockholm: Norstedts.

Kramer, S. N. (1981). *History begins at Sumer.* Philadelphia, PA: The University of Pennsylvania Press.

Sandin, B. (1986). *Hemmet, gatan, fabriken eller skolan. Folkundervisning och barnuppfostran i svenska städer 1600-1850* [The home, the street, the factory or the school. Popular education and child-rearing in Swedish cities 1600-1850]. Lund: Arkiv förlag.

Shannon, G. S., & Bylsma, P. (2003). *Helping students finish school: Why students drop out and how to help them graduate.* Olympia, WA: Office of the Superintendent of Public Instruction.

13

Zetterqvist Nelson, K., & Sandin, B. (2005). The politics of reading and writing problems: Changing definitions in Swedish schooling during the twentieth century. *History of Education, 34*(2), 189-205.

Roger Säljö
Department of Education, Communication and Learning
University of Gothenburg &
Centre for Learning Research
University of Turku

MICHÈLE GROSSEN, TANIA ZITTOUN AND JENNY ROS

3. BOUNDARY CROSSING EVENTS AND POTENTIAL APPROPRIATION SPACE IN PHILOSOPHY, LITERATURE AND GENERAL KNOWLEDGE

INTRODUCTION

Teaching cultural elements, such as literary texts, pieces of music, films, sculptures, and other similar artefacts, is one of the educational aims of a school. As part of our past and present society, cultural elements are considered to be fundamental. At a social level, they belong to shared bodies of knowledge which might foster social cohesion; at the level of individuals, they are expected to play a fundamental role in the students' intellectual and emotional development and in their capacity to act as future citizens. In the present state-of-the-art, however, more research is needed into the way in which the cultural elements taught at school are used by students as *resources* for emotional elaboration and developmental processes.

Starting from this consideration, the research project on which this contribution is based examines how secondary school students make sense of cultural elements taught in three different disciplines: philosophy, literature and general knowledge. Drawing upon socio-cultural and dialogical approaches inspired by Vygotsky and Bakhtin (Grossen & Salazar Orvig, 2011; Marková, 2003; Valsiner, 2007; Wertsch, 1991; Zittoun, 2006), we address two complementary questions: Do students make sense of a cultural element taught in class by referring to cultural elements they know from other contexts? Conversely, do they make sense of personal or social phenomena occurring outside the school by referring to cultural elements taught at school?

Assuming that cultural elements at school have some connection with cultural elements in other contexts, we begin by a brief presentation of our theoretical framework and focus upon what we call *boundary crossing events,* that is a connection (made either by the teacher or by a student) between a cultural element that is part of the lesson, and other elements that belong to the outside world. Then we examine whether these boundary crossing events foster the creation of a *potential appropriation space*, in which students can give a personal sense to the bodies of knowledge taught in class. After presenting the study from which our data is taken, we report three contrasting examples of boundary crossing events and their subsequent potential appropriation spaces.

E. Hjörne et al. (eds.), Learning, Social Interaction and Diversity – Exploring Identities in School Practices, 15–33.

DIALOGICAL AND SOCIO-CULTURAL PERSPECTIVE ON EDUCATION

Our research project is located at the intersection of two research strands. The first examines the interactional and discursive processes involved in teaching and learning. An impressive body of research into classroom interactions has shown that part of the teaching-learning process consists of the teacher's and students' joint construction of a shared meaning of the school subject matter (e.g. Grossen, 2009; Grossen & Bachmann, 2000; Kumpulainen, Hmelo-Silver, & Margarida, 2009; Littleton, 2000; Renshaw, 1998; Rojas-Drummond, Mazón, Fernandez, & Wegerif, 2006). Thus, part of the students' activity is to make sense of the ground rules at work in the situation and to decipher the teacher's point of view about the subject matter (Mercer, 2000). Further development has focused upon the personal sense that the students give to school in general, or to certain school subject matters (for example grammar or mathematics) (Rochex, 1998, 2004). It has also been shown that making sense of school or, for example, mathematics or a piece of literature, is mediated by significant others (parents, teachers, et cetera.) and is fundamental in being successful at school.

The second research strand concerns the role of semiotic mediation in thinking and development (Valsiner, 2007, 2009). Studies in this field have shown that people engaged in the daily work of making sense of problematic situations usually draw on a variety of available resources (Zittoun, 2006). In this context, cultural elements (such as complex cultural artefacts that are primarily intended to carry meaning) can, in some situations, be used by people to develop new understandings, redefine themselves, or make sense of an event. For example, a picture can help them to maintain an experience of self-continuity although they change their place of residence; a novel might help them to define future plans; or a song can bring them to reflect upon some historical issue. Such uses of cultural elements have been called *symbolic resources* (Zittoun, Duveen, Gillespie, Ivinson, & Psaltis, 2003; Zittoun, 2006). A cultural element is used as symbolic resource when it is mobilised by a person, who intentionally links it with something which is beyond its normal, shared meaning: for example, when a novel is not only read by a person in order to follow the fiction or analyse 19th century's language, but also because it enables her to reflect upon her life choices. In other words, the notion of *symbolic resource* captures the fact that under certain conditions cultural elements might participate in the young person's development and socialisation. It refers to the fact that a person uses a cultural element *in connection with* an experience made in her personal life that turns it into a symbolic resource; uses of symbolic resources are always personal.

Beyond their differences, these research strands converge on two points: (a) Both see interpersonal relationships as mediating the personal sense that a learner gives to an object of knowledge (Perret-Clermont, Carugati, & Oates, 2004). Emotionally significant others play a fundamental role in the process of making sense of a cultural element. For example, a parent who acknowledges that a child likes a specific story might facilitate his/her further internalisation of the story (Miller, Hoogstra, Mintz, Fung, & Williams, 1993; Zittoun, 2010). Social interactions are thus constitutive of the process of appropriation and internalisation of knowledge.[3] (b) Both see learning as a socially and institutionally situated process (Grossen, 2000; Resnick, Säljö, Pontecorvo, & Burge, 1997; Valsiner, 2008, Zittoun, 2008). Consequently, a certain body of knowledge (for example a cultural element) may take on various meanings depending on the sphere of activity in which it is embedded and the representations that the participants have of its aims and of the task to be carried out.

Applied to our research object, this view also implies that, as has been shown in the field of mathematics for example (Abreu, 1995), there might be some tensions between various spheres of activity, outside and inside school, in which the apparently "same" cultural element is mobilised. We can therefore form the hypothesis that part of the students' practice consists of identifying whether these two worlds could or should be connected, and if so, in which ways. In other words, learning at school and making sense of a cultural element taught at school might imply a process of crossing boundaries between the inside and the outside of a given learning-teaching situation.

TENSIONS IN THE TEACHING-LEARNING FRAMEWORK

From a socio-cultural perspective, a school is a culturally and historically situated social institution. The school's policies, organisation, curricula, pedagogical practices, modes of communication with parents and other communities, goals and values, frame the teaching-learning activities in the classroom. In turn, they are also framed by broader social and institutional practices. A school can thus be seen as a *community of practice* (Brown, 1997) in which the participants develop shared practices that contribute to the reconfiguration of the context in which they occur. Hence, the context is both a framework and a result of the participants' activity.

Since teachers and students are also participants of other communities of practice, teaching and learning at school require them to position themselves as members both of the school community and of these other communities. From this standpoint a teaching-learning situation appears to be a concentrate of elements pertaining to the here and now of the classroom and to the *there and then* (other classrooms, other communities of practice), which give rise to tensions that the participants have to manage.

The tension between everyday and formal knowledge is one of them. By everyday knowledge, we refer to objects of knowledge, competence, skills, etcetera that are not part of the school curriculum and are not submitted to explicit teaching at school. By formal knowledge, we refer not only to the subject matters and object

---

[3] Here we do not oppose appropriation and internalization, as has been done by various authors (Rogoff, 1995; Toomela, 1996); rather, we consider appropriation as a socially situated activity of progressive mastery and sense-making, and internalisation as its mental phase – the process whereby signs and meaning in the world find some psychic translation (Lawrence & Valsiner, 1993, 2003; Wertsch & Stone, 1985).

of knowledge that belong to the school curriculum, but also to the fact that knowledge, competence, skills, etc. that are taught at school require specific modes of thinking, including formal conceptualisation, hypothetico-deductive reasoning, and reflecting about the implicit rules organising knowledge (Rochex, 2004; Vygotsky, 1986). On the other hand, bodies of knowledge taught at school should enable students to orient themselves in their social and professional environment, and are aimed at becoming a form of daily knowledge (that is, equip them to be integrated in the society in which they live). Some schools can favour the links between everyday and formal knowledge, for example by anchoring the formal curricula in the students' everyday knowledge (Hedegaard, 2009; Hedegaard & Chaiklin, 2005). Other schools rather disregard the links between formal and everyday knowledge and keep them distinct (Rochex, 1998). Students themselves might draw upon everyday knowledge or knowledge learned in another context, to make sense of the school subject matter.

A second source of tensions concerns the respective importance conferred by the participants to the subject matter or to interpersonal relationships. We shall call it object-focused vs. relation-focused interactions. In fact, teacher-students interactions might focus upon the subject matter, whereas in other cases, they might focus upon the quality of interpersonal relationship at the expanse of the subject matter. For instance, with students who have had a difficult school career, teachers might want to establish a good relationship (Zittoun, 2004) before focusing upon the teaching of a certain subject matter. In contrast, in the context of University education, teaching-learning situations mostly focus upon the object of knowledge and tend to neglect interpersonal relationships in a way that might lead the students to feel anonymous and uneasy (Coulon, 2005).

A third source of tensions might arise from the various social identities involved within the students' various spheres of experience (Hermans, 2002; Perret-Clermont, 2009). Outside school, they might have developed competences, skills and knowledge (language speaking, games, sports, theatre, et cetera) that are part of their identities and give them a certain kind of expertise. Within the school context, these various types of experience may or may not be acknowledged; they might be valorised and contribute to the construction of a positive self image, or, on the contrary, be experienced as a private matter that should be carefully kept away from the school context. Thus, a classroom community might, or might not, leave some room for more symmetric relationships in which the students refer to their competence, skills or knowledge in fields other than school disciplines themselves. The students might also be more or less liable to negotiate various facets of their identity. Moreover, in the internalisation process, students, as well as teachers, may find school subject matters that correspond to their private experience and give them a personal sense (Rochex, 1998). Within a classroom community, students and teachers may disclose this personal commitment and make it a *res publica* (Bruner, 2002), or on the contrary, keep it hidden as something belonging to their private life.

These three types of tensions (formal vs. informal knowledge; object-focused vs. relation-focused interactions; identities inside vs. outside school) are of course not exhaustive. However, they show that teaching-learning situations as a concentrate of a here and now and a *there and then*, include discontinuities, divergences and tensions between various communities of practice and the various positionings of individuals within these communities. They can be considered as three indicators, which, taken together, inform us about the specificity of the teaching-learning framework created in the classroom.

BOUNDARY CROSSING EVENTS AND POTENTIAL APPROPRIATION SPACE

Any teaching-learning framework implies boundary crossing practices, by which students and teachers make connections between various communities of practice in which they participate (Wenger, 1998; see also in a slightly different way Tuomi-Gröhn & Engeström, 2003). With the notion of boundary crossing events, our intention is to emphasize, firstly, the uniqueness of the teaching-learning framework characterized by modalities of various types of tensions. Secondly, we want to highlight the semiotic processes and uses of artefacts (Walker & Nocoon, 2007) that people activate as they move from one sphere of experience to another in order to make sense of events in different contexts and communities of practices (an issue related to transfer; cf. Beach, 2003; Säljö, 2003).

At a methodological level, our suggestion is that the way in which students make sense of philosophy, literature and general knowledge by connecting cultural elements taught in these classes with elements from outside, and by using them to make sense of their personal everyday life or of social phenomena, may be captured through boundary crossing events.

We identified two types of boundary crossing events (BCE): in the first, the teacher or a student imports a cultural element, a social event, or a personal experience occurring outside the context of the classroom and connects it with a cultural element currently taught in the classroom. Excerpt [1], taken from a philosophy class given by Paul, the regular teacher, offers an illustration (in italics the BCE, original in Appendix):

[1]   *Paul_14 (School B, translated from French)*
The students have read a text by the philosopher Bertrand Russell. The teacher, Paul, is commenting on it, when Ralph raises his hand:
Ralph   yes but couldn't there be some exceptions to what he ((Russell)) says?
Paul   well, that's, err? […]
Ralph   I don't know, for example the stories of Robin Hood

As he attempts to make sense of Russell's text, Ralph recalls an alien cultural element, *Robin Hood*, a fictional character made famous mainly through literature and films, and lets it cross the borders of the present lesson. *Robin Hood* belongs to popular, everyday culture, that is, to a different sphere of experience than Russell's text in a formal philosophy lesson; in that sense, the mention of *Robin Hood* is here a BCE.

The second type of BCE consists of exporting a school subject matter outside the class in order to make sense of elements, events, or experiences that take place in everyday life. This is for example the case when a student connects texts on racism that have been read in class with the fact that some newspapers report an aggressor's nationality only when he or she is a foreigner (see Excerpt [4]).

In line with our theoretical framework, we assume that by connecting elements from outside and inside the class, BCE indicate how the participants manage the tensions between the two contexts. The occurrence of a BCE is a privileged moment to observe how the tensions between formal and informal knowledge, between object-focused vs. relation-focused interactions, and between identities outside and inside school are handled, and to observe what teaching-learning framework is locally and temporarily achieved. More specifically, our hypothesis is that the way in which these BCE reconfigure the teaching-learning framework may encourage the emergence of what we call a *potential appropriation space* —a space in which learning and change can occur—both at the level of shared activities, and at the level of each person involved (Zittoun, 2004). The term 'potential' is intended to stress that a teaching-learning situation may, under certain conditions, offer an opportunity (potentiality) for learning, or a thinking space Perret-Clermont (2004). It also refers to Winnicott's notion of potential space (1971): provided firstly by 'good enough' interpersonal relationship, and then by cultural traditions, a potential space is experienced when people feel safe enough to engage in playing and creative processes, in adopting different points of view, engaging in counterfactual thinking, etcetera.[4] Thus, the term 'potential' is meant to emphasise that learning involves both collaboration and creativity (Littleton, Rojas-Drummond, & Miell, 2008). In other words, when BCE open a potential appropriation space, the cultural elements under discussion are liable to become symbolic resources for learning and for making a personal sense of learning. Therefore, the general aim of our study is to analyse the characteristics of BCE, to examine how they reshape the teaching-learning framework and to explore their role in the creation of a potential appropriation space.

DATA, METHOD OF ANALYSIS AND RESEARCH QUESTIONS

The data was collected in three Swiss upper-secondary schools (mostly 17-19 year-old students): School A and School B offer pre-academic tracks, whereas School C offers vocational tracks. We observed 14 teachers and their students, in 16 different classrooms, and in three disciplines: literature, philosophy (in Schools A and B), and general knowledge, which is specific to School C and consists of the study of

---

[4] Although Winnicott was mainly interested in the changes leading to the development of the self, it should be noted that the potential space hence defined is extremely close to that of "zone of proximal development" (Vygotsky, 1986) more familiar in studies of learning, which can be created by others, in play or in fiction, and that is the zone in which new understanding can emerge through exploration and counterfactual thinking (or "as-if" processes, see Valsiner, 2008).

various themes in the field of cinema, art, history, literature, etcetera. In total, 56 lessons (27 in literature, 16 in philosophy and 13 in general knowledge,) were videotaped and analysed, all in French. These classroom observations were part of a broader collection of data consisting, among others, of interviews with the teachers.

In a first analytical step, we identified all the BCE occurring in these lessons: 144 BCE were found and the elements outside the classroom that were bridged to the cultural element taught in class were attributed to one of three thematic categories: (a) social, political or historical facts, for example, racism; (b) personal experience or reference to an autobiographical element; (c) cultural elements that were not part of the lesson, such as "Robin Hood" in Excerpt [1]. We also found that these BCE were included in sequences (BCE sequences) made up of four parts: introduction, opening, thematisation of the BCE, and closing. Since, some BCE were directly linked to each others, the 144 BCE identified corresponded to 125 BCE sequences.

In a second step, various aspects of these BCE sequences were analysed, for example: who provoked the BCE, who made it, what reactions did it elicit from whom and of what type. This enabled us to categorise these BCE sequences in eight profiles, according to who made the BCE (teacher or student), who provoked it, and what type of reaction it triggered.

Our third analytical step aimed at answering our hypothesis: do BCE play a role in the creation of a potential space of learning? To explore this question, we focused on the reaction provoked by a BCE: was there a thematic development, that is, some sort of discussion? If so, did this thematic development open a potential space of learning? In other terms, the quality of the thematic development following the BCE was taken as an analytical clue to infer whether a potential space of learning was opened or not.

Due to length limitations, we only present three excerpts: two were taken in School C, in two different classrooms in which a teacher (Elisabeth and Eric) gave a class of general knowledge, and one excerpt was taken in School A in a class of philosophy given by Patrick. These three excerpts correspond to three different profiles of BCE sequences. The first is an example of a profile in which the teacher introduces a BCE that does not give way to any thematic development. The second excerpt exemplifies a profile in which the teacher makes a BCE that gives way to a thematic development. The third excerpt illustrates a profile in which a student makes a BCE that gives way to a thematic development. In each case, we show how the three types of tensions identified above to characterize the teaching-learning framework were handled, and their effects on the construction of a potential appropriation space.

BOUNDARY CROSSING EVENTS AND POTENTIAL APPROPRIATION SPACE

Example 1

Excerpt [2] belongs to the most frequent profile (28 BCE sequences out of 125): The teacher introduces a BCE on his or her own initiative, that is, it is self-elicited; it prompts minimal feedback and the teacher closes the sequence. Thus, the BCE is completely integrated within the teacher's flow of discourse while she holds the floor.

Excerpt [2] is taken from a general knowledge class (School C) about the historical evolution of communication media. The class is given by their teacher, Elisabeth. Under the teacher's guidance, the students are trying to answer various questions in a written exercise. At a certain point, Elisabeth, makes a connection between the school subject matter (the functioning of a telegraph) and a cultural element supposed to be known by the students (in italics the BCE):

[2]   Elisabeth_16 (School C, translated from French)
1 Elisabeth   in comparison with today what is the difference?
2 Student 1   today it's direct
3 Elisabeth   SMS, internet mails, now it's direct, there is no interlocutor between (.) at that time even to call there was- did anybody see *Little House on the Prairie* when the shrew of the village runs the post office, there is a phone and she has to take all the calls and redirect them for example (.) don't you see ?
4 Students   yes yes
5 Elisabeth   well again the generation who saw *Little House on the Prairie*
6 Student 2   yes I have seen it
7 Elisabeth   and then she has small cables and then she puts the calls through to people but she's obliged to be there (.) the telegram it's a little bit the same except that from the post office [...] from the post office somebody had to go to the person

The BCE introduced by the teacher is a well-known and popular TV series (*Little House on the Prairie*), that has not been shown on TV for a long time. The students' feedback is limited to confirming that they know this TV series, and the exercise continues.

Let us take our three types of tensions as indicators of the way in which the teaching-learning framework is reconfigured by the BCE. Looking first at the tension between formal and informal knowledge, we see that the teacher borrowed a cultural element from outside the classroom and connected it with the school subject matter. *Little House on the Prairie* was taken as an illustration of the subject matter on which the lesson was focused; it anchored the history of communication media into something that was supposed to be known by the students and anticipated misunderstandings. By putting a familiar object at the service of an unfamiliar subject matter, the BCE created a bridge between two spheres of experience and was meant to facilitate the students' understanding of the subject matter.[5]

In so doing, the teacher focused on the subject matter, kept control over her own didactical goal and positioned herself as a teacher. Thus, as regards the second type of tension (object-focused vs. interaction-focused interactions), the framework was clearly on the side of object-focused interactions.

Considering finally the tension between identities outside and inside school, we see that by referring to a popular TV series within the classroom, the teacher did not only assume that her students were TV viewers who watched popular TV series, but also implicitly positioned herself, as well as her students, within a certain social space where these cultural elements had an implicit value. She let the students' identities outside school enter the classroom and used them as a support to make sense of the subject matter.

Briefly put, the teaching-learning framework that emerges from this BCE is focused on the subject matter, controlled by the teacher and acknowledges some aspects of the students' cultural practices outside the school. However, the BCE does not give way to a discussion. Therefore, from an observer's standpoint, it is difficult to tell whether or not it opened a potential appropriation space in which the students might use a TV series as a symbolic resource and appropriate the knowledge at stake. An observation of a longer time scale would be necessary to answer this question.

Example 2

The second example also belongs to a frequent profile (30 BCE sequences): the BCE is self-elicited and introduced by the teacher, and it gives way to a thematic development. Excerpt [3] is taken from a general knowledge class given by Eric, a teacher who puts great emphasis upon the quality of his relationships with his students. Just before this excerpt, the students watched a film called "War Photographer" (a documentary about the American photographer James Nachtwey), an activity that belongs to a teaching module concerning cinema. Before the projection, Eric confessed that each time he sees this movie, he is moved. After the projection, he questions his students about the film. A student gives his opinion (in italics the BCE):

[3]   Eric_151 (School C, translated from French)
1   Fabien   well I think that except for two or three images nothing was really
                very very shocking

---

[5] In the literature, a frequent assumption is that such a link is likely to help the student understand and make sense of the situation (Hedegaard & Chaiklin, 2005). However, there is also extensive literature that shows that "familiarity" is not always a facilitating factor and that it may also create confusions between various frames of reference (Rochex, 1998).

2	Eric	yeah it didn't move you to see for example this woman at the beginning in Kosovo who arrives and finds her house completely devastated?
3	Fabien	well I was rather moved to see people starving on the ground
4	Eric	yeah ?
5	Fabien	it happens in any country that's the way it is
6	Eric	*do you come from Italy?*
7	Fabien	yeah
8	Eric	north of Italy?
9	Fabien	yeah
10	Eric	do you have a house there?
11	Fabien	yes my grand-parents
12	Eric	yeah to what are you attached?
13	Fabien	oh not much because I don't go very often
14	Eric	yeah and here?
15	Fabien	here well yes it's my house
16	Eric	are you attached to your house?
17	Fabien	yes because I was born in it, I have been living there since I was very small
18	Eric	yeah what would you feel? Can't you put yourself in the place of this woman for example?
19	Fabien	yeah:: I could
20	Eric	but you're not moved, don't you give a damn about the other person's distress?
21	Fabien	it's not that I don't give a damn but it can happen to anybody, can't it.
22	Eric	(Student 2 raises his hand) yeah ?
23	Student 2	but what I'm saying is that this shocks me less than people who starve because now we've seen so much on the Iraq war, there were a lot of images of this, it's all – it's less shocking
24	Eric	you say on TV? The images you see?
25	Student 2	exactly, with the Iraq war yeah these images came again and again while images of persons who starve, we see them less
26	Eric	yeah so you were struck by images you're not used to seeing, is that right?
27	Student 2	yeah
28	Eric	and you ((name of a third student)) did you already see it last year?

Here, the BCE consists of a teacher's question about the student's biographical data (6: "Do you come from Italy?"). The teacher then asks further questions that gradually invite the student to adopt the point of view of a character in the film (a woman who lost her house during the war in Kosovo) and to justify the "morality" of his feelings.

How does this BCE reconfigure the teaching-learning framework? As regards the tension between informal and formal knowledge, we observe that the movie is not discussed as a cultural artefact that may be subjected to an analysis of, for example, the form of the film, the approach and ethics of a war photographer, the role of the images on public opinion, etc. It is not treated as a formal object of knowledge or, put differently, it is not conceptualised in a way that allows the student to apprehend it on a different way than in everyday life.

If we consider now the second type of tensions, the discussion between the teacher and the student is dominated both by the asymmetry of their status and, on a pragmatic level, by the power of questions (asking a question obliges the addressee to answer). However, there is a discrepancy between the highly asymmetrical management of their roles and the topic of the discussion: personal judgements and feelings. The teacher focuses upon the emotions that the student *should* feel and, consequently, gives a compulsory character to the very fact of feeling certain emotions. The focus of the discussion is not the film anymore but shifts on personal matters so that interpersonal relationships predominate. What happens here is more dominated by relation-focused interactions than by object-focused interactions.

This observation is directly linked to our third level of tensions. In fact, by questioning the student's personal life, the teacher refers to the student's identity outside school and threatens what Goffman (1971) calls the student's "territory" of the self (in this case, the student's home in Switzerland, his grand-parents' house in Italy). The teacher's and the student's personal identities are so deeply involved, their interpersonal relationships come so much to the forefront that for the student, criticising the movie amounts to a criticism of the teacher. Instead of treating the movie as a cultural element, the discussion concentrates on personal feelings and develops a slightly conflictual tone. In this context, the classmate's intervention (23) appears as a social and cognitive mediation. By inviting the teacher to shift his point of view and to adopt instead the role of a TV watcher who is regularly confronted with similar images (23, 25), the student brings new arguments that support his classmate's opinion and, indirectly, invites the teacher to share it.

This analysis shows that although in that case the BCE opened a discussion between the teacher and the students, the participants' emotional involvement did not open a space of reflection on the film itself, or even prevented the creation of such a space.

Example 3

The third example illustrates another frequent profile (23 BCE sequences): a student makes a BCE which is, directly or indirectly, elicited by the teacher and this BCE gives rise to a thematic development.

Excerpt [4] is taken from a philosophy class (School A). The class is given by their philosophy teacher Patrick. The lesson belongs to a teaching module on racism in which the teacher used a philosophical text by Jean-Paul Sartre, as well as a TV broadcast and newspaper articles. This blending of various sources reflected the teacher's goal: to use philosophy to stimulate the students' reflection in their everyday life. Just before Excerpt [4], Patrick and the students finished analysing a newspaper article about a proposed French law against racism. Patrick is about to move on to another activity when he notices two students talking together (in italics the BCE):

[4]   Patrick_89 (School A, translated from French)
1 Patrick   yeah! Were you on racism or what err …
2 Student 1
   Student 2   yeah, yeah !
3 Patrick   yeah ! (he smiles)
4 Student 1   we were talking about newspaper articles
5 Patrick   yeah law articles? ((mishearing))
6 Student 1   no, newspaper
7 Patrick   yeah, and then?
8 Student 1   we were talking about the fact that when we often read about people who are attacked, in Switzerland, just attacked in the street, often they write "by two Kosovars", "by two Albanese", etc. and then they don't specify it when they talk about Swiss people ((on the lips of the student sitting behind we can read "it's normal" and he smiles while looking at the video camera))
9 Patrick   definitely! Definitely! Hmm it's never written "attacked by an inhabitant of the ((name of a place in the region))" (everybody laughs) no but it's true, it's true, does it upset you?
10 Student 1   yeah, one should actually see how it is said, because if we make a difference between saying "I've been attacked by two Kosovars" xx and that we could also say "I've been attacked by two Swiss people", there is a difference saying "I have been attacked by two Kosovars" in the sense that it's just because they are two foreigners
11 Patrick   yeah, yeah I mean and the mass media in my opinion they have a terrible responsibility. I think it is very unjust it should be forbidden. Or one should give the origin every time. and even so, what does it mean? One induces a lot of things. Here I mean, err, the mass media, in order to create a sensation, they induce very strongly err.. provoke xenophobia, hmm, by giving this detail when it involves a foreigner, and at the end we see only this, hmm we see the titles "kosovar", "kosovar", "kosovar" (he looks at everybody) hmm, err, imagine the ((name of the local newspaper)): "bevaisan" ((inhabitants of a small village)), "bevaisan", "bevaisan", hmm after three years you say: "they are all crazy these "Bevaisans!" Hmm, no but I mean it's.. (long pause, he seems to be moved) yeah, yeah it strikes me also, that this is allowed by the law (…) because here we do exactly the thing that Sartre denounces, we put labels and we reduce individuals to their national label. And consequently we induce in the population a rejection of these nationalities

Contrary to Excerpt [3], the BCE introduced by the student consists of exporting a school subject matter outside the school context to make sense of a social phenomenon: racism. It reconfigures the teaching-learning framework in the following way: the informal object of knowledge introduced in the lesson (that is, the reference to how some newspapers report aggression acts, turn 8) goes beyond the subject matter but fulfils the teacher's aim (as we know from an interview with the teacher), that is, using philosophy to involve his students in a deeper reflection on the world and themselves. Discussing this informal piece of knowledge is not an end in itself, but is at the service of the subject matter.

Consequently, as regards the tension between object-focused interactions and relation-focused interactions, the balance is clearly on the side of the former, since the whole discussion remains focused on the topic of the lesson: racism. Moreover, the management of their roles is quite symmetric, as shows the fact that the teacher takes up the students' ideas as a matter for his own reflection.

Considering finally the tensions of identities inside and outside the school, the BCE introduced by the student leads both the teacher and the student to disclose their opinions towards media and racism, and to acknowledge their respective position on this topic. In so doing, they partly stray out of their institutional roles and publicly display other facets of their social identity. However, the fact that the discussion concerns the way in which newspapers report acts of violence does not lead them to disclose their opinions beyond this topic and the discussion is framed by the school situation in which they act. The fact that at a certain point (turn 8) a student makes a comment sotto voce ("it's normal") and smiles without being noticed (except by the video camera) shows that such BCE may also easily become face-threatening, either because all the students do not share the same opinion, or because some students might be tempted to tease the teacher and their classmates on such a sensitive topic.

In this case, the BCE reconfigures the teaching-learning framework in such a way that the dialogue between the teacher and the student becomes a potential appropriation space. Cultural elements mobilised in the whole teaching module (Sartre's text, the text of a new law) have been used as resources that create opportunities for both the students and the teacher to construct new representations, and to share them.

DISCUSSION AND OPENING

The aim of the study reported in this chapter was to examine the way in which cultural elements which are taught in three disciplines, literature, philosophy and general knowledge, may be used as symbolic resources by students to aid learning and development. In order to do so, we analysed boundary crossing events, namely links between a cultural element taught in the class and an external element. According to our hypothesis, these BCE are part of a sequence that allows us to observe how the teacher and the students manage the tensions between, on the one hand activities, identities and bodies of knowledge that exist within the class framework and, on the other hand, those existing in different social contexts. More specifically, our aim was to examine how these BCE contribute to reshaping the teaching-learning framework and to opening a potential appropriation space, a space where learning may occur.

Our observations of classroom interactions showed that there are two different types of BCE: the first consists of connecting a school subject matter with a cultural element, a personal experience or a social phenomenon, that are relevant for the student outside the class, and may be used to confer a personal sense to the taught element. The second type, which has received less attention in the literature, consists of using the cultural element taught in the class to make sense of a personal experience, knowledge or skill, or a social phenomenon. To identify situations in which the BCE might enable the students to engage in personal sense-making of the issues at stake, we were attentive to potential appropriation spaces thereby created.

The first type of BCE was presented in our first example, where a teacher referred to a cultural element assumed to be known by the students and invited them to use it as a resource in order to make sense of a school subject matter. This BCE was entirely managed and controlled by the teacher and did not provoke the students' participation. There was no obvious way in which the students made sense of the cultural elements brought by the teacher, so that it was difficult to tell whether a potential appropriation space had been opened at all.

The two other cases belonged to the second type of BCE, in which the cultural element taught at school was used to make sense of an event out of school. In the second example, we reported a case in which a BCE threatened the participants' face. The cultural element presented in the lesson (a documentary) had a very strong personal sense for the teacher but not for one of the students. It opened a discussion that was not far from conflictual and did not lead to a reflection on the documentary as a cultural artefact. The fact that the BCE involved a strong emotional dimension seems to have hindered the development of a potential appropriation space. In contrast, in the third example, the BCE was introduced by two students, and it opened a discussion between the teacher and one of the students. The students connected the cultural element studied in class (the text of a proposed law against racism) with a social phenomenon, the way in which newspapers sometimes report aggressive incidents involving foreigners. This BCE opened a discussion between the students and the teacher, and led to what seemed to be a potential space of appropriation in which the teacher and the students engaged in a joint reflection.

We thus hope to have shown that BCE sequences are privileged moments to observe how a teaching-learning framework is reconfigured and may, under some conditions, enable students to use cultural elements taught at school as symbolic resources and open a potential appropriation space. Further analysis of these conditions is also required to understand how these results might be used in the teaching-learning practices.

APPENDIX: EXCERPTS IN ORIGINAL FRENCH LANGUAGE

[1]

Ralph	ouais mais il n'y aurait pas certaines exceptions dans ce qu'il dit ?
Paul	ben c'est-à-dire euh [...]
Ralph	je sais pas par exemple les histoires comme Robin des Bois

[2]

1	Elisabeth	par rapport à maintenant c'est quoi la différence ?
2	Elève1	maintenant c'est direct
3	Elisabeth	sms internet mails, maintenant c'est direct il n'y a pas d'interlocuteur entre (.) à l'époque même pour téléphoner il y avait- personne n'as vu dans La petite maison dans la prairie quand la mégère du village elle tient le bureau de post qu'il y a le téléphone et puis elle doit prendre tous les appels et les rediriger par exemple (.) vous voyez pas ?
4	Elèves	si oui oui
5	Elisabeth	ben de nouveau les générations qui ont vu « La Petite maison dans la prairie »
6	Elève 2	si j'ai vu
7	Elisabeth	et puis elle a des petits câbles et puis elle fait passer le téléphone chez les gens mais elle est obligée d'être là (.) le télégramme c'est un peu la même chose sauf qu'il faut qu'en plus du bureau de poste (s'interrompt et interpelle un élève qui parle) sauf qu'il faut en plus que depuis le bureau de poste quelqu'un ait chez la personne

[3]

1	Patrick	ouais ! Vous étiez au racisme ou bien euh..
2	Elèves 1+2	ouais, ouais !
3	Patrick	ouais ! (il sourit)
4	Elève 1	on parlait des articles de journaux
5	Patrick	ouais des articles de loi ? (il a mal compris)
6	Elève 1	non de journaux
7	Patrick	ouais c'est-à-dire ?
8	Elève 1	on parlait de quand on voit souvent des gens qui se font attaquer, en Suisse, agressés comme ça dans la rue, souvent ils mettent « par deux Kosovars », « par deux Albanais », etc., et puis ils ne précisent pas quand ils parlent de Suisses ((un élève au fond de la classe fait une remarque que l'on peut lire sur ses lèvres « c'est normal », le maître ne le remarque pas))
9	Patrick	tout à fait ! tout à fait ! hein, c'est jamais marqué « agressé par un habitant du Val de Travers » (tout le monde rit) non mais c'est vrai, c'est vrai, et ça vous choque ça ?
10	Elève 1	ben ouais, en fait faut voir comment c'est dit, parce que si, on fait la différence par exemple en disant euh « on s'est fait agresser par deux Kosovars xx pis que on pourrait aussi dire « on s'est fait agresser par deux Suisses », il y a une différence de dire « je me suis fait agresser par deux Kosovars » dans le sens que c'est juste parce que c'est deux étrangers
11	Patrick	ouais ouais j'entends, et les mass mes à mon avis là ont une sacrée responsabilité. Moi je trouve ça très malsain ça devrait être interdit. Ou alors il faudrait donner à chaque fois l'origine.. et même qu'est-ce que ça veut dire hein ? On induit pas mal de choses. Là j'entends euh, les mass mes, pour faire du sensationnel, induisent très fortement euh.. provoquent la xénophobie, hein, en mettant cette précision-là quand il s'agit d'un étranger, et on ne voit plus que ça finalement, hein on voit les titres « kosovar », « kosovar », « kosovar » (il regarde tout le monde dans un mouvement circulaire puisque les bureaux sont en U), hein euh, imaginez-vous dans l'Express: « bevaisan », « bevaisan », « bevaisan », hein au bout de trois ans vous dites : « ils sont tous fous ces Bevaisans ! ». Hein, non mais j'entends c'est.. (il regarde l'élève qui a soulevé la question) (longue pause, il réfléchit, semble touché) ouais ouais ça me frappe aussi ça, que ça soit permis par la loi (...) parce que là, on fait exactement hein quelque chose que dénonce Sartre, on met des étiquettes et on réduit les individus à

29

leur étiquette nationale. Et donc, on induit par là dans la population, un rejet de ces nationalités-là

[4]

1	Elève 1	ben je trouve qu'à part deux trois images il n'y avait rien de vraiment très très choquant
2	Eric	ouais ça vous a pas ému de voir par exemple cette femme au début au Kosovo qui arrive et qui trouve sa maison complètement dévastée ?
3	Elève 1	ben :: non ça m'a plutôt ému de voir les gens qui mourraient de faim parterre
4	Eric	ouais ?
5	Elève 1	ça arrive dans chaque pays donc voilà quoi
6	Eric	vous êtes italien d'origine vous ?
7	Elève 1	ouais
8	Eric	du nord de l'Italie
9	Elève 1	ouais
10	Eric	vous avez une maison là-bas ?
11	Elève 1	ouais mes grands-parents
12	Eric	ouais vous êtes attaché à quoi ?
13	Elève 1	oh pas grand chose parce que j'y vais pas souvent
14	Eric	ouais et puis ici ?
15	Elève 1	ici ben ouais c'est ma maison
16	Eric	vous êtes attaché à votre maison ?
17	Elève 1	ben ouais parce que je suis né dedans je suis là-bas depuis que je suis tout petit
18	Eric	ouais qu'est-ce que ça vous ferait vous ? vous arrivez pas à vous mettre à la place de cette femme par exemple ?
19	Elève 1	ouais :: oui je pourrais
20	Eric	mais ça vous émeut pas la détresse des autres vous vous en foutez ?
21	Elève 1	C'est pas une question que je m'en fous mais ça arrive à tout le monde voilà
22	Eric	(Elève 2 lève la main) ouais ?
23	Elève 2	mais moi je dis que moi ça me choque moins ça que des personnes qui meurent de faim parce que surtout maintenant on voyait la guerre en Irak il y avait beaucoup d'images de ça c'est tout c'était moins choquant
24	Eric	vous dites à la télé les images que vous voyez
25	Elève 2	voilà avec la guerre en Irak ouais ces images qui revenaient souvent tandis que des images de personnes qui meurent de faim on voit moins.
26	Eric	ouais donc vous, vous avez été frappé par des images que vous aviez pas l'habitude de voir c'est ça ?
27	Elève 2	ouais
28	Eric	et vous, vous l'avez déjà vu l'an dernier ?

ACKNOWLEDGEMENTS

The research project "Uses of literary and philosophical texts as symbolic resources: socialisation and development of young people in secondary school", was funded by the Swiss National Research Foundation (project 100013-116040/1), led by Tania Zittoun and Michèle Grossen, with the collaboration of Christophe Matthey and Sheila Padiglia (University of Neuchâtel). The authors would also like to thank Olivia Lempen (University of Lausanne) who participated in the collection of the data, as well as the school authorities, the teachers who agreed to participate in this study, and the students.

Correspondence should be addressed to Michèle Grossen, Department of Psychology, University of Lausanne, BFSH 2, CH-1015 Lausanne, Switzerland; e-mail: michele.grossen@unil.ch.

REFERENCES

Abreu, G. de (1995). Understanding how children experience the relationship between home and school mathematics. *Mind, Culture and Activity Theory: An International Journal, 2,* 119-142.

Beach, K. (2003). Consequential transitions: A developmental view of knowledge propagation through social organizations. In T. Tuomi-Grohn & Y. Engeström (Eds.), *Between school and work: New perspectives on transfer and instruction. The meaning of discourse for the construction of knowledge* (pp. 21-34). Amsterdam: Elsevier Science.

Brown, A. L. (1997). Transforming schools into communities of thinking and learning about serious matters. *American Psychologist, 52,* 399-413.

Bruner, J. (2002). Making stories: Law, literature, life. London: Farrar, Straus & Giroux.

Coulon, A. (2005). *Le métier d'étudiant* [The student's job]. Paris: Economica/Anthropos.

Goffman, E. (1971). *Relations in public: Microstudies of the public order.* New York: Harper and Row.

Grossen, M. (2000). Institutional framing in thinking, learning and teaching. In H. Cowie & G. van der Aalsvoort (Eds.), *Social interaction in learning and instruction: The meaning of discourse for the construction of knowledge* (pp. 21-34). Permagon Press.

Grossen, M. (2009). Social interaction, discourse and learning. Methodological challenges of an emergent transdisciplinary field. In K. Kumpulainen, C. E. Hmelo-Silver, & M. César (Eds.), *Investigating classroom interactions. Methodologies in action* (pp. 263-275). Rotterdam: Sense.

Grossen, M., & Bachmann, K. (2000). Learning to collaborate in a peer-tutoring situation: Who learns? What is learned? *European Journal of Psychology of Education, 15*(4), 491-508.

Grossen, M., & Salazar Orvig, A. (2011). Third parties' voices in a therapeutic interview. *Text & Talk, 31*(1), 53-76.

Hedegaard, M. (2009). Children's development from a cultural–historical approach: Children's activity in everyday local settings as foundation for their development. *Mind, Culture and Activity, 16*(1), 64-82.

Hedegaard, M., & Chaiklin, S. (2005). *Radical-local teaching and learning.* Aarhus: Aarhus University Press.

Hermans, H. J. M. (2002). The dialogical self as a society of mind. *Theory & Psychology, 12*(2), 147–160.

Kumpulainen, K., Hmelo-Silver, C. E., & César, M. (2009). *Investigating classroom interaction: Methodologies in action.* Rotterdam: Sense.

Littleton, K. (2000). Rethinking collaborative learning: An overview. In R. Joiner, K. Littleton, D. Faulkner, & D. Miell (Eds.), *Rethinking collaborative learning* (pp. 248-258). London: Free association books.

Littleton, K., Rojas-Drummond, S. M., & Miell, D. (2008). Creative collaborations: Sociocultural perspectives [Special issue]. *Journal of Thinking Skills and Creativity, 3*(3).

Marková, I. (2003). *Dialogicality and social representations. The dynamics of mind.* Cambridge, MA: Cambridge University Press.

Mercer, N. (2000). *Words and minds: How we use language to think together.* London: Routledge.

Miller, P. J., Hoogstra, L., Mintz, J., Fung, H., & Williams, K. (1993). Troubles in the garden and how they get resolved: A young child's transformation of his favourite story. In C. A. Nelson (Ed.), *Memory and affect in development* (Vol. 26, pp. 87-114). Hillsdale, NJ: Lawrence Erlbaum.

Perret-Clermont, A. (2004). The thinking spaces of the young. In A. Perret-Clermont, C. Pontecorvo, L. Resnick, T. Zittoun, & B. Burge (Eds.), *Joining society: Social interactions and learning in adolescence and youth* (pp. 3-10). Cambridge, MA: Cambridge University Press.

Perret-Clermont, A. (2009). Introduction. In M. César & K. Kumpulainen (Eds.), *Social interactions in multicultural settings* (pp. 1-12). Rotterdam: Sense.

Perret-Clermont, A.-N., Carugati, F., & Oates, J. (2004). A socio-cognitive perspective on learning and cognitive development. In J. Oates & A. Grayson (Eds.), *Cognitive and language development in children* (pp. 303-332). London: The Open University & Blackwell.

Renshaw, P. D. (1998). Community of practice classrooms and the new capitalism-alignment or resistance. *Discourse: Studies in the Cultural Politics of Education, 19*(3), 365-370.

Resnick, L. B., Säljö, R., Pontecorvo, C., & Burge, B. (Eds.). (1997). *Discourse, tools and reasoning: Essays on situated cognition.* Berlin: Springer.

Rochex, J. (1998). *Le sens de l'expérience scolaire* [Making sense of school experience]. Paris: Presses Universitaires de France.

Rochex, J. (2004). *La notion de rapport au savoir: Convergences et débats théoriques* [The notion of representation of knowing: Convergences and theoretical debates]. *Pratiques Psychologiques, 10*(2), 93-106.

Rojas-Drummond, S. M., Mazón, N., Fernandez, M., & Wegerif, R. (2006). Explicit reasoning, creativity and co-construction in primary school children's collaborative activities. *Journal of Thinking Skills and Creativity, 1*(2), 84-94.

Säljö, R. (2003). Epilogue: From transfer to boundary-crossing. In T. Tuomi-Gröhn, & Y. Engström (Eds.), *Between school and work: New perspectives on transfer and boundary-crossing* (pp. 311-321). Amsterdam: Pergamon.

Tuomi-Gröhn, T., Engeström, Y., & Young, M. (2003). From transfer to boundary-crossing between school and work. In T. Tuomi-Gröhn, & Y. Engström (Eds.) *Between school and work: New perspectives on transfer and boundary-crossing* (pp. 1-15). Kidlington, UK: Elsevier Science.

Valsiner, J. (2007). *Culture in minds and societies: Foundations of cultural psychology.* New Delhi: Sage.

Valsiner, J. (2008). Open intransitivity cycles in development and education: Pathways to synthesis. *European Journal of Psychology of Education, 23*(2), 131-147.

Valsiner, J. (2009). Cultural psychology today: Innovations and oversights. *Culture Psychology, 15*(1), 5-39.

Vygotsky, L. S. (1986). *Thought and language* (Revised edition). Cambridge, MA: The MIT Press. (original publication 1934).

Walker, D., & Nocon, H. (2007). Boundary-crossing competence: Theoretical considerations and educational design. *Mind, Culture, and Activity, 14*(3), 178.

Wenger, J. E. (1998). *Communities of practice: Learning, meaning, and identity.* Cambridge: Cambridge University Press.

Wertsch, J. (1991). *Voices of the mind: A socio-cultural approach to mediated action.* London: Harvester Wheatsheaf.

Winnicott, D. W. (2001). *Playing and reality.* Philadelphia, Sussex: Routledge (original publication 1971).

Zittoun, T. (2004). Pre apprenticeship as a transitional space. In A.-N. Perret-Clermont, C. Pontecorvo, L. Resnick, T. Zittoun, & B. Burge (Eds.), *Joining Society: Social interaction and learning in adolescence and youth* (pp. 153-176). Cambridge, NY: Cambridge University Press.

Zittoun, T. (2006). *Transitions. Development through symbolic resources.* Greenwich (CT): Information Age Publishing.

Zittoun, T. (2008). Development through transitions. *European Journal of Psychology of Education, 23*(2), 165-182.

Zittoun, T. (2010). How does an object become symbolic? Rooting semiotic artefacts in dynamic shared experiences. In B. Wagoner (Ed.), *Symbolic transformations. The mind in movement through culture and society* (pp. 173-192). London: Routledge.

Zittoun, T., Duveen, G., Gillespie, A., Ivinson, G., & Psaltis, C. (2003). The uses of symbolic resources in transitions. *Culture & Psychology, 9(4)*, 415-448.

Michèle Grossen
Department of Psychology
University of Lausanne, Switzerland

Tania Zittoun
Institute of Psychology of Education
University of Neuchâtel, Switzerland

Jenny Ros
Department of Psychology
University of Lausanne, Switzerland

EVANGELIA PROKOPIOU, TONY CLINE AND GUIDA DE ABREU

4. RETHINKING ETHNIC MINORITY YOUNG PEOPLE'S PARTICIPATION IN MULTIPLE SOCIOCULTURAL CONTEXTS AND ITS IMPACT ON THEIR CULTURAL IDENTITIES

INTRODUCTION

Back in 1979, Urie Bronfenbrenner proposed his ecological model of human development, a multi-level system which describes how individuals relate with their multiple social contexts. In 1991, Carl Ratner proposed a modification of Bronfenbrenner's basic model in which the layers are pictured as interpenetrating. This illustrates how the macrosystem passes through an individual's exosystems and microsystems and how the impacts of all these systems influence the development of an individual. However, although both versions of the model illustrate well how individuals are connected with their multiple contexts they are still models that have a monolithic image of society. What happens in the case of ethnic minority children and young people who are members of a pluralistic society?

To illustrate the complexity of the macrosystem in pluralistic societies and its impact on the development of identities of young people from minority ethnic background in this chapter we explore how second and third generation British-born young people of Pakistani and Greek-Cypriot origin perceive themselves as ethnic minority pupils in both community and mainstream education as well as in their role as members of the wider society. More specifically, we are interested to understand the dialogues that are established between the young people and their school and cultural communities' contexts and the impact these may have on the young people's developing cultural identities.

Community schooling is extra voluntary education developed and run by ethnic minority communities outside of mainstream provision. Community schools are organized mainly on Saturdays and Sundays but can be held on weekdays after mainstream school. These schools are to be found mainly in accommodation that is rented or made available in mainstream school settings, community centres, mosques or churches. Although community schools have been an important component of the educational experience of many ethnic minority children for as long as each ethnic minority community has been settled in Britain, they only gained governmental recognition in the 1970s and 1980s (Robertson, 2005). In

E. Hjörne et al. (eds.), Learning, Social Interaction and Diversity – Exploring Identities in School Practices, 35–52.

2006, the Department for Children, Schools and Families estimated that there were at least 5,000 community schools operating nationally. However, as there is no national community schools' directory, it is not possible to give an accurate figure for the number of community schools in Britain (Strand, 2002).

As never before in our world's history, most individuals and groups live in multicultural contexts and more and more people from various cultural groups are constantly crossing cultural boundaries and coming to intercultural contact through travelling, immigrating, et cetera (Anthias, 2001; Bhatia & Ram, 2001, 2004; Dien, 2000; Ferdman, 2000; Hermans & Kempen, 1998; Hermans, 2001; Rassool, 1999). In this context, the concept of cultural identity and questions regarding its development within such multicultural contexts have attracted a good deal of attention from theorists in the last two decades. Britain, for example, has experienced the growth of diverse immigrant groups, especially groups of Commonwealth immigrants, who came over during the post-war period. Their children comprise successive generations of British-born young people from ethnic minority backgrounds who in turn are now an important and permanent feature of contemporary British society (Anthias, 2001). Rassool (1999) emphasized the heterogeneity of ethnic minority groups in Britain who as he argues "comprise a rich tapestry of cultural, linguistic and historical experiences grounded in different diasporas that, in turn, have developed within specific socio-historic contexts" (Rassool, 1999, p. 26). Moghaddam (2002) argues that for the ethnic minority people who come to live in a new host society, the construction of a new identity is fundamentally important for them and part of a process of integration within the mainstream society. In the same line of argument we can argue that for second or third generation young people- that is, "children of immigrants born and brought up in host countries" (Vertovec, 2001, p. 577) and children of children of immigrants born and raised in their grandparents' host countries respectively- the constant construction and re-construction of their cultural identities through their interaction with the multiple cultural communities they belong to, is of equal paramount importance.

A common characteristic of the research on community schools in the UK to date (Martin, Creese & Bhatt, 2003; Bhatt, Bhojani, Creese & Martin, 2004; Robertson, 2005; Creese & Martin, 2006; Creese, Bhatt, Bhojani & Martin, 2006; Prokopiou & Cline, 2010) is that these studies have referred to these schools' contribution both to education and to the sociocultural development of ethnic minority children and young people. The analysis of the findings in Greek and Pakistani schools that is reported here highlights the value of examining community schools within contrasting communities. When we think of community schools, we should also contextualize them within their communities and take into consideration each community's own developmental trajectory in relation to both its origins and mainstream society. By acknowledging the different developmental pathways taken by different minority communities in mainstream society, this chapter suggests that community schools in Britain are developing in different ways in response to the distinctive needs and goals of each minority community.

THEORETICAL BACKGROUND

To theorise the influence of multiple heterogeneous contexts we revisit and elaborate Bonfrenbrenner's model. In addition, we will draw on dialogical self theory (Hermans 2001) and cultural developmental theory (Valsiner 2000) to understand the cultural and dialogical nature of the processes through which ethnic minority young people develop their identities in community schools.

Cultural Developmental Theory

The co-constructivist cultural developmental theory views a person's psychological development as co-constructed by individuals and their sociocultural worlds or jointly constructed by the two (Valsiner, 2000). For Valsiner (1989), the developmental process can be distinguished into the social and the individual level which "proceed over time in a mutually interdependent way" (Valsiner, 1989, p. 507) and change can be promoted by their transaction. This perspective views human development as a dynamic process that involves multiple levels of bi-directional transactions between individuals and the multiple heterogenous contexts in which they participate. Valsiner (2000) points out that it is necessary to examine the history of complex psychological phenomena in order to understand how they have come to be developed in their present forms and how they may be developed in the future. In a similar vein, Ferdman (2000) argued that the construction of identities should be studied in a framework of specific historic and cultural realities. In effect, Ferdman defined the task as not only asking "who am I?" but also "*why* am I who I am"? This point is important because it helps to clarify why minority individuals from different groups make sense of themselves in the way they do. In other words, *why* did they come to have the identities that they do? In what ways do those individuals' place in a specific historical context influence the way they make sense of themselves?

Dialogical Self Theory

Dialogical self theory (Hermans, 2001) offers a dynamic view of identities development by paying attention to the interaction between individuals and their sociocultural environments. It offers a very useful conceptual tool to understand the cultural and dialogical nature of the processes through which ethnic minority young people develop their identities in both community and mainstream schools. Identity construction is viewed as a process which an individual constantly constructs and reconstructs through an ongoing dialogue between the person and others, a process characterized by being subject to changes in the sociocultural as well as historical contexts.

From a dialogical self theory standpoint the traditional identity question of "who am I?" should be rephrased as "who am I in relation to the other?", and "who is the other in relation to me?" (Hermans, 2003, p. 104). These rephrased questions imply that one's sense of identity is influenced by his or her relationships with others. Our understanding of this process of influence is increased when the importance of others in one's sense of identity is acknowledged and explored as being part of one's self-system (Hermans, 2003). From a dialogical self theoretical perspective, a theory of personal and cultural positioning, Hermans (2001) conceptualized self or identity and culture in terms of a multiplicity of voiced positions among which dialogical relationships can develop. In his account, internal positions are positions that are perceived by the individuals as part of themselves (e.g. I as an ethnic minority child) and external positions are positions that are perceived by the individuals as part of the environment (e.g. my community school becomes important to me because it helps me to feel proud of my cultural background). External positions refer to other people and objects in the environment that the individuals perceive as relevant from the perspective of some of their internal positions (e.g., I feel an ethnic minority child because I am attending a community school) and they usually are considered as *mine* (Hermans, 2003). In this theory internal positions receive their relevance from their relation to some of the external positions. All these internal and external positions are part of the self (I-positions) and their significance is derived from their mutual transactions over time. Thus there is a hypothesized process in which:

a) The self is constructed within the landscape of *self-in-relations* both internal and external and populated by other people's voices (Hermans, 2003; Valsiner, 2004; Ho, Chan, Peng & Ng, 2001).
b) The self is divided into functional constituent parts of mutually related components (I-positions) (Valsiner, 2004).
c) These I-positions create voices which relate to other voices which in turn are linked with other I-positions (multivoiced identity).
d) Within this *dialogical arena*, I-positions are constantly constructed, reconstructed and relocated by the individual within a specific space-time field which is historically and culturally contextualized and characterized by power differences (Hermans & Kempen, 1993; Hermans, 2003; Valsiner, 2004).

Many authors from both a cultural developmental and dialogical perspective (e.g., Bhatia & Ram 2001, 2004; Hermans & Kempen, 1998) have argued that much of the literature on immigrant identity has tended to see ethnic minority young people as being in between their two cultures (minority and host). In contrast, the standpoint of cultural developmental and dialogical theories entails a dynamic perspective on the identities of ethnic minority young people. From this standpoint, their identities should not be studied just as static comparisons between various "beings" (Valsiner 2004, p. 9), i.e. being Pakistani or Greek versus being British, but rather as a process through which they are in a constant negotiation of the many aspects that constitute their multiple cultural identities, e.g. I as a Muslim, I as a Pakistani, I as British, etc.

THE CONTEXT AND METHODOLOGICAL APPROACH

The Schools and the Communities

In order to explore how second and third generation British-born young people of Pakistani and Greek-Cypriot origin perceive themselves as ethnic minority pupils in both community and mainstream schools as well as members of their society, we draw on field work conducted in a Pakistani school and a Greek-Cypriot school in England.

The Pakistani school was founded more than 10 years ago and is based at a large mainstream school in a small multiethnic south midlands town in England with a student population of over 60 pupils at the time the research took place. The school works with 4 to 18 year old pupils, mainly of Pakistani origin but also from other Muslim backgrounds such as Bangladeshi, Turkish and Somali. It offers Arabic, GCSE Urdu, GCSE Islamic Studies and a range of mainstream curricular subjects, mainly English and mathematics as well as preparation for 11+ entrance exams and annual national assessments in mainstream schools (SATs). Additional subjects include arts and crafts, study skills and a variety of PSE topics all presented within a culturally relevant context. The school runs every Saturday. A group of 10 to 12 teachers and volunteers make up the staff team, supported by an active management and parents' committee. The school has been partially funded through the local authority that supports the work of other ethnic minority voluntary and community based schools and classes in this town.

The Greek school was founded over 20 years ago in a metropolitan area in England and operates in a large mainstream school. Almost 300 children from 4 to 17 years of age attended the school at the time of the research. The teachers come from Cyprus and Greece and there are classes from nursery up to and including A-Level classes (Greek literature and language). The school follows a syllabus which has been prepared by the Ministries of Education of Cyprus and Greece designed specifically for Greeks who live abroad. The leaving certificates issued by the school are recognised by the ministries of Cyprus and Greece. The school runs every Saturday and on a weekday and is partially self-funded through tuition fees but mainly supported, especially in terms of teaching staff salaries, by the Greek and Cypriot Educational Missions.

In the following paragraphs a brief overview of the migration histories is presented with the aim of supporting the interpretation of the analysis later in this chapter. The mass migration of Pakistanis to Britain started in the late 1950s and early 1960s (Anwar, 1979). The main reasons for their migration were, on the one hand, Britain's need for manual unskilled workers and on the other hand the immigrants' need to find employment and economic security as well as the colonial links with the host country (Anwar, 1979). The Pakistani community is a heterogeneous community which differs with regards to the areas of Pakistan (e.g., Punjab, Kashmir) with which families most closely identify. Nearly all British Pakistanis are Muslims but they vary in the ways they practice Islam. The Pakistani community is also a diverse community in terms of socio-economic status. In London and the South East, some of the Pakistani communities are well established and their educational achievement is on the same level with, or higher than, the national average. In the West Midlands and the North, many communities have been affected by unemployment, poverty, and social exclusion, and the educational achievement in Pakistani communities is much lower than the national average (RAISE Project). Recent reports (e.g. Ahmad 2006; Stone, Muir & Smith, 2004) indicate the impact of the rise in Islamophobia in Britain after the terrorist attacks in New York on 9/11/2001 on British-Muslims. As Ahmad (2006) pointed out "within minutes of the planes crashing into the twin towns in New York, Islam and terrorism became inseparable, inextricably linked" (Ahmad, 2006, p. 962).

Large-scale Greek-Cypriot migration to Britain started during the last decade of British colonial rule on the island, in the 1950s and 1960s, mainly for economic reasons. However, the Greek-Cypriot community in Britain expanded significantly after the Turkish invasion of the island of Cyprus in 1974. In general, the Greek-Cypriot community is considered to be a well-established and socio-economically successful community with the majority of Greek-Cypriots in business and the professions (Papapavlou & Pavlou, 2001).

The Research Method

The main tool for data collection was episodic interviewing (Flick, 2000) which was used to assess the pupils' experiences and perceptions and to understand the underlying dynamics of their community schools and their impact on the pupils' developing identities. Individual drawings and group work were used as complementary tools. Interviews took place either on the schools' premises or at participants' homes, depending on their preference. The interviews started by familiarizing the interviewee with this specific form of interview, e.g. "In this interview, I will ask you to recount situations in your community school" (Flick, 2000) and a clarification of the interview procedure including information regarding the duration of the interview and ethical issues such as confidentiality, anonymity and the right to withdraw.

The participants were 16 students of Pakistani and Greek/Greek-Cypriot origin with a record of long term attendance at these schools. The students, both girls and boys, were adolescents aged 13 to 18 years, eight in each school. In the Pakistani school, of the eight participants, for five of them both parents were born overseas while for three of them one of the parents was born in England and the other overseas. In the Greek school, of the eight participants, two were second generation and two were third generation ethnic minority young persons while for two, one of the parents was born in England and the other in Greece and for the other two, one of the parents was born in England and the other in Cyprus.

The Analytical Framework

The data presented here are selective and draw on the episodic interviews with the young people in both schools. The participants' views were analysed based on their responses to the following three I-positions:

(a) I as an ethnic minority student in my Pakistani/ Greek community school;
(b) I as an ethnic minority student in my mainstream school;
(c) I as being of a Pakistani/Greek background in the UK.

We then present selectively the most dominant voices that were created through that positioning. The final step was to abstract the *import* (see Todoulou-Polemi, Vassiliou & Vassiliou, 1998; Vassiliou & Vassiliou, 1981) of each extract, that is the minimum description of it, which preserves the essence of what the young people said, and arrange these imports in sequence, in order, by presenting their views rather than our interpretation, to reveal the dialogical character of their voices.

The voice is a phenomenological construct with theoretical implications which allows us to identify the various relations between parts, I-positions, with the whole, self (Valsiner, 2004). Thus the voices act as characters interacting in a story, unfolding their experiences from their own standpoint while they agree, disagree and negotiate with each other (Hermans, 2003). All these oppositions and conflicts indicate the discontinuity of self but at the same time they are still part of the same continuous self (Hermans, 2003).

THE ANALYSIS

Pakistani school

School Contexts
In the following section we will explore an internal position of these young persons – "I as an ethnic minority person" and its relation to their external position – "my community/mainstream school" – and identify the important processes that take place within the arena of dialogue of those I-positions.

I-position: I as an ethnic minority student in my Pakistani community school
For the young people in this school the voice of being *similar* to their community school's cultural community has emerged as a powerful voice which has taken centre stage. The majority of them talked through the I-position of being Muslims and thus they highly valued the religious aspect of their cultural identities. For them, being a Muslim at their community school helps them to define themselves in contrast to the multicultural context of the mainstream school and facilitates their identity development by encouraging the sharing of their common cultural and religious practices among others who are familiar with them.

Voice 1: the similar
I: and to be, you know, British of a Pakistani origin in your X. school how is it for you?

Bibi: I think it's … sometimes I can be like … umm … like 'yeah' because sometimes in the schools [we] are used to surrounded by other people who aren't like British-Pakistanis or something and they just sometimes they just don't get you so sometimes it's like be like "oh, I wish I wasn't here, I have to explain this over and over again" so when you go to that school like the next day at community school it's like "oh … [happy …] I think these people are like me …" so especially like in Eid times and Ramadan times it's just … feel happy with people there because they just know what are you're doing, what you are about, you don't be constantly explain so yeah …

I-Position: I as an ethnic minority student in my mainstream school
One of the most important voices that were created through their position "I as an ethnic minority student in my mainstream school" was the voice of *normality* which was approached through different I-positioning. To give an example, one young person perceived herself as a "normal" person in her mainstream school by positioning herself within her minority community's context and relating herself to her community's religious and cultural practices, even when others found that odd.

Voice 2: being normal but weird for others
I: and what do the other young people in the English school like?
Nahid: They are … because they are not like the same culture as me … sometimes, some of the stuff I might like do like … they find it a bit weird, like … say if we had a […] day, then say someone is like … like … no it may be not like … you know … but … but like when I wear henna sometimes, I find that […] and they say like "Oh why did you put on henna?" or like "where did you get it from? Where did you buy it from?" … they would say like … "Oh, why do you put on henna and how long does it last?" and that stuff … I'll find that a bit, like, normal to wear henna because I can always like mainly on Eid and […] I do tend to wear some … it's just too normal …

As seen above, Nahid thought that it is normal for her as a British-Muslim young person to wear henna while she is at her mainstream school. However, her fellow classmates think that she is weird. If Nahid was only living within her minority community context or in a Muslim country this conflict would not have been present because it is normal to wear henna. In a British school however, Nahid is projecting the general attitude (Abbey, 2004) towards her situation which creates the classifications *weird* and *normal*. Thus, this young girl within that context felt confusion in her identity construction through going back and forth with different symbolic meanings about her identity. From that position, Nahid's internal position "I'll find that a bit, like, normal to wear henna" is discrepant with her external position that her classmates "find it a bit weird", something that might be an indication of internal conflict in relation to her developing identities.

Community context
In the following section we will explore an internal position of these young people – "I as an ethnic minority person" and its relation to their external position – "my mainstream community" -and identify the important processes that take place within the arena of dialogue of those I-positions.

I-Position: I as being of a Pakistani background in the UK

When the young people talked through their I-positions of being members of their minority community, they voiced their views about being members of a minority community which is negatively stereotyped and discriminated against. In general, they thought that the mainstream community have stereotypical views of Pakistanis as underachievers who lack the competence to speak English, have low income, lack education, create cultural barriers and are associated with high crime and terrorism.

Voice 3: the negatively stereotyped person

I: and, if I'll ask you now how do you feel living in England, in this country?

Fahim: good … yeah, okay, good … probably … apart from like a bit of racism….apart from that it's okay.

I: do you have an example, you know, can you give me a situation where you … could be personal or not personal …

Fahim: well, it's … like be harder for me to find a job than a white person with the same qualifications …

I: are you afraid of that?

Fahim: not really … but probably when I get there they might be … obstacles in the way plus there're … there're *lot* of anti-Muslim feelings emerging.

I: and how this makes you feel?

Fahim: it's always … sometimes is like … I don't want to make it obvious, say I'm a Muslim … well, like terrorism

As is evident in the above interview extract, Fahim chose to hide his Muslim identity when this identity was threatened. For him, being negatively stereotyped generated fears resulting in the need for the religious aspect of his cultural identity to become "invisible". At this point we could argue that Fahim's need is in accordance with Stuart Hall's suggestion that when a struggle starts against "otherness" some people choose not to be visible as "other" (Hall, 2006). As is evident in his interview extract, Fahim's response to the conflict between his internal and external positions was to "choose" not to make it obvious that he is a Muslim.

Voice 4: The multiple "I"

Fahim: If I was white I'd lack a certain group of friends so certain like *a set* of like opportunities and experiences, by being Pakistani and British so increases that a bit, it's like a whole new script of possibilities …

As seen above, Fahim this time talks through his I-position of belonging to both his mainstream and minority communities. Through such a positioning, he emotionally and cognitively integrates his multiple identities.

Unfolding the dialogue between the different settings
(Voice 1) Being of a Pakistani background in my community school becomes important because all the students are similar and share the same religious and cultural values which people from other backgrounds can't understand … (voice 2) … so while as a Pakistani in the mainstream school you feel normal when you exercise your cultural practices, you are seen as weird by the others … (voice 3) … and within the mainstream society you are sometimes treated with racism and you are afraid that you will not have the same opportunities as others with the same qualifications and when you experience religious discrimination you sometimes want to be invisible as a Muslim … (voice 4) … although for you being Pakistani and British it's like a whole new script of possibilities and experiences.

Greek school

School contexts

I-Position: I an ethnic minority student in my Greek community school
For the participants in the Greek school, being *similar* to their school's cultural community has also emerged as a powerful voice. For these students cultural similarity with their community school's community was represented by the shared cultural and family values.

Voice 1: the similar

I: and to be of Greek-Cypriot background in this school how is it for you?
Lydia: it … this doesn't matter really, I think because you're all the same anyway so it doesn't really matter …
I: and how do you feel for being you know around with other people from the same background … what does it means for you to have other friends …
Lydia: because there are …there are certain things that are like people from a different background wouldn't understand … like … just little things … like families and stuff are generally quite similar and similar ways of like thinking sometimes about certain things …
I: Would you give me an example?
Lydia: like … I don't know the way you act towards like a family member … they … people generally are closer probably …

As seen in the above interview extract, Lydia's voice of being similar to her community school's cultural community was linked with other I-positions, namely, that of being of a Greek cultural background and living in the dominant society which created the voice of sharing the same cultural and family meanings and values with other members of her cultural group in contrast to the multicultural context in which she is situated and where these meanings and values cannot be understood.

I-Position: I as an ethnic minority student in my mainstream school
When the young people talked as members of their minority community in their mainstream school, many of them positioned themselves as members of a group which is positively stereotyped and emphasized the importance of feeling proud of their background.

Voice 2: the person who is proud of his/her cultural background
I: and to be of a Greek-Cypriot origin in the English school is …?
Stella: is good (laugh) because it's quite a lot of us and also quite a lot of things originated from the Greeks so you feel proud when you are in a lesson and they are talking about something that Greeks invented.

I-Position: I as being of a Greek background in the UK
In general, the young people in this school thought that their majority community perceived their minority community in positive terms e.g. having a civilised background with a world contribution, bringing their cultural elements into British society and enriching it, being a close knit, interesting community as well as lively, cheery, happy and loud people.

Voice 3: the accepted
I: How to you think people in British society think of Greeks or Greek-Cypriots?
Thalia: umm … I don't think they … they look at us badly as they would with others because we don't come from an uncivilized background, you know, because we were the ones who invented science and philosophy and everything else, so they can't say 'Oh! You stupid people' whatever … because we are not and, you know, lots of things like the Olympics and stuff they wouldn't been around without us, if we hadn't invented them.

Voice 4: The multiple "I"
I: How do you feel, you were born here … how do you feel living in this country?
Lydia: I like … I like living here ... I wouldn't live anywhere else … I don't think
         …
I: And in which ways do you feel, you know, similar with the rest of British society …
Lydia: Because I am … I am entirely … I am British really in a way … I think in a way I act as British so … I feel more at home here than I do in Cyprus
         …
I: and in which ways do you feel different, if you feel different?
Lydia: umm … I don't really … I don't feel different.
I: and, in general, you know, to be of Greek –Cypriot background in England, how do you experience that?
Lydia: umm … it's nice because there is no like … separate British culture … it's nice to have another culture and then being British …

Unfolding the dialogue between the different settings
(Voice 1) Being of a Greek background in my community school becomes indifferent because all the students are similar and share the same family values and way of thinking something that people from other backgrounds can't understand ... (voice 2) ... but as a Greek in the mainstream school you are accepted because of the cultural contribution of Greece to the world and you feel proud of your background ... (voice 3) ... and within the mainstream society you are not seen as badly as others because you come from a civilized background ... (voice 4) ... and it is nice to have that background and being British at the same time.

REVISITING BRONFENBRENNER'S MODEL TO ACCOUNT FOR THE MULTIPLE HETEROGENEOUS SOCIOCULTURAL CONTEXTS

Even before the emergence of cultural psychology as a movement Bronfenbrenner (1979) had tried to explain how these multiple contexts for human development are organized when he proposed his ecological model of human development, a multi-level system which describes how individuals relate to their multiple social contexts. This model conceived the societal influences as a set of four nested mutually inclusive systems. The microsystem represents what an individual experiences in a specific setting. For a child, for example, one microsystem may be the school environment with teachers and peers. Another microsystem may be the home environment with parents and siblings. At the next level is the mesosystem which refers to links amongst given settings in which the individual directly participates. For example, if a child does not speak the mother tongue with parents in the home environment, this might affect his/her achievement at the language course at his community school. The third level is the exosystem which refers to links to given settings in which the individual does not participate directly but which have an impact on the individual. For example, the decision of the local council to ban funding for a community school may lead the child to be ignorant of his/her mother tongue. Finally, the fourth level, the macrosystem, refers to the wider ideology, belief systems, laws etc and organization of social institutions in the society the individual is in. For example, if the dominant ideology endorses monolingualism, parents and children may be affected by factors such as negative social attitudes towards multilingualism. Bronfenbrenner's model explains how a change in the macrosystem may affect the exosystem and hence a child's mesosystem and microsystem. This is a systemic model which illustrates how individuals move from lower to greater levels of complexity and make the ways persons-contexts are connected visible (Smith & Cowie, 1991; Ratner, 1991; Valsiner, 2000).

Ratner (1991) argued that although Bronfenbrenner's model has been widely valued for including many societal influences or layers in relation to the individual, it gives the misleading impression that these social layers are outside the individual and not related to each other. Thus, he proposed a modified depiction of

Bronfenbrenner's basic point in which the layers are pictured as interpenetrating and illustrated how the macrosystem passes through an individual's exosystems and microsystems and how the impacts of all these systems influence the development of an individual (see Figure 1).

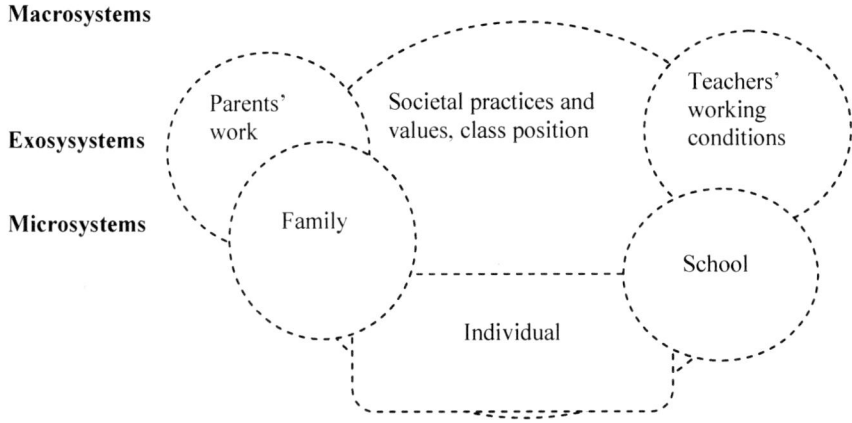

Figure 1. Representation of the individual and social relations (Ratner, 1991, p. 173).

Earlier in this chapter, we criticized Bronfenbrenner's (1979) model and Ratner's (1991) adaptation of it, as models that depict a monolithic image of society and could not be applied to the situation of ethnic minority young people who are members of a pluralistic society. In the following section a model will be introduced which we hope will offer a more appropriate conceptualization for a diverse society by illustrating the complexity of an ethnic minority young person's macrosystems and microsystems.

RETHINKING ETHNIC MINORITY YOUNG PEOPLE'S PARTICIPATION IN
MULTIPLE SOCIOCULTURAL CONTEXTS AND ITS IMPACT ON THEIR
CULTURAL IDENTITIES: A NEW MODEL

As can be seen in Figure 2, for an ethnic minority child a macrosystem is not only the practices represented by the dominant society but also the practices (e.g. religious and language practices), values and beliefs represented by the minority community that also have an impact on his/her development.

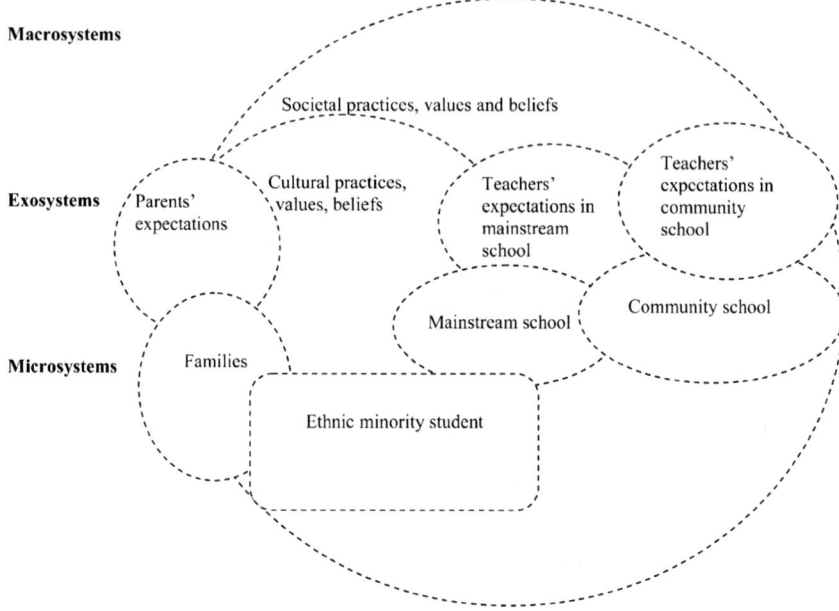

Figure 2. Representations of the social and educational worlds of ethnic minority students.

Similarly, for an ethnic minority child who attends both a mainstream and community school (microsystems) his/her educational worlds are even more complex. Valsiner (2000) referred to education as having a double function; the first function is to foster the acquisition of skills and knowledge and the second is to provide indirect guidance towards socially expected ways of acting, thinking and feeling towards the others. In this sense, he pointed out that mainstream formal education has the effect of distancing some young people from their minority cultural context and reinforcing the development of their identities in accordance with values and ways of thinking relevant to the expectations of the society at large. This would be an outcome of the bonding of persons' identities to the social goals of the mainstream schools. For an ethnic minority person who attends a community school, it could be argued that community education is a similar process which directs young people in the opposite direction by guiding them towards culturally expected ways of acting, thinking and feeling towards the others. In this sense, community education can be expected to have the effect of bringing young people closer to their cultural contexts and reinforcing the development of their identities in accordance with values and ways of thinking relevant to the expectations of their minority community. This would be the outcome of the bonding of persons' identities to the sociocultural goals of the community schools.

As the findings presented in this chapter suggest, both community schools aimed at empowering the minority cultural identity of the young people through offering a sense of belonging and of minority identity and through encouraging participation in common cultural celebrations and activities. Thus, both community schools were moving towards the development of these young peoples' cultural identities in terms of values and ways of thinking that are in accordance with the expectations of the minority communities in which the schools were embedded. Although both schools aimed to foster a cultural closeness of the young people with their minority communities, on the one hand, the Pakistani community school intended to influence their cultural identity development mainly through the teaching of the religion by providing the space for meeting other Muslim young people and guiding young people's way of life in accordance with their religious and cultural values and duties. This school also aimed to increase self-confidence and strengthen the students' sense of minority identity in order to combat negative stereotypes and racism in the dominant society and mainstream schools. In this context, a strong minority identity is related not only to the minority community but also to the mainstream community which both constitute these young people's macrosystems. On the other hand, the Greek school intended to influence their students' minority cultural identity development mainly through sharing similar family and cultural values with other members of the minority community and through learning the community language which was perceived as a "safety valve" to an already threatened minority identity. In this sense, the main aim was the preservation of the community's cultural identity and therefore it was mainly related to the minority community itself.

The findings also suggest that the different experiences of the young people in the Pakistani and Greek schools within their majority community (a discriminated versus an accepted group respectively) positioned them in very different worlds, and their reactions to the ways they believed they were perceived in the mainstream community and school contexts differed significantly. The findings also illustrate how difficult and complex a process integration could be for many non/White, non/European/Western children of immigrants. Thus, for the participants in the Pakistani school the negotiation was a struggle shaped by issues of racism and religious discrimination and characterised by the exercise of power and dominance by others. For the Greek students dialogical oppositions (ie different and accepted) did not reduce the multivoiced and dialogical character of their identity. For the Pakistani students their inter-construction process was mainly characterized by conflicts between what they felt about themselves and how they thought others in the majority community perceived them. The dialogue between their intra-construction and inter-construction processes was blocked because the opposites were not dialogically related. Such a dialogue reduces the multivoiced character of the identity and moves towards a monological direction (Hermans, 2003). Thus, being discriminated against by their majority community generated fears for their future and cast a shadow over the minority aspect of their cultural identity.

Finally, the young people in both groups were moving towards multiple identities through a dialogical negotiation of aspects of differences/ similarities and belonging within their majority and minority communities and community and mainstream school settings as well as living in a multicultural society and in a wider international context that encourages trends towards globalization. These negotiations resulted in multivoiced identities which emerged through a constant positioning and re-positioning within their communities and school contexts.

CONCLUDING THOUGHTS

While the importance of the multiple social contexts in which individuals participate had been acknowledged in the past, the ways that ethnic minority young people, who live in diverse societies, relate to their multiple sociocultural and educational contexts have not been similarly examined. It has been illustrated here that for ethnic minority young people both their microsystems and macrosystems are even more complex. It is essential that this complexity is addressed in research since contemporary societies are becoming more and more diverse and many more young people are living in multicultural contexts. Within such contexts, the concept of cultural identities and questions regarding their development require models that would leave the way open for new holistic conceptual developments with multidirectional influences that cross many levels of analysis, including the child, the family, the school, and the wider cultural communities.

REFERENCES

Abbey, E. (2004). Circumventing ambivalence in identity: The importance of latent and overt aspects of symbolic meaning. *Culture and Psychology, 10*(3), 331-336.

Ahmad, F. (2006). British Muslim perceptions and opinions on news coverage of September 11. *Journal of Ethnic and Migration Studies, 32*(6), 961-982.

Anthias, F. (2001). New hybridities, old concepts: The limits of 'culture'. *Ethnic and Racial Studies, 24*(4), 619-641.

Anwar, M. (1979). *The myth of return: Pakistanis in Britain.* UK: Heinemann.

Bhatia, S., & Ram, A. (2001). Locating the dialogical self in the age of transnational migrations, border crossings and diasporas. *Culture and Psychology, 7*(3), 297-309.

Bhatia, S., & Ram, A. (2004). Culture, hybridity, and the dialogical self: Cases from the South Asian diaspora. *Mind, Culture and Activity, 11*(3), 224-240.

Bhatt, A, Bhojani, N, Creese, A., & Martin, P. W. (2004). Complementary and mainstream schooling: A case for reciprocity? *NALDIC Publications Group: Occasional Paper 18.*

Bronfenbrenner, U. (1979). *The ecology of human development.* Cambridge, MA: Harvard University Press.

Creese, A., & Martin, P. W. (2006). Interaction in complementary school contexts: Developing identities of choice-an introduction. *Language and Education, 20*(1), 1-4.

Creese, A., Bhatt, A., Bhojani, N., & Martin, P. W. (2006). Multicultural, heritage and learner identities in complementary schools. *Language and Education, 20*(1), 23-43.

Dien, F. S. D. (2000). The evolving nature of self-identity across four levels of history. *Human Development, 43*(1), 1-18.

Ferdman, B. (2000). "Why am I who I am?" constructing the cultural self in multicultural perspective. *Human Development, 43* (1), 19-23.

Flick, U. (2000). Episodic interviewing. In M. W. Bauer, & G. Gaskell (Eds.), *Qualitative Researching with Text, Image and Sound: a practical handbook*. London: Sage Publications, 75-92.

Hall, S. (2006). Once more around the 'identity' question. *Paper Presented at Queen Mary's University of London*, 15 November, 2006.

Hermans, H. J. M. (2001). The dialogical self: Toward a theory of personal and cultural positioning. *Culture and Psychology, 7*(3), 243-281.

Hermans, H. J. M. (2003). The construction and reconstruction of a dialogical self. *Journal of Constructivist Psychology, 16*(2), 89-130.

Hermans, H. J. M., & Kempen, H. J. G. (1993). *The dialogical self: Meaning as movement*. San Diego, CA: Academic Press.

Hermans, H. J. M., & Kempen, H. J. G. (1998). Moving cultures: The perilous problems of cultural dichotomies in a globalizing society. *American Psychologist, 22*(10), 1111-1120.

Ho, D. Y. F., Chan, S. F. F., Peng, S. Q., & Ng, A. K. (2001). The dialogical self: Converging East-West constructions. *Culture and Psychology, 7*(3), 393-407.

Martin, P. W., Creese, A., & Bhatt, A. (2003). Complementary schools and their communities in Leicester. Final Report for the ESRC Project for Project No: R000223949. Available at: http://www.ue/ac.uk/education/staff/finalreport.pdf.

Moghaddam, M. F. (2002). Cultural surplus and social mobility among minorities. *Culture and Psychology, 8*(4), 401-407.

Papapavlou, A., & Pavlou, P. (2001). The interplay of language use and language maintenance and the cultural identity of Greek Cypriots in the UK. *International Journal of Applied Linguistics, 11*(1), 92-113.

Prokopiou, E., & Cline, T. (2010). Constructing cultural and academic identities in community schools: A socio-cultural and dialogical approach. In V. Lytra, & P. Martin (Eds.), *Sites of multilingualism: Complementary schools in Britain today*, 71-83. Trentham Books.

RAISE Project. The achievement of British Pakistani learners. Available at: www.insted.co.uk/raise.html (last accessed 30th May, 2007)

Rassool, N. (1999). Flexible identities: Exploring race and gender issues among a group of immigrant pupils in an inner-city comprehensive school. *British Journal of Sociology of Education, 20*(1), 23-36.

Ratner, C. (1991). *Vygotsky's sociohistorical psychology and its contemporary applications*. New York: Plenum Press.

Robertson, H. L. (2005). Teaching and learning in community language schools. NALDIC Publications Group: Occasional Paper 19.

Smith, K. P., & Cowie, H. (1991). *Understanding children's development*. Oxford: Blackwell Publishers.

Stone, R., Muir, H., & Smith, L. (2004). Islamophobia: Issues, challenges and action. A Report by the Commission on British Muslims and Islamophobia. Trentham Books: Stroke-on-Trent: UK.

Strand, S. (2002). Surveying the views of pupils attending supplementary schools in England in 2001. A Report for CfBT and the African Schools Association (ASA) relating to the Supplementary Schools Support Service (S4).

Todoulou-Polemi, M., Vassiliou, V., & Vassiliou, G. (1998). The grouping process across cultural change. *Group, 22*(2), 105-119.

Valsiner, J. (1989). From group comparisons to knowledge: A lesson from cross-cultural psychology. In J. P. Forgas, & J. M. Innes (Eds.), *Recent advances in social psychology: An international perspective*, 501-510. Amsterdam: Elsevier Science.

Valsiner, J. (2000). *Culture and human development*. London: Sage Publications.

Valsiner, J. (2004). Temporal integration of structures within the dialogical self. Paper presented at the Third International Conference on the Dialogical Self. Warsaw, Poland, 28 August 2004.

Vassiliou, G., & Vassiliou, V. G. (1981). Outlining the synallactic collective image technique as used within a systemic, dialectic approach. In J. E. Durkin (Ed.), *Living groups*, 216-227. New York: Brunner/Mazel.

Vertovec, S. (2001). Transnationalism and identity. *Journal of Ethnic and Migration Studies, 27*(4), 573-582.

Evangelia Prokopiou
Arachne Greek-Cypriot Women's Group
London, UK

Tony Cline
Educational Psychology Group
University College London

Guida de Abreu
Psychology Department
Oxford Brookes University

SARAH CRAFTER

5. MAKING SENSE OF HOMEWORK: PARENTAL RESOURCES FOR UNDERSTANDING MATHEMATICAL HOMEWORK IN MULTICULTURAL SETTINGS

Parental involvement in children's homework is strongly endorsed and encouraged by political and educational policy in the UK. However, involvement in mathematics homework is said to be particularly problematic for parents because of changes to the curriculum since their own schooling, the introduction of multitudinous mathematical strategies at school, and in the case of multicultural communities, an ever-increasing heterogeneity of learning experiences amongst parents. Using the theoretical framework of cultural models and cultural settings this chapter examines the kinds of resources parents use to make sense of their child's mathematics homework. Two parental resources for making sense of mathematics homework are scrutinized: (a) the child, and (b) cultural models of child development. The interviews with twenty-two parents revealed that these resources were highly intangible and often symbolic models which were open to misunderstandings, resistances and transformations. Also, the child could be an active or resistant co-constructor of these resources which subsequently informed the homework setting.

INTRODUCTION

Educational and political policy in England has for some time promoted the idea that parental involvement in children's homework is a powerful indicator of achievement success in school (Department for Children, Schools and Families, 2008) despite mixed evidence from the academic research literature (Farrow, Tymms, & Henderson, 1999). This has led to a dual understanding in the way the relationship between home and school learning is perceived. On the one hand home and school are placed as very separate institutions in that parents are prescribed the main responsibility for shaping and moulding the child into an educated and economically viable adult. On the other hand children are seen as both active and passive harbingers of school values which the child takes home through their transitions between contexts (Edwards & Alldred, 2000). In the case of the research study reported here, children take home to their parents, mathematical material learnt in the classroom in the form of mathematics homework. In

E. Hjörne et al. (eds.), Learning, Social Interaction and Diversity – Exploring Identities in School Practices, 53–68.

multicultural settings the parents must try to make sense of the mathematical material sent home from school when their own past educational experiences are the most obvious provider of information (O'Toole & Abreu, 2005). This chapter examines what resources parents, with a variety of educational experiences, use to understand their child's mathematics homework. Resources are meaningful constructs for understanding and making sense of particular phenomena, like homework. Resource is a concept which refers to the way in which the individual is simultaneously a seeker and provider of information which is open to resistance, interpretation and multiple representations (Crafter, 2009).

This examination takes place within a framework which supposes that mathematical learning is not a neutral or culture-free subject (Swanson, 2005; Abreu & Cline, 2003). Sociocultural theorising of mathematical activity links both social and cultural context with cognition (Abreu, Bishop & Presmeg, 2002) and the two most predominant contexts for children's mathematical learning are home and school. In other studies with ethnic minority communities looking at mathematical learning, researchers like González, Moll and Amanti (2005) have noted that home and school learning has traditionally been a one-way street. Mathematical information often goes from school to home but there is little expectation for home traditions, representations and practices in mathematics to be returned. School as an institution is culturally constructed and its practices are based on the colonisation of those who are not in white, middle class positions (Rogoff, 2003). However, the knowledge that parents bring to the home learning situation is heterogeneous because of their own varied educational and cultural experiences.

Shifting levels of migrancy and increasing heterogeneous populations implies new challenges for educational systems across Europe. Despite this, there is still a strong political drive to have parents involved as a partner in their children's learning (Crozier, 2000). However, the messages sent out to parents on behalf of the government tend to be somewhat ambivalent in that parents (and teachers) are blamed if standards fail to be raised but must also be allies to the government to raise standards (Cullingford & Morrison, 1999). Whatever mixed messages come from the state; the school continues to view itself as the champion of parental involvement. This political machine continues unabated in the UK as the William's Report recently proposed that parents are a powerful and enduring force in their children's education. This was taken one step further when it was stated: "Parents should be at the centre of any plan to improve children's outcomes, starting with the early years and continuing right through schooling" (Department for Children, Schools and Families, 2008, p. 69). This raises complex questions – which parents and whose knowledge is most advantageously applied?

What it means to be parentally involved is fairly far-reaching and altogether ill-defined (Solomon, Warin, & Lewis, 2002). To be involved could refer to maintaining contact with the school, attending consultations with the teacher, watching sports days and plays, or taking on more active roles like belonging to the governing body. This chapter will focus on the most obvious form of parental involvement which is homework. In this instance, homework refers to the tasks set by teachers based on classroom practices and sent home for pupils to carry out in nonschool hours (Cooper, 1989). Evidence surrounding the advantages of having parents involved specifically with mathematics homework is ambivalent. In a study by Sheldon and Epstein (2005, p. 204) schools that "effectively implemented" activities to support mathematics homework were said to have a beneficial effect on achievement. However, a more recent and extensive synthesis of parental involvement in homework concluded that while this was true for other subjects it was not the case for mathematics (Patall, Cooper, & Civey Robinson, 2008). For one, major educational and curriculum changes means that parents have very different experiences of mathematics learning compared to their children (O'Toole & Abreu, 2005; McMullen & Abreu, 2009). Moreover, the variety of mathematical strategies available may make the homework situation too complex.

Expectations for children's schooling, particularly in countries like the UK, USA and much of Western Europe centre on providing children with unifying representations and values around what "education" means and what types of learning should take place (Goodnow, 1990). In the mathematics classroom this requires both the teacher and pupils to share a world view of the colonisation of number and in turn, the colonisation of mathematical practice in all settings (Bauchspies, 2005). The "colonization" of the home by school practices does not attempt to reflect or value family practice but marginalises practices which are not represented by White, middle-class groups (Edwards & Warin, 1999). Reay and Lucey (2000; cited in Street, Baker & Tomlin, 2008) argue that the middle classes have aligned their discourses with the school to create an advantage, whilst working classes may (or may not) resist such colonisation within the home. Similar arguments can be made in relation to ethnicity.

From the schools' point of view, if parents are to play a key role in their children's mathematics learning at home and if homework as an extension of classroom practice is to succeed, then practices in the home must be normalised (Crozier, 2000). However, homogeneity in home communities cannot be assured. The UK context is complicated in that in many of the larger towns there is a substantial degree of diversity around ethnicity, language, class, practices, traditions and representations of education and learning. Studies in the US that borrow from a sociocultural perspective tend to rely on homogenous communities (Andrews & Yee, 2006) such as Mexican immigrants (González et al., 2005) or specific Latino communities (Gallimore & Goldenberg, 2001). The same cannot necessarily be said for studies in the UK.

Given these complexities it is not surprising that some parents find it difficult to understand their child's mathematical homework but draw on a variety of resources to make sense of their child's school learning to help them succeed. A 'source' provides information, often in the form a book or person and suggests passivity on the part of the receiver. Parents can also seek out information in an active fashion. Parents operate in both of these ways to explore and examine the educational world of their child. Of particular note is that parents can use a resource in different ways; they may be resisted, reinterpreted or misunderstood. One might suppose that mathematical homework, particularly work sheets and booklets are a fairly concrete resource. However, it is argued here that resources which seem very concrete and "objective" may also be susceptible to miscommunication or interpretation because individual past educational experiences can lead to multiple representations (Crafter, 2009).

As such, resources may be influenced by pre-existing or developing Cultural Models (Gallimore & Goldenberg, 2001). Cultural models can be understood in terms of a shared understanding of how the individual perceives the way the world works, or should work. A cultural model is described as:

> Encoded shared environmental and event interpretations, what is valued and ideal, what settings should be enacted and avoided, who should participate, the rules of interaction, and the purpose of the interactions. (Gallimore & Goldenberg, 2001, p. 47)

Cultural models are often hidden and unrecognisable to the individual and quite often assumed to be shared by others around them. Mathematical learning also comes with a knowledge structure which is a reflection of the family or community practices (Abreu, 2008). Parents draw on their own understandings of mathematics learning to make sense of mathematical homework or conceptualisations of "education." Cultural settings refer to those activities, which cause people to come together to perform a joint activity. These activities are frequently mundane and played out in the repetitious routines of everyday life, such as the parent who counts the items on a shopping list with the help of a child or the family sitting down together to watch a favourite TV programme. For example, a parental cultural model that teaching is the schools responsibility and should not be done in the home will influence the practices within that cultural setting. Or, the parent who has a model that their own mathematics is very bad could influence the cultural setting during homework.

STUDYING PARENTAL RESOURCES FOR UNDERSTANDING MATHEMATICAL HOMEWORK AND 'EDUCATION'

Respondents

The twenty-two parents participating in this study had children in primary schools (ages 5-11 years) situated in a town in the South East of England. Eleven of the 22 parents were from ethnic minority backgrounds and the remaining participants were White and British born. The children are characterised as being either high or low achievers in mathematics and were placed as such by their teachers using examination results data and teachers' own representations of achievement.

Collecting and Analysing the Data

Data collection took place in three multiethnic schools that are known as school A (mainly White), school B (ethnically mixed) and school C (mainly South Asian). Data from parents was collected using the episodic interview (Flick, 2000), a method which assumes a shared common knowledge on behalf of the participants about the subject under study. It specifically facilitates the exploration of meanings and representations in combination with examples of experientially based concrete circumstances. The question is posed in two parts, the first part seeking to elucidate the narrative/semantic aspects of the phenomenon under study and the second asking for a concrete episode by way of an example. Some examples from the interview which are relevant to this analysis are:

– Does your child bring any maths homework home? Can you tell me about what she/he has been doing recently?
– Is there any type of homework you would like to see more of? Can you tell me about that if there is.
– Is the way you help with their homework different now from when they were younger? Can you tell me about that?
– Would you say that on the whole your child enjoys their maths homework? Describe to me a situation when that was the case.

Thematic coding was the procedure used for analysing the interviews (Flick Fischer, Neuber, Wilhelm Schwartz & Walter, 2003) which began with the transcribing and thorough reading of the data. Coding was then conducted in two steps and 'data-driven' (Braun & Clarke, 2006) which involves collecting data relevant to a particular phenomenon (in this instance 'understandings of homework'). The first step involved extracting text where parents made mention of their understandings of their children's homework. The second step involved taking this data and sorting it into various foci of understanding in the form of resources. In their accounts, parents utilised a varied number of resources to help them understand their child's homework. The two dominating resources were: (a) "the child" and (b) cultural models of child development and for reasons of space, these have become the focus on this analysis.

ANALYSING RESOURCES FOR UNDERSTANDING HOMEWORK

Although the study was specifically about mathematics, parents within the sample used this opportunity to talk about their child's education as a whole and therefore the data is highly inclusive of other educational issues. For parents, making sense of their children's mathematics education is like fixing together the pieces of a puzzle and this is managed in a holistic way. Homework was particularly crucial to parents as a means of constructing cultural models and formed part of the 'puzzle' in understanding their child's learning on a week-by-week basis. Homework operates to connect classroom practices with home learning. However, taking into account the changes to the mathematics curriculum since parents were at school (see McMullen & Abreu, 2009), the multiple strategies available to solve mathematical problems (Patall et al., 2008) and the difficulties this raises for helping with their child's home mathematics learning, it is not surprising that it could be a source of conflict (Edwards & Warin, 1999) and misunderstandings. Resources were necessary for making sense of the mathematics homework.

Using 'the child' as a resource for understanding homework

As the only figure regularly making the transition between home and school it is not surprising that 'the child' was a key resource for parental cultural models of homework. It is not simply that the child provides information about homework which the parents then utilise during homework activities; though this may be the case. Rather, parents' cultural models around mathematics homework are informed, developed and maintained with the child in mind. What is crucial here is that these resources may have little to do with direct tuition and mathematical strategy. Also, cultural models of homework and the child as a resource are reciprocally supporting one another in a regular process of maintenance and transformation (Zittoun, 2008). Parents considered that there were two major purposes to having homework, and they had little to do with the direct advancement in learning. The first purpose parents thought homework served was to increase their child's levels of independence and responsibility in their learning. The following two quotes reveal how homework for independence and responsibility is conveyed through the parents' talk:

> James' mother: We always try as much as possible to make him, or to get him to do it on his own cause that's the whole point of the homework. (White British: school A, 5/6 years, HA)

> Amira's mother: If they give them homework the children feel they have to be more responsible, they think they have to do this and take it back and they're more excited ... and if they don't do homework they have to stay back or something, then they will sit down and do it, they will worry about it more, feel more responsibly that they have to do that. (Pakistani: school A, 10/11 years, LA)

Both of these parents have a cultural model of homework as a learning skills tool. The mathematical content does not, at this juncture, take centre stage. With the child in mind, homework is a tool for personal enhancement; to create learner independence and responsibility. James' mother takes personal ownership of the homework setting in a way that aligns her cultural model for the purpose of homework with the school. As an explanation for her daughter's lack of independence, Amira's mother puts the onus on the school to encourage and create a culture of responsibility in her own child. This is not because she lacks this commitment as a parent, but simply because the struggle to encourage her daughter to take responsibility keeps failing. She told me:

> Amira's mother: Amira's a bit lazy, she doesn't like to give her brain hard work, she doesn't like to use her brain much. She would rather have me do it; most of the time she'll say "mum, can you do this for me"? and I say "it's not my homework, you do it." I tell [her] which way to go about but she'll keep on pushing until I really do tell her, so I'll get fed-up and I'll give her the answers, until I have to really put her in her place and say "look, this is your homework, not mine." (Pakistani: school A, 10/11 years, LA)

Here, "the child" is an active resource in driving the homework setting and in this case, an active resister for what her mother would consider to be an appropriate cultural model for doing homework. Amira's mother's model around the purpose of homework, namely her child's development of responsibility, is not arbitrary. It follows on from interactions with her daughter where she (the child) has become the resource for the cultural model of homework. The conflict brought about by homework raised by Amira's mother was a problem for some of the other parents sampled. Mathematical homework as a particular harbinger of conflict and tension has been raised in previous research (Hughes & Greenhough, 2007; Lange & Meaney, 2011; Patall et al., 2008). When conflict occurs, cultural models around the purpose of homework become clouded. The parent needs the child as a resource to complete the homework successfully but at the same time must take on the role of teacher to help sustain their child's concentration. The next quote is from Amy's mother:

> Amy's mother: Amy is somebody who; like some children like to do homework but she doesn't really like to do homework at all, it's like a job to get her to do anything really. I mean if you really, really encourage her then she'll do reading and that but to get her to do anything else is a bit of a chore I must admit
>
> Sarah: Do you end up having a bit of a struggle?
>
> Amy's mother: We do actually, I mean, if my husband tries to do it with her she just really, really plays him up. But as I encourage him to make it sound a bit fun then she'll do it with you … she just don't really like homework, she'll mess about with anything rather than do her homework really. (White British: school B, 5/6 years, LA)

Amy appears to actively resist her home learning which in turn means she resists her mother's cultural model of the 'ideal' homework setting. Amy's mother has understood that to enact the role of teacher in the homework setting leads to conflict. Therefore, the homework setting cannot be an extension of their daughter's classroom practices. Instead it is necessary for her to develop alternative strategies in order to "make it sound a bit fun." This parent has had to develop new resources leading to the alteration of her previous cultural model of homework practices. This highlights problems with employing parents as holders of expert knowledge (Crozier, 2000).

Dale's parents (White British: school A, 10/11 years, LA) also reported a similar struggle with him at home:

> Dale's mother: I've not seen him bring very much maths homework home, but having said that, he tends to do his homework with his Nanny, that's his grandma, rather than somebody who just looks after him. But as far as maths recently is concerned, he's still quite, he's still at quite low levels on it, you know, where we have been talking to him about maths he still finds multiplication difficult. He still finds some fairly simple mental arithmetic

quite difficult … he's not good at doing homework, it's a real battle with him, a real sit down and that's why we tend to get Nanny to do it; as soon as he gets out of school because he's still in "school mind" before he's got home and the Play station and the Tele [television] and all that have taken over. So he goes to the library to do it …

Dale's parents try to reconcile their cultural models of his low mathematical achievement (confirmed by being in the lowest mathematics set at school and doing poorly in examinations) whilst trying to comply with institutional expectations to be involved with homework. Although Dale's parents cared about his success in school his active resistance in being a resource for mathematical homework meant that his parents drew on other strategies to manage the setting. In this case they enlisted the help of the Grandmother to ensure he did his homework. We do not have the full information here, but the suggestion is that he went to the local library to do his homework alone. This would be at odds with the institutional models for parental involvement in homework. Furthermore, Dale's parents presented a model that if they pushed him too much, it might "turn him off" to learning.

This next parent spoke about how the teacher actively encouraged the child to be a resource in the homework setting. The teacher orchestrates a cultural model for the parent that homework is an interactional event with the child as a pseudo-teacher:

Sarah: Does Jamal bring any maths homework home? Can you tell me what he's been doing recently?

Jamal's mother: He does, yeah. The last homework was adding, three digit numbers. The one previous to that was some puzzles, he was set a puzzle and he had to work it out for himself. Like he had, "someone went to the beach and he had thirty pebbles, divided by, I mean, if they collected those pebbles how many would there be?" something like that. With them, he needed help, but I spoke to the teacher and she said "this homework was set so the parents and children could get involved and help each other," so. (Bangladeshi: school A, 5/6 years, HA)

Historical changes to the curriculum have meant that difficulties arise for both parents who have and have not been educated in the UK (McMullen & Abreu, 2011; O'Toole & Abreu, 2005). However, parents' own past educational experiences make salient certain elements of their experience for their current cultural models of homework. For example, Jamal's mother, who was a British born Bangladeshi with a high achieving child, described no feelings of discomfort in using her child as a resource for helping with homework. However, for Elena's mother, her education in a different country (France) is at the forefront of her cultural model:

Elena's mother: For me it's hard to explain to her when she says "mum, I don't understand" because I've never done that before and unless I know what they're talking about I can't help her because to me, it's such a long time ago since I've been to school, it's so different. I've been in a different country as well, it's just so hard for me to explain to her when she doesn't understand; just guess I suppose. (Mixed-heritage; school C, 10/11 years, LA)

If the child is not able to explain school mathematical strategies then parents find it difficult to use the child as a resource. For Elena's mother her education outside of England compounded the feeling that she could not help her daughter. However, British born and highly educated parents can face similar difficulties because of changes to mathematical strategies introduced through the National Numeracy Strategy in 1999. For example, difficulties arose for Lee and his mother (White British: school B, 10/11 years, LA) when he couldn't be used as a resource for understanding long division homework. Lee couldn't explain to his mother how to do long division using classroom strategies so he could not act as a useful Resource in the joint homework setting. In the end his mother spoke to the teacher.

Rajesh's mother supplemented homework from the school with sums which she wrote out herself based on the types of worksheets sent home by the school. She considered these a compliment to what the teacher supplied because she tried to build on her son's mathematical weaknesses. Despite being placed in the lowest set at school and being cited by the teacher as a low achiever, Rajesh was an enthusiastic and willing home learner. In the first part of the quote his mother talks about providing a list of additions and subtractions mixed up, which she showed me during the interview:

Rajesh's mother: So he comes home right, like one day we do maths and he's like "yeah, yeah I wanna do maths" so I give him that and then he just does it. I keep on doing the basics with him because they said at school he had problems doing the three numbers, because he got confused adding the three numbers [e.g. 10+5+3]. So now he's better like, he does make mistakes so then we go over it again ... I try and confuse, I try and put a take away in with the add, cause he tends to just zoom past without realising what ...

Sarah: And then you've done here little lines for the numbers? [a number line]

Rajesh's mother: He does that, that's his, that's how he works it out. I just write it out and then the normal, and he's still a bit confused with the changing around so I do that once every week, I just give him one now. So now he's got the hang of it.

While Rajesh's mother and Rajesh both enact a homework situation which is reflective of the cultural practices of the classroom, it is Rajesh who provides the resource for completing the mathematics. He brought from the classroom the number line which was learnt at school but used at home to complete his additions and subtractions.

There are three emergent patterns here for how "the child" is used as a resource for constructing a cultural model of homework. The child may be an active resource, like Jamal, who is happy to be co-teacher with his mother in the homework setting. He was a high achieving pupil who could clearly explain mathematical strategies used in the classroom in the home setting. The child may be an active resister for being a resource, which was the case Amira, Amy and Dale. In Amira's case her apparent "laziness" helped her mother construct a cultural model of mathematics homework as a tool for developing independence and responsibility. She coupled this with a cultural model that school should be responsible for instilling this ethos of responsibility towards home learning. Amy's mother could not use her child as an active resource because of her resistance in being part of a joint homework setting. Parents also talked about the child as a passive resource, so the cultural model of homework is developed with the child in mind but the model is imposed on them, which was the case for James' mother.

Using Cultural Models of Child Development as a Resource for Understanding Homework

Cultural models of child development, whilst used pervasively as a resource (see Crafter, 2009, for models of achievement) were also symbolic constructs which fed into models of homework. At times the parents were specifically asked by me to comment on age but at other times spontaneously evoked cultural models of child development to make sense of homework learning. For some of the parents in this study the cultural settings of the homework interactions had changed as their children grew older, even for those parents who had children as young as six and seven years old (Year 2 in the English school system). Parents enjoyed the increasing independence their children experienced with age during the homework learning. Jamal's mother explained how the resources she needed for helping with homework altered as her son aged:

> Jamal's mother: When he was younger I think we had to go into it in more depth, like explain it word for word. Whereas now, he does understand what needs doing but it's just a matter of how to work it out. (Bangladeshi: school A, 5/6 years, HA)

The skills a parent needs for helping a child with homework can be multitudinous and the investment that parents make potentially far-reaching (Solomon et al., 2002). The data in this study suggests that those skills are tested as much with a young child as they are with an older child. It is not necessarily the advanced stage of mathematics that counts, but the ways in which parents need to find explanations for the mathematics that can be problematic. Even though Jamal was only six years old, his mother's cultural model of child development is tied with the homework setting in that there was a growing autonomy on the part of her son.

Parents' use of models of child development as a resource to help with homework formed part of the approach adopted by Samuel's mother. She described the way she learnt to adapt her communication skills with her son during their homework settings. I asked her whether the way she helped with her son's homework was different from when he was younger:

> Samuel's mother: Well I suppose in a way because I don't sit as much with him and also in the younger days I was like "no, no, no, mustn't do it like that, no, no, no" and I've learnt not to do that and I've stepped back. What he's done and completed I would say "oh that's good, what do you think you can do to improve it?" so I've changed, yes I've changed the way I might approach the same problem, my attitudes different. (Mixed Heritage: school B, 5/6 years, HA)

This mother had used her models of child development as a resource for developing new interactional strategies in homework settings. This mother found different ways of conversing with her son to aid his mathematical learning (Smith, 2003).

Equally, it is notable that both Jamal and Samuel were high achieving children. We may surmise that models of child development were a salient resource for these parents because they afforded a less conflictual homework setting. One of the aspects of the homework scenario, which seemed to set apart the parents of high achieving and low achieving children in this sample was the adaptability and strategies used to deal with the homework setting. In contrast to the parents above, Amy's mother described the homework setting with her daughter as altogether different:

> Sarah: Is the way you help with her homework different now from when she was younger? Can you tell me about that?

> Amy's mother: Probably a bit more, if she's got homework it's got to be done, obviously wouldn't get her to do it when she was younger, if she didn't want to do it when she was younger I didn't force the issue but now, if she has got homework and it's got to be done then I have to sort of try and make her do it really. So it's probably more stricter to do it. (White British: school B, 5/6 years, LA)

Amy's mother struggled to get her daughter to engage in many educational activities at home but the institutional pressure to do the work had increased alongside changing cultural models of child development. The demands from political and institutional contexts on parents' means that Amy's mother had gone from avoiding the homework setting in her daughter's younger years, to forcing her to do the homework as she had grown.

Cultural models of child development also work as a resistant resource for homework. Not all parents were happy to have mathematics homework and cited models of child development as one of the contributing issues:

Jennifer's mother: I don't think seven year olds should have to bring homework. I think they're at school from nine till three thirty and I think that for a seven year old that is probably quite enough really. White British: school B, 5/6 years, HA)

Sarah: Is there any type of homework you would like to see more of? Can you tell me about that if there is?

Simon's mother: Um, the other way really. I just, like I say I don't want, I think, they're children, they're little; he's in the infants still. I just think, just now and again to encourage them and get them going but I don't want to see too much put on them at this stage because I think their childhood is taken away with the pressure of sitting down and doing homework ... I don't want to put too much on them and I think, let them have their playtime and be with their friends and not too much homework and things like that. I want them to be children, they grow too quick . (White British: school B, 5/6 years, HA)

The cultural models about child development held by these parents are at odds with those held by the school institution. As one teacher commented "I still think some parents haven't quite caught onto the idea that they're seven so we should be expecting quite a lot of them." These vying cultural models between home and school can create conflicts between the values and positions represented there (Hedegaard, 2005).

Up until this point, the quotations from parents about models of child development as a resource for understanding homework have all been from parents of Year 2 (aged 6/7 years) children. The parents of Year 6 (aged 10/11 years) children also drew on child development as a resource for developing/ reconstructing cultural models about homework. The issues raised by the parents of the older children were very similar to those of the Year 2 parents. With age there comes an increased level of independence, which some parents found helpful in the homework setting. The following quote is an exemplification of this point and was described by other parents of both high and low achieving children:

Sarah: Is the way you help with their homework different now from when she was younger? Can you tell me about that?

Elena's mother: It is yeah, because she knows more about it than I do, if you know what I mean. Most of the time she just asks because she's not sure but she'll tell me more about her homework than I can tell her. When she was younger it was so much easier for me to tell her what to do, and how to do it and now I think "what are they talking about?" (Mixed Heritage: school C, 10/11 years, LA)

As her child grows Elena's mother sees the gap between her own knowledge and that of her child growing wider. Fleer and Richardson (2008) argue that Vygotsky proposed a pedagogy which looked forward in child development rather than to the past, which is often the case in current educational realms like school. However, the home is also a site where, particularly for mathematics learning, views of the future can be fraught with insecurities. For Elena's mother, being able to help with mathematics at home becomes increasingly difficult.

Dale's parents, like some of the year 2 parents, were against homework altogether for the primary years:

Dale's mother: I'm against it personally. I'm not happy that they have so much homework at his age really, I think it just turns kids off school sometimes if you're giving it to them at six, seven, eight, nine. When they get to high school, twelve, thirteen, perhaps give them homework but at that age … I just think the schools dump a lot on the parents, 'oh, you're behind, do it at home', you know.

Sarah: So you feel there's a bit of pressure on you to make up for?

Dale's father: Shortfalls of the schools, yeah. (White British: school A, 10/11 years, LA)

It must be noted that Dale's parents were the only ones in the sample to feel that a Year 6 pupil should not have so much homework. One might interpret from the quote above that the issue is not just one of child development however, but of the parents' representation that school as an institution struggles to meet a standard of education and uses the parent as a pseudo-teacher – something (Crozier, 2000) coined as the ethos of "self-helpism" (p. 10). As parents, their opinion may be more pronounced because they have a child who is struggling to achieve in the educational system.

Three fundamental issues were raised when looking at models of child development as a resource for feeding models of homework. Firstly, that as their children grow parents are both relieved to see increasing levels of independence which makes explaining mathematics easier, alongside fear about keeping up with mathematical complexities in the future. Secondly, Amy's mother felt an omnipresent pressure from the school institution to make her child do her homework even she was actively resistant. When her child was younger she did not feel the need to pressure her to complete homework but this model had altered as her daughter developed. Other parents, particularly those with children in Year 2 (5/6 years old) were resistant to the imposed cultural model of child development held by the school and closely linked with the model of homework.

IN SUMMARY

When parents spoke about their children's mathematics homework it was clear that parents used the homework setting to make sense of wider educational issues. The resources written about in this chapter were borne out of this sense making through data-driven coding of parental understandings of homework. In other words, the resources acted as a mechanism for making meaning. As argued earlier in the paper, resources and cultural models have a reciprocal relationship with one another. Resources can be influenced by pre-existing cultural models or cultural models can be drawn on as a resource; as was the case of models of child development. This is because resources themselves are not necessarily stable but transformative, and seemingly concrete resources like examination results are open to misunderstandings and interpretations (Crafter, in press).

Even when parents spoke about "the child" as a resource for their cultural models of homework, descriptions of *how* the child was a resource varied. The child could either be active, passive or resistors to being used as a resource. Those who are achieving well appear to bring classroom mathematical strategies into the home setting with ease and therefore seem comfortable to be used as a resource. Other pupils took on a resistant role in the cultural homework setting perhaps because they found the work difficult and could understand little about the benefits. There has been scarce evidence which looks the meanings of homework held by students and even less to suggest that they perceive the benefits of homework to be the same as they are for adults (Warton, 2001).

Cultural models of child development were an interesting resource in the sense that they are themselves highly symbolic and intangible. Models of child development are inextricably linked with mathematical homework in determining what parents think children should be able to do and how the homework setting is played out. Parents can also use these models as resources for resistance by considering them too young for receiving any mathematical homework at all. A few spoke of the relief that came with increasing independence in their child's homework setting as they grew older. This provides some indication for the difficulties that are particularly reported around the subject of mathematics and parental involvement (Patall et al., 2008).

Through all of the analysis on parental resources for understanding the homework setting what is perhaps most telling is what parents did *not* talk about. Namely, that the teacher as a resource of information for models of mathematical homework had little sway in the talk of the parents in this study. That is not to say that parents did not speak about interactions with teachers concerning homework, they were however relatively rare. So why did parents rely on the child, or models of child development as a resource to construct their meanings of homework? The first reason might simply be a matter of ease and frequency. In other words, the parent sees the child on a daily basis and therefore they are the most regular provider of information. For the Year 6 (ages 10/11 years of age) parents in school A, gaining access to the teacher was difficult because of the spatial barriers the school had erected - parents were not allowed on to the school grounds unless they had made a prior appointment. Some of the parents described how some teachers were more difficult to approach than others. These are both issues, which might lead a parent to seek less concrete resources for their meaning constructs.

In some instances school had encouraged the use of "the child" as a resource for collaboration in the homework situation. Richard, a teacher in school B (teaching 5/6 year olds) for example, liked parents to ask the child questions about their homework if the parent lacked an understanding about what the child should be doing. In engaging in this interaction, Richard believed the child increased its own level of understanding about the homework. However, as already discussed, the child can also be an active resister, sit on a fairly wide spectrum of achievement and in most instances, be doing mathematics in a different way to their parents. While in theory having the child as an active resource in collaboration may seem a positive idea and tended to be endorsed by the teachers, it makes life difficult for parents when the child is unable to access classroom-based mathematical knowledge in the home setting.

The advantages of having parents involved in mathematics homework is not nearly so clear-cut as government policy endorsed by documents such as the Williams Report (Department for Children, Schools and Families, 2008) suggests. Major educational and curriculum changes makes mathematics homework particularly difficult as an extension to classroom-based practices because it requires learning practices in the home to be normalised (Crozier, 2000). Parents, who are far from being a homogenous group, must try and make sense of mathematical homework with the resources that are available to them. The resources that they choose may be open to resistance and misunderstandings and act in a reciprocal way to be both influencing, and influenced by, cultural models surrounding learning.

REFERENCES

Abreu, G., de, & Cline, T. (2003). Schooled mathematics and cultural knowledge. *Pedagogy, Culture and Society, 11*(1), 11-30.

Abreu, G., de, Bishop, A., & Presmeg, N. (2002). *Transitions between contexts of mathematical practices*. Dordrecht: Kluwer.

Abreu, G., de (2008). From mathematics learning out-of-school to multicultural classrooms: A cultural psychological perspective. In L. English (Ed.), *Handbooks of international research in mathematics education* (pp. 352-383). USA: Lawrence Erlbaum Associates.

Andrews, J., & Yee, W. C. (2006). Children's 'funds of knowledge' and their real life activities: Two minority ethnic children learning in out-of-school contexts in the UK. *Educational Review, 58*(4), 435-449.

Bauchspies, W. K. (2005). Sharing shoes and counting years: Mathematics, colonization, and communication. In A. Chronaki, & I. M. Christiansen (Eds.), *Challenging perspectives on mathematical classroom communication* (pp. 237-259). US: Information Age Publishing.

Braun, V., & Clarke, V. (2006). Using thematic analysis in psychology. *Qualitative Research in Psychology, 3*, 77-101.

Cooper, H. (1989). Synthesis of research on homework. *Educational Readership, 47*, 85-91.

Crafter, S. (in press). Parental resources for understanding mathematical achievement in multiethnic settings. Paper presented at the *6th Conference of the European Society for Research in Mathematics Education* (pp. 14-22). Lyon, France.

Crozier, G. (2000). *Parents and schools: Partners or protagonists?* Staffordshire: Trentham Books.

Cullingford, C., & Morrison, M. (1999). Relationships between parents and schools: A case study. *Educational Review, 51*(3), 253-262.

Department for Children, Schools and Families (2008). *The Williams Report of the independent review of mathematical teaching in early years settings and primary schools*. DCSF Publications.

Edwards, R., & Alldred, P. (2000). A typology of parental involvement in education centring on children and young people: Negotiating familiarisation, institutionalisation and individualisation. *British Journal of the Sociology of Education, 21*(3), 435-455.

Edwards, A., & Warin, J. (1999). Parental involvement in raising the achievement of primary school pupils: why bother? *Oxford Review of Education, 25*(3), 325-342.

Farrow, S., Tymms, P., & Henderson, B. (1999). Homework and attainment in primary schools. *British Educational Research Journal, 25*(3), 323-342.

Flick, U., Fischer, C., Neuber, A., Wilhelm Schwartz, F., & Walter, U. (2003). Health in the context of growing old: Social representations of health. *Journal of Health Psychology, 8*(5), 539-556.

Flick, U. (2000). Episodic interviewing. In M. Bauer & G. Gaskell (Eds.), *Qualitative researching with text, image and sound: A practical handbook* (pp. 75-92). UK: Sage Publications.

Gallimore, R., & Goldenberg, C. (2001). Analysing cultural models and settings to connect minority achievement and school improvement research. *Educational Psychologist, 36*(1), 45-56.

González, N., Moll, L. C., & Amanti, C. (2005). *Funds of knowledge: Theorizing practices in households, communities, and classrooms*. New Jersey: Lawrence Erlbaum Associates.

Goodnow, J. J. (1990). The socialization of cognition: What's involved. In J. W. Stigler, R. S. Shweder, & G. Herdt (Eds.), *Cultural Psychology: Essays on comparative human development* (pp. 259-286). UK: Cambridge University Press.

Hedegaard, M. (2005). Strategies for dealing with conflicts in value positions between home and school: influences on ethnic minority students' development of motives and identity. *Culture & Psychology, 11*(2), 87-205.

Hughes, M., & Greenhough, P. (2007). 'We do it a different way at my school': Mathematics homework as a site for tension and conflict. In A.Watson, & P.Winbourne (Eds.). *New directions for situated cognition in mathematics education* (pp. 127-150). Springer.

Lange, T., & Meaney, T. (2011). I actually started to scream: Emotional and mathematical trauma from doing school mathematics homework. *Education Studies in Mathematics, 77*, 35-51.

McMullen, R., & Abreu, de. G. (2011). Mothers' experiences of their children's school mathematics at home: The impact of being a parent-teacher. *Research in Mathematics Education, 13*(1), 59-74.

O'Toole [now Crafter], S., & Abreu, G., de (2005). Parents' past experiences as resources for mediation in the child's current mathematical learning. *European Journal of Psychology of Education, 20*(1), 75-89.

Patall, E. A., Cooper, H., & Civey Robinson, J. (2008). Parental involvement in homework: A research synthesis. *Review of Educational Research, 78*(4), 1039-1101.

Rogoff, B. (2003). *The cultural nature of human development*. Oxford: OUP.

Sheldon, S. B., & Epstein, J. L. (2005). Involvement counts: Family and community partnerships and mathematics achievement. *The Journal of Educational Research, 98*(4), 196-206.

Smith, T. J. (2003, September). Pedagogy as conversation: A metaphor for learning together. *Mathematics Association of Victoria Annual Conference*. Melbourne: Monash University.

Solomon, Y., Warin, J., & Lewis, C. (2002). Helping with homework? Homework as a site of tension for parents and teenagers. *British Educational Research Journal, 28*(4), 603-622.

Street, B., Baker, D., & Tomlin, A. (2008). *Navigating numeracies: Home/school numeracy practices*. UK: Springer Science.

Swanson, D. M. (2005). Schooled mathematics: discourse and the politics of context. In A. Chronaki, & I. M. Christiansen (Eds.), *Challenging perspectives on mathematics classroom communication* (pp. 261-294). US: Information Age Publishing.

Warton, P. M. (2001). The forgotten voices in homework: Views of students. *Educational Psychologist, 36*(3), 155-165.

Zittoun, T. (2008). Learning through transitions: The role of instutions. *European Journal of Psychology of Education, 23*(2), 165-181.

Sarah Crafter
Centre for Children and Youth & the Division of Psychology
University of Northampton

WEN-CHUAN LIN AND GABRIELLE IVINSON

6. ETHNIC CULTURAL LEGACIES AND LEARNING ENGLISH AS A FOREIGN LANGUAGE

A Social-Cultural Study in Taiwan

INTRODUCTION

Learning English in Taiwan has become a primary economic concern as industries have recognized the need to compete within global markets in which trade is predominantly carried out in English. The growth in demand for, and supply of, English language education in school settings is escalating. The National Curriculum of Primary and Secondary Schools (Grades 1-9) in Taiwan designated English as a school subject as early as primary level grade 5 (age 10) in 2001 and introduced it even earlier, in grade 3 in 2005 reflecting a public recognition of the importance of learning English. Although English has gained in prestige in Taiwan, pupils from different geographical regions and various social groups achieve differently in learning English as a foreign language (EFL) measured by national tests. National data from the Basic Competence Test for Junior High Pupils taken at age 14, consistently demonstrate a substantial gap in English achievement between candidates living in urban and rural locales. For decades, the dominant explanation of the 'urban-rural divide' guiding policy debates was of resource disparity between urban and rural regions. This study will challenge this simplistic explanation of groups' differential achievement in EFL.

This study was guided by socio-cultural work (Abreu, 1995; Lave & Wenger, 1991; Rogoff, 1995; Rogoff & Lave, 1984; Wenger, 1998) which recognizes that EFL involves situated practices that cannot be dislocated from local as well as wider cultural arenas. It intents to broaden theories of EFL learning by recognizing that pupils' learning has to be situated within broader frames of analysis including the political, institutional, local and ethnic cultural contexts in which individuals encounter English. The paper explores two substantive issues; (1) differences between ethnic groups' situated experiences of, and access to, English, (2) the relationship between ethnic group cultures in four groups (Hokkien, Chinese Mainlander, Hakka and indigenous people) and experiences of American and Anglo culture.

Research on pupils' experiences of learning English from a socio-cultural perspective requires an investigation of different planes of analysis (Rogoff, 1995, 2003) in order to uncover the complex issues, such as ethnic, home and community

E. Hjörne et al. (eds.), Learning, Social Interaction and Diversity – Exploring Identities in School Practices, 69–84.

culture that influence access to English language learning. This chapter will argue that ethnic cultures provide pupils in Taiwan with different socio-cultural resources that influence their access to Anglo-American English language in schools. First, the paper begins with a brief overview of EFL learning in Taiwan. It will then describe aspects of the ethnic culture of four groups and its impact on learning English. Third, a description of the socio-cultural methodological approach employed in this study will be provided and will focus primarily on one of the instruments, a questionnaire adapted from Scribner and Cole's (1981) study of language use in Liberia. Findings will be used to explore how some groups come to school already better equipped to access Anglo-American English than other groups. Implications for this will be discussed for EFL teaching and learning in Taiwan.

CONTEXT OF EFL IN TAIWAN

English has played a pivotal role in the education history of Taiwan (Huang, 1993). In recent years, Taiwanese society has been subjected to far reaching, rapid economic change; for example, its entry into WTO (World Trade Organization) in 2002 has led to increased economic cooperation and trade exchange between Taiwan and the other 145 countries in the world community (WTO News, 2001). It became the world's fifteenth largest trading country in 2004 (BFT, Taiwan, 2004). Learning English as an international language has become vital to its economy in terms of providing access to the world community, viewed as one of the keys to success in Taiwan's economic globalization and modernization. It is generally believed that speaking better English fuels upward occupational and social mobility. The pressure to develop better English competence is fierce among learners at each school level. At pre-school stages, common slogans, such as 'do not fail your children at the starting point in learning English' have fuelled growth in 'bilingual' or 'whole English' kindergartens. The Curriculum of Elementary and Junior High School Education (Grade 1-9) required by the Ministry of Education (MOE) in Taiwan in 2001 has designated English as a school subject as early as primary level grade 5 and lowered it further to grade 3 and 4 in 2005 (MOE, Taiwan, 2005) although some schools have taught English at grade 1 and 2 for some time in response to parental expectation and pressure.

ETHNIC CULTURES IN TAIWAN

Taiwan is an island with an ethnically mixed population composed mainly of Hokkien (69%), Hakka (15%), Chinese Mainlander (14%), and indigenous people (2%). These social groups have specific ethnic cultural variations that are particularly pivotal for our understanding of how value is attached to English language learning. The four social groups, which will be considered in turn, have different geographic and historical roots.

The Hokkien people (or called '*Minan Zen*') migrated from China some three hundred years ago. They are the largest social and business-trading group in

Taiwan. They settled in the plains and developed sea or river ports which provided good living conditions and close trade networks with China. Being a Hokkien, as Greenhalgh (1984) suggested, has meant aiming to move from small to large-scale enterprises and climbing the commercial ladder. Due to their historical-cultural legacy of business trading contributing to economic growth and success, the Hokkien have become one of the most distinctive ethnic groups in Taiwan. Given that global business is undertaken in English, the Hokkien value learning English highly.

Chinese Mainlanders migrated from Chinese mainland in 1949 and settled in cities. They brought with them their own traditions, political influences and Mandarin language. Their lifestyles as predominantly urbanites working either in the military or the civil service gave them what was generally considered to be relatively high political and social status. 'White-collar Mainlanders' (Greenhalgh, 1984) became distinct from other ethnic groups, because they valued social mobility which they achieved by rising from low to higher public sector jobs with higher salaries and greater responsibility. Descendants of 'business Hokkien' and 'white-collar Mainlanders' tend to live in urban areas where access to English language resources is greater than in rural areas. The children of these ethnic groups are encouraged to engage in English language learning and to take advantage of after-school learning in, for example, the numerous 'cram schools' ('*bu-xi-ban*').

Hakka ethnic groups migrated from southern China later than Hokkien groups and settled in rugged hills, working in labor-intensive agricultural production. They brought with them a strong pride in the literary accomplishments of their ancestors including a tradition that valued literary study. One of the participating schools in the study was located in Hakka Meinung which had a reputation for being 'the town of PhDs.' The community continued the cultural legacy of valuing and encouraging 'academic study'. Inspired by this cultural legacy, hundreds of PhDs and thousands of Masters' and Bachelors' degrees have been produced in Meinung over the past three decades. Despite Hakka Meniung's rural location, the number of cram schools and after-school activities is increasing. In contrast to other rural communities, schools in Hakka Meinung have a culture of strong academic achievement and English is highly valued.

Recent statistics indicate that there are fourteen indigenous ethnic groups in Taiwan which make up approximately two per cent of its population. The Paiwan tribe (hereafter termed 'indigenous people') is the third largest indigenous group with a population of some 78,000 (GIO, 2010). Along with other rural tribes it has a strong cultural legacy of athletic prowess which is celebrated and highly valued. Successful models of international, athletic performance such as Mr. Chuan-Guang Yang (1933-2007) of the indigenous Ami tribe, known as the 'Iron Man of Asia', inspire young indigenous people to develop their athletic potential as do the numerous athletic coaches and professional sports players. For some indigenous pupils who come from lower socio-economic backgrounds, achievement in sport provides a possible route out of poverty. Local school culture is influenced by these historical roots and pupils are encouraged more to engage in athletic training than in academic learning. There is little after-school provision for EFL learning in these rural areas.

SOCIO-CULTURAL APPROACHES TO LEARNING

Neo-Vygotskian socio-cultural approaches to learning start with the social. Vygotsky's famous dictum states that everything that appears within the child first appeared outside in the socio-cultural and historical plane.

> Any function in the child's cultural development appears twice, or on two planes. First, it appears on the social plane, and then on the psychological plane. First, it appears between people as an interpsychological category, and then within the child as an intrapsychological category [...] It goes without saying that internalization transforms the process itself and changes its structure and functions. Social relations or relations among people genetically underlie all higher functions and their relationships. (Vygotsky, 1981, p. 163)

According to socio-cultural approaches, learning occurs through participation in practice as people together engage in ongoing activity using the tools and resources of their cultural community (Rogoff, 2003). These cultural tools shape activity so that individual action has to be seen as always enacted with mediational means (Wertsch, 1991). Learning English takes place in a variety of contexts even though formal schooling is the primary one. However, what pupils bring with them from their encounters with English in the home, through the media or by walking on the streets of their local community can not be disassociated from the way they undertake classroom activities. Classroom activities can be viewed as situated activities that are undertaken with what Brown and Duguid (1993) called 'stolen knowledge' gained from contexts outside formal classrooms settings. The study investigated the socio-cultural resources that may have aided English language learning for the four ethnic groups in this study.

METHODS

The Four Participant Schools

The study investigated grade 8 (pupils aged 13 years old) English classrooms in four schools chosen to represent a range of groups according to their ethnic and social class background within Taiwanese society. Case study schools were chosen to represent geographical diversity including city centre, suburban, rural and remote areas. The predominant ethnic group in Urbany School was Hokkein whilst in Suburbany School was Hokkien with some Mainlander. In Hakka Rural School was Hakka and in Mountainside School was mainly indigenous Paiwan. The ethnic mix and the languages spoken by pupils in each school are summarized in Table 1.

Table 1. Predominant language and ethnicity in the four schools

Locales	Languages	Pupils' ethnicity	
Urbany	Mandarin & Taiwanese	Hokkien	(70%)
		Mainlander	(19%)
		Hakka	(10%)
Suburbany	Mandarin & Taiwanese	Hokkien	(74%)
		Mainlander	(26%)
Hakka Rural	Mandarin & Hakka	Hakka	(88%)
		Non-Hakka	(12%)
Mountainside	Mandarin & Paiwan	Indigenous Paiwan	(97%)

All schools followed the Grade 1-9 national curriculum which involved 3-4 hours for English per week. There was one supplementary period, which compromised an official after-school revision class in the four schools. Given the national emphasis on EFL, some used time dedicated to lessons considered not to be important for EFL in addition to the standard provision. Urbany School, which claimed to have a bilingual culture, had five hours of English classes per week including one supplementary lesson every weekday afternoon and a further 'Daily Life English' where pupils learned colloquial English with the aid of a school magazine called '*Life ABC*'. There was in addition a 'Lunch Time English' session in which English DJs, chosen from pupils with marked English proficiency, undertook bilingual broadcasts.

Suburbany School had five hours of English classes per week, including a supplementary period. However, given its elite school status, Suburbany School has replaced the two-hour extracurricular activities with English sessions, and provided Saturday classes for high-ability pupils fortnightly. English, like other core subjects (Mandarin and Math), was allocated morning sessions because pupils are expected to have better concentration than in the afternoon. In Suburbany School, as in Urbany School, a large group of pupils stayed behind after school or attended neighboring cram schools ('*bu-shi-ban*'). Cram schools were private-run language institutes popular with pupils in Taiwan. Cram schools taught English grammar and conversational skills. Many pupils had up to nine hours of EFL classes per week.

Hakka Rural School had five hours of English lessons per week and the structure of the school day was similar to that in the two urban schools. Nevertheless, despite its rural nature, many Hakka Rural School pupils attended cram schools which taught grammar and had high academic expectations.

In Mountainside School, there were five hours of English lessons per week including one in a supplementary period. Unlike other schools, core subjects were not allocated to morning sessions but were spread evenly throughout the day. In Mountainside School, as in Hakka Rural School, no specific lessons were taught by foreign teachers. A two-hour 'Extra Curriculum' (Friday) session dedicated to sport exemplified Mountainside's school vision. Few pupils were interested in going to cram school and in any case none was locally available. The time allocated to English in school and the lack of cram schools suggested that English was less valued in the indigenous than in other cultural groups.

Research Instruments and Analysis

This study relied on multiple forms of data collection investigating different 'planes of analysis'. Methods include historical analysis, questionnaires, classroom observation and semi-structured interviews. Documentary analysis and informal visits to local people in the communities provided an understanding of English learning as a historical, social and culturally constituted practice. This paper focuses primarily on findings from the questionnaires.

Questionnaires were modified from Scribner and Cole's (1981) seminal research in Liberia and administered to pupils in Mandarin. The questions fell into three major parts. The first part '*learning the language*' asked about pupils' experiences of learning English across their schooling careers, the presence of others' such as family, school friends or peers who had encouraged or helped them to learn English, and resources available in the locales such as foreign English teachers and cram schools. The second section '*use of the language*' asked about use of English in everyday life such as access to newspapers, Web information or signs written in English in towns, homes and schools. Further questions asked about writing in English such as keeping diary or writing E-mails. The third section '*demographic details*' asked about age, ethnicity, ethnicity of family members, parental education and career patterns, and pupils' foreign culture experiences. 268 participant pupils in the four schools completed questionnaires of which there were 253 valid returns. Questionnaires were coded into an SPSS database. There were 269 variables, which were analyzed using descriptive statistics. Classroom observation was employed to investigate teachers' pedagogic practice in two classrooms in each school. Teacher-student interactions were audio recorded and observational data gained from 28 one-hour sessions in the eight classrooms were analyzed. A coding scheme was designed to characterize different forms of teacher-pupil interaction. Semi-structured interviews were carried out with teachers and pupils to explore English language teaching and learning in depth.

Analysis of the questionnaire provided insight into why some pupils came to school already better equipped to access Anglo-American English than others. Findings have been divided into four sections: The first three draw on data from the student questionnaires and are divided into historical legacies, everyday access to English and socio-cultural resources in the communities. The fourth section illustrates an example of a teacher using pupils' ethnic knowledge to bridge between pupils' everyday experiences and academic English learning.

PARENT'S ETHNIC AND CULTURAL CAPITAL

Parental encouragement, engagement and arrangements play pivotal roles in students' access to English. Parental education and occupational backgrounds seem to be associated with pupils' engagement with English language learning in this study. Hokkien and Mainlander parents had higher, overall educational levels than indigenous and Hakka groups as can be seen in Table 2.

Table 2. Occupations of pupils' parents

	Urban		Rural		
Father's occupation	Hokkien (n=98)	Mainlander (n=28)	Hakka (n=64)	Indigenous (n=53)	All pupils (n=243)
Labor (unskilled)	24 %	11 %	49 %	65 %	37 %
Business	48 %	37 %	22 %	6 %	28 %
Government official	14 %	30 %	11 %	6 %	15 %
Military / police	1 %	15 %	2 %	6 %	6 %
Mother's occupation					
Labor (unskilled)	9 %	4 %	19 %	28 %	15 %
Business	35 %	35 %	35 %	8 %	28 %
*Government official	19 %	23 %	4 %	2 %	12 %
Temporary work	8 %	0 %	9 %	20 %	9 %
*Military / police	0 %	8 %	0 %	2 %	3 %

Note. 1. 'Government official' includes teachers.
2. Percentages do not always add up to 100 due to missing values.

65% of indigenous and 49% of the Hakka fathers were reported to occupy unskilled labor jobs and were severely under represented in business, government and police/military sectors. In contrast, almost half of Hokkien fathers were reported to work in 'business' while 30% of Mainlander fathers worked as 'government officials'. Looking at the distribution of male parental occupations from a historical perspective, the prevalence of 'business Hokkien' and 'white-collar Mainlander' supports Greenhalgh's (1984) anthropological description of two distinct pathways followed by these groups to the top of the commercial and social ladders. The better educated Mainlanders parents; fathers (30%) and mothers (23%), were reported to have civil servant or teaching jobs. The distribution of well paid and less well paid jobs along ethnic divides is referred to in Taiwan as 'iron rice bowls' (*tie-fan-wan*). The term recognizes that parents from Hokkien and Mainlander groups provide children with the benefits that come from having high social status and economic resources. Ethnic divisions in economic capital also mark an unequal access to socio-cultural resources that support English learning such as paying for cram school lessons.

Another aspect of ethnic cultural legacies in the four groups is their religious belief revealed from the questionnaire.

Table 3. Pupils' religious belief

| | Urban | | | Rural | |
Religion	Hokkien (n=98)	Mainlander (n=28)	Hakka n=64)	Indigenous (n=53)	All pupils (n=243)
(Yes)	60 %	50 %	36 %	67 %	53 %
Buddhism	35 %	18 %	29 %	0 %	21 %
Taoism	21 %	25 %	7 %	0 %	13 %
Christian	2 %	7 %	0 %	39 %	12 %
Catholic	2 %	0 %	0 %	28 %	8 %

Note. Percentages do not always add up to 100 due to missing values.

As can be seen in Table 3, more than half of Hokkien (56%) and more than 40 per cent of Mainlander (43%) reported that they held either Buddhist or Taoist religious beliefs. This is in line with Greenhalgh's observation that the majority of Taiwanese historically 'identified themselves as Buddhists' (Greenhalgh, 1984: 537). Indigenous pupils, in contrast, claimed to hold Western religious beliefs, with nearly 40 per cent self reporting as Christian and almost 30 per cent as Catholic.

Western religions for indigenous people within Taiwanese society have their own historical roots. Following Han immigration the footprints of foreign missionaries (mainly Christian) brought Western customs to the mountains, alongside religious doctrine, which interweaved with tribal culture. It might be speculated that a historico-cultural legacy of Western religion might support indigenous pupils positive approach to foreign culture such as an initial interest in learning English. One of the participant indigenous teacher in Mountainside school certainly described herself as a '*xenophile*', saying that '*most Paiwan pupils, including myself, are churchgoers [...]. We tend to recognize Western culture rather than Han Chinese culture*'. Nevertheless, despite their knowledge of Western religious systems, indigenous pupils did not seem to get enough chances to practice English in their day to day lives, as will be addressed in the following section.

EVERYDAY ACCESS TO ENGLISH

The questionnaire asked about pupils' experiences of English in everyday life such as reading practice, perceiving objects written in English, teaching or being helped byothers with English homework. Table 4 provides data on some everyday activities that gave pupils access to English.

As shown in Table 4, when pupils were asked in what circumstances they would read English, nearly 50 per cent of them read English on 'TV programs' (N= 253, 48%) or on 'websites' (N=253, 47%). Indigenous and, to a lesser degree, Hakka respondents, reported having less everyday access to English than urban,

Table 4. Everyday English practices

Categories of practice	Urban			Rural	
	Hokkien (n=98)	Mainlander (n=28)	Hakka (n=64)	Indigenous (n=53)	All pupils (n=243)
TV programs (reading)	42 %	64 %	47 %	40 %	48 %
Websites (reading)	60 %	46 %	47 %	34 %	47 %
House (visible signs)	62 %	71 %	41 %	37 %	53 %
In town (visible signs)	64 %	82 %	53 %	42 %	60 %
Help from others	47 %	71 %	37 %	45 %	50 %
Teaching others	64 %	82 %	15 %	10 %	43 %

particularly Mainlander pupils. When pupils were probed as to the existence of visible signs of English in their house or town more than half (average 53%) reported the existence of household objects written in English, such as labels on electronic products or instructions for taking medicine (see Table 4). Almost twice as many Mainlander (N=28, 71%) as indigenous (N=53, 37%) pupils reported coming across English in everyday settings. Twice as many mainlanders (N=28, 82%) as indigenous (N=53, 42%) pupils reported seeing things in town written in English, such as road or shop signs. 50 per cent of all pupils reported that they had friends or family who could speak, read, or write English and could help them with English homework. 43 percent of all pupils reported having taught someone how to speak, read, or write English. While 82 per cent of Mainlanders reported they had helped someone with English only 10 per cent of indigenous pupils reported they had. Very few Hakka (N=64, 15%) reported having taught others.

This picture of pupils' access to English in everyday life reveals large differences between ethnic groups. More Mainlander pupils than other groups reported having seen or practiced English in everyday settings and it is likely that their experience of towns rather than rural countryside and villages had contributed to this finding. These pupils also gained access to English through families, cram schools and school classrooms. We could ask whether or not schools can compensate for the lack of exposure to English experienced by the Hakka and indigenous groups in everyday life. The following section throws light on this.

ACCESS TO ENGLISH IN RELATION TO EDUCATIONAL CONTEXTS

The questionnaire included questions on parental encouragement, availability of traveling abroad and extra provisions such as cram school lessons.

Table 5. English in relation to formal educational contexts

Parental Encouragement, arrangements	Urban			Rural	
	Hokkien (n=98)	Mainlander (n=28)	Hakka (n=64)	Indigenous (n=53)	All pupils (n=243)
Encouragement	72 %	75 %	72 %	67 %	72 %
Parents know English	44 %	46 %	25 %	21 %	34 %
Cram school English practices					
Commenced from here	89 %	89 %	61 %	27%	67 %
Listening to teachers here	68 %	75 %	47 %	17 %	52 %
Starting level of learning English					
Kindergarten	19 %	29 %	3 %	0 %	13 %
Primary School	79 %	64 %	95 %	100 %	85 %
Experience of foreign teachers					
(Yes)	90 %	93 %	33 %	13 %	57 %
Enjoy it	66 %	58 %	71 %	86 %	70 %
Experience of foreign culture					
Been abroad	34 %	52 %	22 %	4 %	28 %
Lived abroad	1 %	11 %	0 %	0 %	3 %

Table 5 demonstrates that more than 70 per cent of all pupils reported being encouraged to learn English by parents. A further question asked if specific family members had knowledge of English. Twice as many urban in comparison to rural pupils reported that their parents knew English and had chances to practice with them at home. Travel abroad to learn English has long been valued by Taiwanese parents.

When pupils were asked where they studied and when they first started to learn English, a high percentage of pupils reported having after-school revision lessons in cram school everyday. More than half (67%) of all pupils reported starting to learn English in cram schools either at pre-school or primary level. 52 per cent of all pupils reported that their first experiences of listening to English being spoken was from their cram school teachers. The popularity and availability of cram schools in urban areas and the Hakka township suggests that they were the institutions outside home and formal schools where pupils were able to receive additional formal instruction in English. A strikingly higher proportion of Hokkien and Mainlanders (both 89%) reported having been given opportunity to learn English from cram schools than rural groups (Hakka 61% and indigenous 27%). When pupils were asked at which level of schooling they first started learning English, 85 per cent of all pupils reported that they started to learn English in primary classrooms. None of the indigenous pupils reported learning English in Kindergarten while almost 30% of the Mainlander pupils did. Questions about whether they were taught by teachers who were not Taiwanese and came from abroad, urban pupils reported more contact with native English speakers than Hakka and indigenous pupils.

Across many questions about access to English learning, a common pattern emerged that revealed the extent to which Hakka and indigenous pupils were distinctly disadvantaged in comparison to the other two groups in terms of resources. A question later in the questionnaire about foreign travel found that half of Mainlander pupils (N=28, 52%) reported having traveled abroad for sight seeing or for study tours, while only 4 per cent of indigenous pupils reported having done so (see Table 5). 11 per cent of Mainlander pupils, in contrast to other groups, reported that they had lived abroad at some time in the past.

Hakka and indigenous pupils started to learn English later, had fewer cram schools and less experience of native English speakers than other ethnic groups. It could be argued that formal institutions can not compensate for the lack of contact with English that Hakka and indigenous pupils encountered in their everyday lives. However, socio-cultural studies have suggested that when teachers are able to draw on local culture they are better able to bridge between pupils' everyday knowledge and academic knowledge (e.g., Heath, 1983; Scribner & Cole, 1981). The following section demonstrates how one teacher drew on pupils' everyday knowledge while teaching English.

PEDAGOGIC PRACTICE: USING ETHNIC CULTURE TO GIVE PUPILS ACCESS TO ENGLISH

The following section describes some of the pedagogic techniques that were used by teachers in Hakka Rural school. Data concerning teachers' knowledge of local community or access to pupils' local culture were predominantly drawn from classroom observations. In general all eight classrooms revealed similarities in instructional style driven by the need to maintain high examination scores that is typical in Taiwanese school culture. Pedagogic practice was dominated by control intending to ensure that pupils undertook the 'teacher's agenda' (Mehan, 1979). However, one of the teachers (Ms. Mei) from Hakka Rural School incorporated pupils' everyday culture into her instructional discourse. It is worth noting that although at times each teacher used illustrations from pupils' everyday experience, such as referring to going to a Taiwanese restaurant or night market, Ms. Mei used them frequently and was found to refer to ethnic Hakka everyday culture even though she was an ethnic Hokkien teacher. The following extract illustrates typical features of her interactional style.

In the afternoon (13:20~14:05 pm) of 1st October, 2004, Ms. Mei was teaching a lesson from the textbook. The text included a dialogue between June and Coco. June was a high school girl from America talking to her Taiwanese friend, Coco about their different experiences of schooling, including cram schools. At the outset of the lesson, Ms. Mei asked pupils to listen to a CD of dialogue between June and Coco's and followed by questions. While introducing the new term 'cram school' Ms. Mei initiated a series of questions concerning Hakka pupils' everyday cram school experience.

Extract

1	T:	After the dialogue about wearing school uniform, Coco changed the
2		topic by asking 'Do you go to cram school?'
3		((writes on board and reads)) 'Do you go to cram school?'
4		Coco changed a topic by asking what?=
5	Ss:	((answer promptly)) = 'Do you go to cram school?'
6	T:	Cram school. 'Cram' is a new word. Read after me. 'Cram'=
7	Ss:	((repeat)) =Cram

((The next few turns are spent in reading and repeating the words 'cram' and 'cram school' between teacher and pupils.))

8	T:	What's cram school? ((expects Chinese translation))
9	Ss:	'bu-shi-ban' (Cram school)
10	T:	Ok, 'go to cram schools' is… ['chi-bu-shi-ban']
11	Ss:	['chi-bu-shi-ban']
12	T:	Wow … 'schools'. We have plural 's' here, meaning lots of them.
13		Do you go to cram schools? […] seem like lots of you do.
14		Please raise your hands if you go to cram schools.
15	Ss:	((Raise hands and make a little noise.))
16	T:	Wow, half of you do. Ok, put down your hands.
17	Ss:	((Some complain about going more than twice a week.))
18	T:	So 'lucky' or so 'poor'! You can imagine it for yourselves.

Hakka culture emphasizes academic study and many Hakka pupils attended 'cram schools. In the questionnaire 61 per cent of Hakka pupils reported attending cram schools (see Table 5 above). In the course of learning the new phrase: '*go to cram schools*' (line 2 in Extract), Ms. Mei asked about pupils' own experiences of cram school. She asked '*do you go to cram schools*' (line 13). This is an example of 'bridging' (Rogoff, 1990) Ms Mei drew on pupils' out of school knowledge as she demonstrated a new linguistic phrase. In response to her question some pupils' complained about being tired of going to cram school (line 17). Ms Mei avoided making judgments and simply responded: '*you can imagine it for yourselves*' (line 18). Her empathetic understanding and awareness of her pupils' everyday lives helped to achieve intersubjective meaning with her pupils. Her pedagogic approach frequently drew on her knowledge of Hakka local culture. The way she incorporated pupils' everyday knowledge into her pedagogic practice gave pupils a message that she valued their indigenous culture and by extension valued them as English language learners.

It could be argued that Ms. Mei's pedagogic approach, by drawing on pupils' everyday experiences, scaffolded their access to English and disrupted rather than reinforced a pattern of disadvantage in this groups' access to English. In comparison to Hokkien and Mainlanders groups Hakka pupils had fewer socio-cultural English related resources that are culturally and locally available to them. The following discussion relates to the relationship between socio-cultural resources and differential patterns of achievement in English language learning.

GOING BEYOND THE URBAN-RURAL DIVIDE

Learning English as an international language has become vital to Taiwan's economic globalization and modernization. People have come to recognize that English proficiency is intimately linked to economic and personal earning potential. However, differences in levels of achievement were found to be related not only to regional but also cultural differences among social groups. The study found that access to English and the value associated with it varied between ethnic cultural groups suggesting why some ethnic groups achieve less well than others in learning English. Findings pertaining to pupils' experiences of English in various settings such as everyday life, informal institutions and in classrooms, demonstrate how patterns of disadvantage accumulated for some ethnic groups and not others. Within school settings, each of the four schools had the same amount of weekly hours learning English within a fixed class timetable, a formalized schedule complying with the national curriculum guidelines. However, flexibility existed across the schools, mirroring either their individual 'school visions' or related commitments. Ethnic cultural variations found in rural locales gave pupils competing values in relation to English language learning. For example, Hakka cultural emphasized academic study (cram schooling) and indigenous people's cultural emphasized athletic prowess. Parental occupations gave children differing access to social and cultural capital in relation to English. The 'business Hokkien' and 'white-collar Mainlander', gave urban pupils advantages. Their parents valued English learning highly yet they also had relevant experience of English that they could pass on financial resources to back this up. While Hakka and indigenous parents valued English learning they often had fewer financial resources, less relevant personal experience of English and sometimes competing value systems such as athletic prowess which was part of a long historical legacy. Mountainside pupils were encouraged to practice sports every afternoon. Formal and informal after-school learning was available in all locations except the mountainous areas where indigenous pupils lived. Although Hakka pupils also inhabited rural areas, their historical legacies placed great value on scholarship and this had led to a better provision of cram schools in Hakka dominated localities in comparison to other rural areas.

Regional differences in access to socio-cultural resources have long been reflected in the annual National Basic Competence exam achievement patterns.

Tests have demonstrated that approximately half of junior high pupils nationwide are low achievers and some appeared to have given up learning English (Chang, 2002). The majority of these live in rural areas. The regional difference in English learning achievement has been widely characterized as the 'urban-rural divide'. However, findings from this study reveal that patterns of underachievement relate to differences in ethnic culture rather than simply to rural and urban locations. Differences in wealth, relations to job-markets, life-styles, child-rearing and other family arrangements underlie cultural traditions. The urban-rural difference is not simply an issue of geography but of socio-cultural resources available in locales arising from ethnic historical legacies and patterns of employment.

TOWARDS A PEDAGOGY OF CULTURAL BRIDGING

The values embedded within the culture of each group ensure that certain activities have high status and that parents guide and encourage their children to participate in the practices that are valued within their ethnic culture and embedded in the community such as cram schools or athletic coaching. Historical cultural legacies interacted with what kinds of resources became locally available in relation to English learning. These interactions positioned pupils differentially with respect to formal school English learning and help to explain the consistent pattern of achievement in English that has been documented as the 'urban-rural divide'. In short, the 'urban-rural divide' assumption cannot be simply interpreted as an issue of geography, except in the sense that different ethnic groups who have fewer resources to scaffold English learning have traditionally resided in specific locales. There are complex socio-historical roots to the pattern of achievement that include cultural values, norms, beliefs and as well as resources.

The Hakka teacher who was able to bridge pupils' ethnic cultural knowledge in her pedagogy was found to be effective in achieving 'intersubjectivity' (Rogoff, 1990, p. 71). Intersubjectivity is when interlocutors find a common ground that allows shared meaning to take place. Following Vygotsky (1987) Rogoff has referred to this as 'bridging' (Rogoff, 1990, p. 70). The study found that Mountainside School children have fewer socio-cultural resources available in their locales to help them to access English than other ethnic groups. Furthermore, highly valued cultural practices privileged the body and sporting prowess rather than practices required for academic learning in schools making pedagogic bridging particularly challenging. Ms. Mei was an exception in this study because she was an ethic Hokkien yet she had made strong efforts to get to know the Hakka culture of her pupils. Many teachers in rural schools do not share or even know about the cultural values of their pupils (cf. Abreu, 1995). If the rural–urban divide is not to widen even further, then teachers will have to search beyond academic cultures to find bridging resources. The study found that Mountainside School pupils have fewer socio-cultural resources available in their locales to help them to access English than other ethnic groups. Much of the indigenous pupils 'stolen knowledge' was unknown and so not used as resources for learning English. Therefore many indigenous pupils could not recognize themselves through the pedagogic practices of their English teachers. One place to start the process of pedagogic bridging may be through a cultural awareness of religion. Even if teachers do not share, for example, the Western religious systems of their pupils there is enough global knowledge available to create the grounds for intersubjectivity, likewise with sport. Once teachers are made aware of the socio-cultural resources that are carried by Mountainside School children's ethnic cultures they can be encouraged to draw on these as resources for cultural bridging. However, cultural bridging requires knowledge of ethnic cultures, the willingness to value such cultures in their own right and a willingness to expand pedagogic practices beyond that narrowly associated with academic culture. In this way teachers may help to disrupt the seemly unbreakable 'urban-rural divide' in English language learning in Taiwan.

ACKNOWLEDGEMENTS

This article was supported by grants from the Economic & Social Research Council (ESRC: PTA-026-27-1522), UK and presented at the 2008 Biennial Meeting at European Association for Research on Learning and Instruction (Earli).

REFERENCES

Abreu, G. de (1995). Understanding how children experience the relationship between home and school mathematics. *Mind, Culture and Activity: An International Journal, 2*(2), 119-142.

BFT, Taiwan (2004). Trade statistics. Retrieved September 28, 2004, from http://cus93.trade.gov.tw/english/FSCE/FSC0011E.ASP.

Brown, J. S., & Duguid, P. (1993). Stolen knowledge. *Educational Technology, 33*(3), 10-15.

Chang, W. C. (2002). Revamping the 'double skewed phenomenon' of English subject in NBC test for junior high school pupils [in Chinese]. Retrieved April 3, 2004, from http://grbsearch.stic.gov.tw/tiff/91/rrpg91120850.pdf.

GIO, Taiwan (2010). Taiwan yearbook: People and language. Retrieved March 22, 2010, from http://www.gio.gov.tw/taiwan-website/5-gp/yearbook/02PeopleandLanguage.htm.

Greenhalgh, S. (1984). Networks and their nodes: Urban society on Taiwan. *China Quarterly, 99*, 529-552.

Heath, S. B. (1983). *Way with words: Language, life, and work in communities and classrooms.* Cambridge: Cambridge University Press.

Huang, T. L. (1993). *The pedagogic innovation and enrichment of EFL* [in Chinese]. Taipei: Crane.

Lave, J., & Wenger, E. (1991). *Situated learning: Legitimate peripheral participation.* Cambridge: Cambridge University Press.

Mehan, H. (1979). *Learning lessons: Social organization in the classroom.* Cambridge, MA: Harvard University Press.

MOE, Taiwan (2005). General guidelines of Grade 1-9 Curriculum of elementary and junior high school education. Retrieved April 2, 2005, from http://english.moe.gov.tw/public/Attachment/66618445071.doc.

Rogoff, B. (1990). *Apprenticeship in thinking: Cognitive development in social context.* Oxford: Oxford University Press.

Rogoff, B. (1995). Observing sociocultural activity on three planes: Participatory appropprication, guided participation, and apprenticeship. In J. V. Wertsch, P. del Rio, & A. Alvarez (Eds.), *Sociocultural studies of mind* (pp.139-164). Cambridge: Cambridge University Press.

Rogoff, B. (2003). *The cultural nature of human development.* Oxford: Oxford University Press.

Rogoff, B., & Lave, J. (Eds.) (1984). *Everyday cognition: Development in social context*. Cambridge, MA: Harvard University Press.

Scribner, S., & Cole, M. (1981). *The psychology of literacy*. Cambridge, MA: Harvard University Press.

Vygotsky, L. S. (1981). The genesis of higher mental functions. In J. V. Wertsch (Ed. and Trans.), *The concept of activity in Soviet psychology* (pp. 144-188). Armonk, New York: Sharpe.

Vygostky, L. S. (1987). Thinking and speech. In R. W. Rieber & A. S. Carton (Eds.) *The collected works of L. S. Vygotsky* (N. Minick, Trans.) New York: Plenum Press.

Wenger, E. (1998). *Communities of practice: Learning, meaning, and identity*. Cambridge: Cambridge University Press.

Wertsch, J. V. (1991). *Voices of mind: A sociocultural approach to mediated action*. Cambridge: Harvard University Press.

WTO News (2001). WTO Ministerial Conference approves accession of Chinese Taipei. Retrieved June 20, 2005, from http://www.wto.org/english/news_ e/pres01_e/pr244_e. htm.

Wen-Chuan Lin
English Department
Wenzao Ursuline College of Languages, Taiwan

Gabrielle Ivinson
School of Social Sciences
Cardiff University, UK

SANGEETA BAGGA-GUPTA

7. CHALLENGING UNDERSTANDINGS OF BILINGUALISM IN THE LANGUAGE SCIENCES FROM THE LENS OF RESEARCH THAT FOCUSES SOCIAL PRACTICES

INTRODUCTION

A number of different languages are present in the linguistic ecology of Sweden including Swedish; sign languages; English and other foreign languages; regional languages or varieties of Swedish; "neighbour languages" like Danish, Norwegian, Icelandic, et cetera; national minority languages; and the immigrant and refugee languages of those who have come to live in Sweden. (Hult, 2004, p. 183)

Swedish society has been a diverse space for a very long time and the meetings of peoples from other spaces with a multitude of linguistic and cultural backgrounds has contributed to and shaped popular images of what we today consider to be *the* "original and authentic" homogenous Swedish culture (see also Bagga-Gupta, 2008). Mass media and IT revolutions during the last quarter of the 20th century have re-vitalized our understandings of this original, core culture and the concomitant (re)conceptualisations of the more recent diversifying processes in the Swedish national context. In other words, the explosive access to contemporary media has given rise to specific understandings where recent diversifying processes are viewed as being more dramatic and as having created a more heterogeneous society. These popular understandings also seep into the academic literature. Issues with a bearing on these types of agendas are raised in this chapter.

Furthermore, critically understanding dimensions of the present language and cultural landscapes that young people are members of, including explicitly recognizing the multilingual and multicultural nature of spaces inside and outside Swedish educational institutions today, constitutes an important democratic issue within research itself. Recognising and making visible the numerous languages that are seen as contributing to complexities in Swedish classrooms is one such focus. At the same time there is need to understand that this scenario is far from unique or peculiar to Swedish. The rise of English as a global language and the concomitant shift in status for nationally dominant languages together with the rise in status of regional or ethnic or heritage or community languages at national levels, are two

E. Hjörne et al. (eds.), Learning, Social Interaction and Diversity – Exploring Identities in School Practices, 85–102.

significant forces that have more recently seriously questioned the one nation-one language myth (Garcia, 2009, Hornberger, 2002).[6]

The complex nature of classroom diversity calls for research to attend to the concerns that professionals experience in institutional settings by both *reframing these concerns* and also through *critical re-searching activities* such that analytically new issues can be raised and present understandings can be challenged. As Hornberger decisively points out:

> The challenge of negotiating across multiple languages, cultures, and identities is a very real one in classrooms all over the world, one not to be lightly dismissed. Yet, on the whole, educational policy and practice continues blithely to disregard the presence of multiple languages, cultures, and identities in today's classrooms. (Homberger, 2002, p. 43)

Thus, highlighting dimensions of equity and difference inside and outside classrooms and re-conceptualising curricula issues are significant for enabling important shifts in positions that have a bearing on everyday practices in the lives of young people in Northern contexts. This, as I have discussed previously, allows attention to be paid to current conceptualisations of language and culture and enables democratic potentials in education to come centre stage (Bagga-Gupta, 2004a).

This chapter revisits some classical studies in the Language Sciences since the 1960s and discusses what kinds of contributions these have made to (re)conceptualizations in academic areas like bilingualism and literacy. Furthermore, this chapter aims to critically explore conceptualisations of language – particularly bi- and multilingualism in the arena of institutional education (i.e. schools and legislation). While the analysis and discussions go beyond issues of linguistic rights and policies, by taking social theories of mind positions and post-colonial perspectives as points of departure, they situate research on language issues in the realm of democratic agendas. The focus is upon the context of institutional education, where schools are not merely understood as operational sites for national and international level policies with a bearing on multilingualism. Schools, it is argued, are sites where we privilege certain understandings of "language and communication" and more specifically, certain understandings of "language learning". A shift in understandings where schools are seen as *one of many sites or locations* where children are socialized into their primary and multiple languages allows us to understand the problems inherent with more narrow selective positions vis-à-vis learning. Such a shift in positions, it is argued, has the potential to contribute towards furthering our understandings regarding pluralistic societies and throwing light on "the ongoing tension of the multilingual balancing act" in education (Hult, 2004, p. 196).

This introductory section has zoomed into the central themes in this chapter. The next section raises conceptual issues related to firstly, the differences between

---

[6] Also pitting the number of nation-states (ca 250) against the most recent estimates of the number of actively used human languages (ca 6000) puts to rest this widespread largely eurocentric myth.

the role and enterprise of research and the institutional field of education, and secondly, between different types of research agendas that can be discerned not least in the literature on bilingualism, literacy and special education. It forms the basis for critically focusing upon the role that research discourses and the organization of research itself plays in the maintenance and reproduction of selective understandings of language and language learning. The third section in this chapter revisits some early studies in addition to more recent research from both the Literacy-cum-Language Studies and the Deaf Studies fields. Here the relevance of the social practices position in the Educational and Language Sciences fields is focused. The kinds of contributions the earlier classical studies have made to (re)conceptualizations in academic areas like bilingualism and literacy are discussed. The second last section highlights commonsense understandings that relate to and frame bilingualism in educational policy and institutional contexts. The ways of understanding and "talking about bilingualism" are juxtaposed and shown to be in disaccord with the ways in which human beings routinely engage in "bilingual talk" in everyday life both inside and outside school settings. The concluding section brings together the salient issues raised in this chapter.

(RE)SEARCH IN THE LANGUAGE AND EDUCATIONAL SCIENCES AND INSTITUTIONAL PERSPECTIVES

Conceptual and Comparative Issues

The organization of institutional education is an enterprise that has strong historical traditions and is based upon accumulated collective knowledge at the societal level. The initiation of mandatory schooling for *all* children in Northern societies after the Second World War brought issues of human diversity and difference centre stage in institutional education. Research endeavours, to a large extent funded by society, have been and continue in large measure to be viewed as important for addressing issues of equity and difference in school settings. Research is thus, not uncommonly understood in terms of a neutral tool which will help us arrive at better and more refined educational methods so that ethnic minorities, functionally disabled and other marginalised groups can be "included" in education.

Recognizing the inherent tension between the agenda of the institutional field of education and what research is expected to deliver, not withstanding, an important distinction needs to be drawn between thematic areas like, for instance, literacy education, bilingual education and/or special education in terms of *research fields* and literacy education, bilingual education and/or special education as *activity and institutional fields*. As a research field or research activity "bilingualism" or "bilingual education", for instance, represents critical analysis and reflections on the institutional activity field of "bilingual education". This means that the analysis of the institutional fields of thematic areas like literacy education or bilingual education or special education is done from explicit scientific perspectives and through the use of analytically driven questions, research methodologies and theories. Here assumptions regarding communication, language, learning and development in the theoretical frameworks that are drawn upon need to be fore fronted in the studies that are conducted.

The distinction mentioned above highlights an important issue and suggests that the activity of reflecting critically upon the institutional field of education (i.e. doing research) is different from the activity of being engaged as a professional within the institutional field of education. Thus, while research is important, it has limited possibilities and cannot be used as a neutral tool from which we can distil or arrive at "educational methods". It may however be interesting to note that while a "compensatory perspective" guides the activity and institutional field of bilingual education, I will argue below that *critical multilingual and participatory perspectives* themselves make up marginal positions in the bilingual research landscape. In other words, there exists both a dominance of monolingual points of departure and a parallel paucity of research that focuses social practices in the bulk of the research that informs the thematic area of bilingual research.

The distinction highlighted above has specific implications in the areas of bilingual or diversity education and also special education. A number of specific models or ideologies of learning and communication are understood as having shaped the organisation of education for functionally disabled pupils and for bi- and multilingual pupils in school settings (see further below). Thus for instance, the label and the explicit communicative rationale of any given bilingual education model tends to be equated with and is seen as representing the everyday communicative-practices in that model. The point that is important here is that there is a fundamental difference between the logic of the institutional field of bilingual education (including policies) or the ideologies of communication that underlie any given model, and the activity of research that highlights the need to reflect upon this institutional field. The studies that are accounted for in the next section of this chapter have focused the study of communicative-practices in different settings both inside and outside educational institutional settings. One can say that a *descriptive-analytical* agenda – and not a *prescriptive* agenda – is the point of departure in such studies. This descriptive-prescriptive distinction is presented through the example of research in the bilingual area in Figure 1.

A point of departure in a descriptive-analytical perspective is highlighting and studying that which is taken for granted or that which is "normal" in bi- and multilingual communication-practices. Here, the primary focus is not the explicit "problem" at the institutional field level. In addition, the significance of the "best methods", the "structure of communication" and the "how" to teach issues become subordinate to issues of "communicative content", who is involved in the teaching, what is being focused, et cetera. in the descriptive-analytical agenda. This type of research concomitantly attempts to (i) throw light upon patterned "ways with words" or ways of communicating in institutional settings and (ii) understanding the underlying central assumptions vis-à-vis communication, learning and development that guide the social practices in a given bilingual educational model.

Descriptive-analytical research agenda	Prescriptive-ideological research agenda
– Studies and analysis of bi- & multilingual communication in everyday life inside and/or outside classroom settings – Focuses on the communication-practices in educational settings and *language use* in a given bilingual educational model – Focuses upon when, how, together with whom and why different modalities and languages are used inside and outside classroom settings – Focuses on the central assumptions regarding language, communication, learning and development in a given educational model	– Aims to identify the most superior model or method of communication which is deemed to be applicable in all subjects and classroom situations – Focuses upon what we or others think we should be doing in schools – An underlying assumption here equates the communicative model with the communicative-practices in that model

Figure 1. Different research agendas – example research in bilingual education

There is growing awareness that a number of thematic areas in the Language Sciences continue to be dominated by prescriptive or ideological agendas. In other words, there is a dearth of empirically focused studies of the everyday lives of human beings generally and young people particularly and their communication repertoires in institutional educational settings and as well as their usage of languages outside classroom settings. This growing awareness and the theoretically significant distinction drawn upon here calls for the need to focus human interaction and participation in educational settings (and not the ideologies or models at the institutional levels). In addition this resonates with implications that arise from taking sociocultural theoretical perspectives as points of departure in the Language Sciences and the Educational Sciences.

The next section revisits some classical studies in the Language Sciences since the 1960's and discusses their impact upon academic thematic areas like bilingualism and literacies in the Language Sciences. New and parallel insights from studies in the Deaf Studies fields are also raised. The common denominator in both is the underlying focus on human social practices and contributions from these fields to areas in the Language Sciences.

(RE)VISITING SOME STUDIES IN MULTILINGUAL SETTINGS

Attending to issues involved in the *communities of users* of one or more language variety – rather than language per se has been previously recognized as having contributed to shifts in understandings related to human communication. Research focused since the 1960s on the *everyday uses* of oral, written and signed languages in settings as diverse as the Vai community in Liberia (Scribner & Cole, 1981), the southern United States during the "desegregation" process (Heath, 1983), villages in Iran (Street, 1984), a Mexican community in northern California (Vasquez, Pease-Alvarez & Shannon, 1994), a NGO that, since the late 1960's, provides services for migrant children and communities in urban South-East Asia (Bagga-Gupta, 1995), deaf and hearing educational communities in Scandinavia (Bagga-Gupta, 2000, 2002, 2004b; Hansen, 2005), deaf home communities in north-eastern USA (Erting, 1999; Erting, Thumann-Prezioso & Benedict, 2000) and multilingual hearing educational settings in Sweden (Carlsson & Bagga-Gupta, 2006; Cromdal, 2000, Gynne & Bagga-Gupta, 2011), has put the spotlight on the *situated, distributed, collective* and *chained* ecology of languages and meaning making.

While some of the early classical studies from the 1960s and 1970s focused upon the uses of *different* languages by children and adults in a range of settings, their contributions have primarily, if not singularly, been acknowledged in the area of Literacy Studies in the Language Sciences. In other words, while, these early studies were conducted in communities where human beings used more than one language variety, code, et cetera. in the course of their daily lives, a shift in understandings in the area of Bilingual Studies does not seem to have taken place. Work by Heath (1983), Scribner and Cole (1981), Street (1984) and others are acknowledged as showing that human beings develop the different languages they use – both oral and written – to the level of competencies required in different domains and arenas in life. Such results have been taken to mean that developing literate skills in a particular language, variety or register, requires contact with mundane tasks that mediate, support and make such skills in a particular language or register functional and necessary (see also empirical accounts in Bagga-Gupta, 1995; Knobel, 1999). These types of early studies in multilingual settings have shown that the capacity to read and write in a specific code or variety cannot be seen as something neutral which an individual carries with him/her for use in social situations across languages. The point here is that, while these kinds of early studies in the Language Sciences were conducted in *multilingual contexts* their contributions have mainly been acknowledged in (re)conceptualizations in the area of Literacy Studies (also known as New Literacy Studies). Their contributions to the field of bi- and multilingualism have, so far, remained more or else eclipsed.

Furthermore, these kinds of studies have demonstrated how formal schooling in Northern types of contexts constitutes an environment that makes extensive use of and reinforces practices in which written language becomes functional. But what is functional *inside* the school setting may not be functional in everyday life, leisure or work settings *outside* schools, since literate activities may play no significant role or an altogether different role in another language or register there. The point that is significant for present purposes is that acknowledgement regarding the domain specificity of competencies in *different language* codes, registers or varieties is seldom attributed to these earlier studies.

Insights derived from another field of bi- and multilingual research within the Language Sciences has relevance here. Attending to issues related to the communities of users in "visually oriented"[7] settings, instead of the prescriptive tendencies in the two dominating perspectives in the large body of literature in the deaf field, has during the last decade or so contributed to a new orientation in the literature (see Bagga-Gupta, 2004c). The deaf research field furthermore is recognised as being heavily polarised with two prescriptive tendencies: a medical-psychological perspective that views deafness and deaf human beings as handicapped and a cultural perspective that views deaf human beings in terms of a linguistic minority. The prescriptive nature of the discussions in the literature, thus for instance, legitimizes one of these two traditions as the norm, that in turn gives rise to a superior or correct method of communication for the deaf (especially in educational contexts). A non-prescriptively oriented third research tradition has, as mentioned above, been identified in the literature more recently. Leaving aside the previous focus upon oralism and manualism, researchers (often themselves users of one of the worlds many different SL's, Signed Languages) have recently started engaging in the analysis of visually oriented human beings' everyday communication in different settings. By focusing upon the social practices in which human beings routinely use a given Signed Language together with one or more spoken and/or written languages has turned attention away from the two different dominating and normalizing discourses that build upon either an "oral tradition" or a "manual/sign language tradition".

The patterned ways of using manual signs from a specific SL, manually representing written words through finger-spelling, visually linking manual signs of a SL to the written signs of a written language system by pointing, underlining or otherwise highlighting, mouthing a word and linking it to other visual representations have, in this body of literature, been identified as being regular features of human communication in visually oriented settings.

Concepts such as chaining, linking, sandwiching, et cetera have emerged in this body of literature to account for the complex and patterned ways in which different language codes and modalities are routinely used by human beings.[8] This parallel and patterned use of at least two languages – American Sign Language, ASL-English or Swedish Sign Language, SSL-Swedish or Norwegian Sign Language, NSL-Norwegian in visually oriented settings in many ways resembles the links between the oral-written uses of language that characterizes communication that have been discussed in the Literacy Studies literature through concepts such as "literacy events" and "literacy practices". Furthermore, both literacy events and bilingual "signed" communication incorporates the use of different modalities. Thus the intertwined use of oral and written modalities or oral/signed and written modalities in one or more languages or varieties constitutes the recurring patterns described in the Literacy Studies and more recently Deaf Studies literature. In other words, it is the linking and patterned ways of chaining in and between the different language codes, varieties and modalities that characterizes meaning making

---

[7] See Bagga-Gupta (2004b) for an exploration of the empirically grounded concept "visually oriented".
[8] For instance visual manual signs, visual written signs, manual finger-spelling, oral language, visual mouthings of oral languages, etc.

processes in human communication where oral, written and/or signed languages are used.

Taken together, these types of studies of communication-practices in bi- and multilingual settings have emerged within relatively newer communicatively oriented positions that challenge the dominant perspective in the Language Sciences where emphases lies upon formalistic and structuralistic approaches. Thus, the "skill focused" and "signal focused" conceptualisations of human communication are under critique in more recent research on *languages and literacies*. The co-construction of meaning, situatedness of meaning, the social as a pivotal, the need to focus communicative-practices, attending to membership issues, taking into account the representative and interpretive nature of language, etc., make up some of the complex – though nevertheless important – issues that have been attended to in the kinds of studies that have been discussed in this section.

However, there appears to exist a gap between the analytical assumptions that are prescribed to in these social theories of mind positions, and the ways in which (i) many branches of the Language Sciences are conceptualized and (ii) the resulting organization of language instruction in educational settings. Linked to this gap is a particular view of learning generally and language learning specifically. One can say that the analytical assumptions in the more recent sociocultural or social theories of mind positions are at odds with, for instance, linear trajectories that dominate current understandings of human intellectual development in general and human language learning and development in particular. In the latter, the "brain as container" metaphor not uncommonly frames understandings of language development and learning. It is these kinds of conceptualisations within the Language Sciences and the organisation of language instruction in school settings that are focused upon in the next section.

SELECTIVE CONCEPTUALISATIONS

Examples from the Language and the Educational Sciences Fields

The term bilingualism has become an important area of study in Northern settings and is perhaps one of the most central concepts in the Language Sciences today. It lies at the center of a *web of understandings* and is connected to a flora of concepts in language education. The latter include both areas of research inquiry and subjects that are taught in schools and in higher education in Sweden: "home language", "mother tongue", "foreign language", "Swedish", "first language", "second language", "Swedish as a second language", "Swedish for the deaf/hard of hearing", etc.

The studies conducted in different types of bi- and multilingual settings discussed in the previous section indicate that, from sociocultural or social theories of mind positions, bilingualism can scarcely be understood in terms of competencies in two language codes. While a growing number of researchers situated within new paradigms in the human sciences acknowledge that a competencies view of two or more language codes, registers, etc. is an idealization, *the misleading nature* and the *monolingual bias* inherent in this conceptualization is more infrequently acknowledged. The first anomaly relates to the fact that – at least in the North – monolingualism continues to be (incorrectly) taken as a point of departure as the human norm. Communication in different codes, registers or modalities is not a central concern for multilingual human beings as they go about mundane chores and activities in the course of their daily lives. As discussed earlier in the introduction, a monolingual Eurocentric position often disregards the fact that the majority of the people in the world live multilingually. This perspective furthermore fails to recognize the fact that patterned ways of meaning making or communication in mundane activities are not only rich sites for research, such communication needs to be understood *from* multilingual points of departure. The monolingual bias in the field of Bilingual Studies (especially in the North) becomes compounded by the scarcity of researchers who themselves live multilingually in their daily lives, and who thereby potentially bring to the research analysis a multilingual point of departure. Creating spaces where multilingual academic voices become mainstreamed in the Bi(multi)lingual Studies field thus is an important way to address the monolingual bias in the literature. The point that is salient for present purposes was appropriately surmised by Grosjean over a decade ago and holds true even today: "Few areas of linguistics are surrounded by as many misconceptions as is bilingualism" (Grosjean, 1996, p. 20).

Furthermore, a basic conceptualisation in the Language Sciences can be exemplified in the organisational and administrative divisions between (i) *different language codes* e.g. Swedish, English, French, Hindi, Turkish, Swedish Sign Language, British Sign Language, American Sign Language, etc., and (ii) *different codes for different learner categories*. These two – administrative and organizational – sets of categories are exemplified in Figure 2 by different language subjects and the concomitant explicit or implied learner category for each in the Swedish national syllabi.

These two primary administrative conceptualisations have a bearing on the organisation of (i) language research within academia, (ii) language areas in higher education and (iii) language instruction at the school level (including policy and legislation) and have been termed the *horizontal division* (i.e. different language codes) and the *vertical division* (i.e. different codes for different learner categories) in previous analysis of the language landscape of the Swedish educational system (see Bagga-Gupta, 2004a). The horizontal and vertical divisions illustrate a reductionistic tendency in the Language and Educational Sciences. The terminology and the divisions that are created mediate and function as structuring resources for specific ways of understanding human identities, learning and development in the institutional field of education. Figure 2 can be critically explored from such a focus.

The horizontal division: language classification through subject titles in syllabi	The vertical division: explicit or implied learner category
Swedish (first compulsory language)	Ethnic Swedish pupils
Swedish as a second language	Ethnic minority or immigrant pupils
Swedish for immigrants	Adult immigrants
Swedish for the deaf/hard of hearing	Deaf & heard of hearing pupils in special schools
English (second compulsory language)	All pupils
Swedish Sign Language	Deaf & Hard of Hearing pupils in special schools
Swedish Sign Language for hearing	Hearing pupils in "regular" schools
Danish, Norwegian, Icelandic (neighbouring language)	All pupils
French, German, Spanish (foreign language)	All pupils
Turkish, Arabic, etc. (home language)	Ethnic minority or immigrant pupils
Nationally recognised minority languages	Pupils who can make a claim to a nationally recognized minority language

Figure 2. Languages and learner-categories in the Swedish education landscape

An administrative/organisational logic, for instance, requires that school sites offer "Swedish as a second language" to ethnic minority Swedes (i.e. immigrants and/or minorities) despite the fact that many of them are already at least bi- and trilingual. In addition, offering "third generation immigrants" (sic) in Sweden the possibility to study the subject "Swedish as a second language" is not only difficult to understand (see also critique in Myndigheten för skolutveckling, 2004) but categorizing human beings in terms of generational backgrounds is highly contentious and defies not just basic democratic doctrines but also analytical understandings of culture and difference. Furthermore, recent work shows that the majority of immigrant pupils, for a number of different reasons, study the subject "Swedish" and not the subject "Swedish as a second language". Another example of this *bilingual web of anomalies* pertains to the administrative and organisational logic wherein the subject "English (second compulsory language)" is offered to both ethnic Swedes and ethnic minority Swedes. Thus, bi- and multilingual pupils are, not uncommonly, offered "Swedish as a second language" in addition to English which also enjoys the status of a second language. These types of categorizations present a mismatch when compared to the lived lives of young people who are members of school settings.

94

Bringing together the issues raised so far in this section, one can say that the recurring use of the concept "bilingual" in everyday life, in the mass-media, in legislature and in academic writings itself needs to be critically examined, not least since multilingual human beings in Swedish society and present day Swedish educational settings are automatically reduced to "bilingual" human beings. The issue raised here was recognized by Heath and her colleagues' in their studies from the late 1960s in southern parts of the United States: "To categorise children and their families on the basis of either socioeconomic class or race and then to link these categories to discrete language differences was to ignore the realities of the communicative patterns of the region" (Heath, 1983, p. 3). The continuing instrumental conceptualisation – the vertical division in the language sciences, generally and the organisation of teaching and learning of languages, i.e. the horizontal division in school settings more specifically – is a selective position (in at least Sweden). The example of the segregated organisation of instruction for deaf bilingual pupils is an explicit illustration of the inherent reductionism that such categorisation implies.

Under the current "one school for all" guiding principle in Swedish education, the continuing negative point of departure in the organization of special schools for a particular group of pupils (i.e. deaf pupils) raises issues that are not commonly discussed in the literature. This segregated school form builds upon category thinking wherein deaf pupils in Sweden are accorded a bilingual status. Legitimacy is granted to the segregated school form because of the "pupils' needs" vis-à-vis their two languages, i.e. SSL as the "first language (of the deaf)" and Swedish in terms of a "second language for the deaf". In other words, the vertical organisational division is seen as naturalizing the need for a segregated school "for the deaf". This type of reductionistic division not only makes the diverse nature of deaf children's language socialization[9] experiences outside schools invisible, but also losses sight of democratic potentials in language education in the Swedish "one school for all" landscape, not least because the division is here based upon audiological levels. A re-interpretation of language and culture in this situation would focus attention on the fallacy of "different language codes for different categories of learners" and allow for the emergence of a school form where SSL and Swedish are the *primary languages* of learning and instruction for all pupils irrespective of their hearing status.[10]

Furthermore, the bilingual web of anomalies can be seen to continue to create other types of simplistic and reductionistic boundaries in the organisation of

---

[9] It is often estimated that 95% of deaf children are born into non-signing, ie. Non-SSL or non-ASL home environments. Furthermore, ethnic minority deaf pupils in Sweden may come from both non-SSL and non-Swedish speaking home environments. Homogenizing such diversity in educational institutional settings is problematic.

[10] As I have argued previously (see for instance Bagga-Gupta, 2004b, 2007), this is far from an utopian idea in that not only have entire societies existed where a SL has been used by hearing, deaf and hard of hearing human beings, but also that individual schools have been and continue to be organised such that "visually oriented" bilingualism opens up for the inclusion of hearing, deaf and hard of hearing pupils in an inverted-inclusive school form (see Teruggi, 2003 for an interesting present day example of such a school form).

languages both within academia and in the institutional educational field (see also Bagga-Gupta, in press-a, in press-b). Thus for instance, boundaries get created in the Language Sciences landscape in other specific ways too: with a *numerical* connotation (e.g. first, second, third, bilingual, etc.), *relational* signification (e.g. my language, your language, their language, mother tongue, native language) and *geographical* emphasis (e.g. national language, home language, foreign language, etc.). These boundaries mediate understandings that are pushed by a selective individual centred tradition vis-à-vis human learning and development that is contentious. Such demarcation processes receive further momentum within academia, for instance with the institutionalisation of narrow subject areas in the Language Sciences. In other words, the horizontal and vertical divisions in the Language Sciences flourish both as administrative categories in (Swedish) school sites and within higher education and research. However, the interesting issue is the fact that all these bounded concepts exist in relation to an assumed static, correct and desired point of departure, i.e. "Swedish language", and/or in relation to particular understandings of how (language) learning occurs. Taking the monolingual native ethnic Swede as a given point of departure, and particular understandings of language learning and human development, has given legitimacy to other areas of language in the curriculum.

Inspired by Wikans' (1999, 2002) research in Norway on the ways in which Northern societies reduce the notion of culture and the instrumental ways in which "culture has run astray"[11] in the streets of at least one particular Northern setting, one can ask whether the selective though dominant web of understanding are symptomatic of the fact that language appears to be lost in Sweden? The dominant perspectives in the Language Sciences within academia and within institutionalized education discussed here are in need of examination from critical social and post-colonial perspectives: "the ways in which we understand both "language" and "culture" contribute and play a prominent role in constructions of Self and Other and the ways in which we talk about learning language and learning culture. However, this *talking about learning to converse* is at odds with how we *learn to converse*" (Bagga-Gupta, 2004a, pp. 14-15).

Furthermore, the social theories of mind positions on learning help (re)formulate issues of language socialization in the following ways: "the central point of the focus on culture as learned behaviour and on language habits as part of that shared learning" (Heath, 1983, p. 11). Key assumptions in such positions enable us to see that the language we use (including the language that we use in academic discourses) creates and mediates in a very potent sense our realities. However, it maybe important to point out that the kinds of studies that have emerged in such new positions lie not only at the margins in the larger academic Language and Educational Sciences landscapes, but lie also in the periphery within the separate thematic areas in the Language and Educational Sciences themselves.

---

[11] Wikan (1999, p. 57).

RESEARCH INTO SITUATED LANGUAGES-CUM-LITERACIES IN USE

Concluding Reflections

Research that juxtaposes and brings together different areas in the Language Sciences and/or attempts to generate knowledge at the intersections of different thematic areas of study is not a common enterprise. The kind of research that has emerged and is emerging indicates that the original epistemological sense of the concept "communication" has in mainstream research been forgotten. This is the case not least in research that focuses upon (i) maintaining boundaries between languages and human beings (and thereby categorizing them), and the (ii) measurement of communicative competencies, skills and learning processes. Recognizing the meaning making nature of human communication or the *fluidity between linguistic varieties* or a *continuum of multilingualism* attends to the empirical realities highlighted in such studies and allows for evoking analytical categories such as chaining, linking, bridging, etc. A parallel line of discussion in the Literacy and Bilingual Studies fields has recently questioned the notion of bilingualism in terms of two separate written codes and analytically proposed the need to attend to a "continua of biliteracy" (Hornberger, 2003). The argument that gets substantiated in such accounts is that not only is the use of two or more languages, linguistic varieties and communication modalities linked and chained in human communication, but that they, in significant ways, shape human identity and culture.

Social theories of mind positions view categorical thinking as essentialist and problematic. In the research agenda this means that the analytical emphasis needs to focus everyday interactions and social practices against the backdrop of sociohistorical processes (Säljö, 2000; Wertsch, 1998). Furthermore, research agendas here regard learning and development to be collective, distributed and situated processes (Lave & Wenger, 1991; Rogoff, 1990; Wenger, 1998). The primacy accorded to language use and communicative-practices has implications for understanding human identity: it is not human characteristics like ethnicity or deafness or age that are significant, but rather issues of human difference in relation to *languages and literacies in use* that are significant.

The specific, dominant traditions that allow us to categorize languages in numerical, relational and geographical terms build upon the "brain as container" model where the underlying assumption is that one's (singular) "mother tongue" or "home language" should automatically form the basis for learning any other language/s.[12] Such quaint Eurocentric and linguacentric ideas disregard, as has been argued earlier, global human realities and the largely ethnographically oriented literature that has, amongst other issues, previously highlighted the fact that the majority of the worlds human beings are multilingual, that language competencies develop throughout the life span and that languages tend to be domain specific in the multilingual lives of most human beings.

---

[12] Children's (and even adults') primary languages need, it is argued here, to be understood in terms of parallel multilingualism, rather than "additive bilingualism" or "subtractive bilingualism".

Research that focuses *everyday social practices* of human beings who *use two or more language varieties* illustrates how adults and children develop the language/s they use to the level of competencies required in different domains and arenas in life. While these types of research findings suggest broader ways of understanding human communication, learning and development, they have perhaps only in limited ways shaped the very institution that is seen as being responsible for the teaching and learning of different languages and literacies.

Such research can potentially raise important issues vis-à-vis the organization of language instruction in school sites. Here previous and ongoing research on communication-practices in Swedish institutional contexts can be illustrative.[13] Results from interactional studies conducted in a diverse range of settings: at pre-school institutional settings for (hearing) children who do not use Swedish as a primary language in their home spheres, in special schools, national upper secondary schools for the deaf, in the middle and secondary levels of hearing schools, adult educational settings for immigrants and for netbased language instruction, for instance, indicate that a demarcation is not uncommonly maintained between the formal teaching of language skills in language focused lessons/activities and uses of languages in other lessons/activities (where language is itself often not in focus).[14] Differences between focusing upon the form and function of languages appears, in some of these studies, to be so clear cut that it has been suggested that pupils unwittingly are afforded more meaningful and dialogical ways of participating in languages in the latter settings. This has, it has been argued, important implications for learning literacy and different languages. The results from these more recent and ongoing studies are similar to the findings of a large scale evaluation project that studied classrooms in one percent of all Swedish pre-schools, schools and upper secondary schools a decade ago (Skolverket, 2000). In particular, the results from such studies and projects in different types of institutional settings seem to suggest that there is a tendency for language practices to become traditional and monological if and when pupils, for any number of reasons, are viewed as deviating from normative understandings of a monolingual, functionally able, ethnic Swedish young person. Thus for instance, multilingual immigrant pupils, deaf pupils in bilingual special school settings, ethnic minority Swedish pupils learning Swedish, all appear to receive more traditional language instruction if and when they are experienced as being weaker in the target language, i.e. Swedish. Such studies continue to demonstrate the dominance of a monological-formalistic bias and the dominance of a traditional and narrow view of language instruction in school sites.

The critique raised vis-à-vis mainstream understandings of language and learning raised here brings to the forefront aspects of the common *monolingual and*

---

[13] The studies referred to here are based at the CCD/KKOM, Communication, Culture and Diversity – Deaf Studies research group at Örebro University in Sweden. This work is informed by the social theories of mind perspectives where the overriding focus is on studies of social practices.

[14] See for instance Bagga-Gupta (2002, in press-a), Carlsson and Bagga-Gupta (2001), Rosén and Bagga-Gupta (2011), Dahlberg and Bagga-Gupta (submitted); compare also with Skolverket (2000).

monoethnical bias that has existed in the field of language pedagogy, especially in the post World War II period. Classifying languages in terms of a horizontal division, i.e. different language codes, in the educational curricula is, it can be argued, important from an institutional and administrative point of view. In other words, curricula, syllabi and the organisation of time and space in school settings require that one pays attention to a differentiation between different language codes. But, furthering this classification and maintaining it in terms of essentialistic categories and in terms of different pupil groups' different learning abilities (i.e. the vertical division) is problematic. These latter conceptualizations draw upon particular assumptions related to views about "how language learning occurs" and "what language and culture are". The work presented in this chapter challenges such categorizations (not least within academics and research itself) since it is argued here that (i) human attributes become meaningful within the context of everyday interactions and in situated social and textual practices, and (ii) language categories need to be freed from the constraints of traditional learning theories and the constraints of human categories themselves.

While schools in Northern contexts like Sweden are traditionally understood as sites that socialise the young into (mono)lingual and (mono)cultural citizenship, I have in this chapter highlighted the fact that research into the social practices of young people with a diverse range of cultural experiences and multiethnic backgrounds seem to have been dominated by four tendencies. *Firstly*, research has focused communication in terms of "different" language categories rather than socialization processes more broadly. *Secondly*, issues related to culture, difference and identity are elaborated in terms of static essentialized understandings of marginalized groups and issues (and here it is not uncommon that language issues come center-stage). *Thirdly*, research inquiry has in large measure primarily focused school arenas and not young peoples' everyday lives more broadly. In other words, there is an important need to critically understand young peoples' social practices (including new literacies, technologies and popular culture) and identities in the changing contexts that currently characterize Northern societies. And *finally*, a critical multilingual perspective is wanting in the bilingual research landscape.

ACKNOWLEDGEMENTS

The research that is reported here has been conducted at different universities in Sweden and in the USA. The bulk of it has been carried out at the CCD/KKOM research group at Örebro University in Sweden. Support by the Educational Sciences Committee of the Swedish Research Council for Project LISA-21, *Languages and Identities in School Arenas in the 21st century* is particularly acknowledged.

REFERENCES

Bagga-Gupta, S. (1995). Human development and institutional practices. Women, child care and the mobile creches. Linköping, Sweden: Linköping Studies in Arts and Science 130. Doctoral dissertation, Linköping University.

Bagga-Gupta, S. (2000). Visual language environments. Exploring everyday life and literacies in Swedish Deaf bilingual schools. *Visual Anthropology Review, 15*(2), 95-120.

Bagga-Gupta, S. (2002). Explorations in bilingual instructional interaction. A sociocultural perspective on literacy. *Journal of the European Association on Learning and Instruction, 5*(2), 557-587.

Bagga-Gupta, S. (2004a). Challenging understandings in pluralistic societies – Language and culture loose in school sites and losing sight of democratic agendas in education? *Utbildning och Demokrati. Tidskrift för didaktik och utbildningspolitik, 13*(3), 11-36.

Bagga-Gupta, S. (2004b). Visually oriented language use. Discursive and technological resources in Swedish Deaf pedagogical arenas. In M. V. Herreweghe, & M. Vermeerbergen (Eds.), *Sociolinguistics in European deaf communities*, The Sociolinguistics in Deaf Communities Series, Vol 10. Washington DC: Gallaudet University Press.

Bagga-Gupta, S. (2004c). Literacies and deaf education. A theoretical analysis of the international and Swedish literature. Research in Focus 23 Series. Stockholm: Swedish National Agency for Education.

Bagga-Gupta, S. (2007). Aspects of diversity, inclusion and democracy within education and research. *Scandinavian Journal of Educational Research, 51*(1), 1-22.

Bagga-Gupta, S. (2008). Understanding communication and identities in culturally diverse school settings in present day Sweden. Conceptual and methodological points of departure & socio-historical reflections on "cultural diversity in Sweden". Presentation at the Bi-annual Earli joint-SIG Social Interaction, Learning and Diversity meeting in Goteborg, Sweden, 19-20 May 2008.

Bagga-Gupta, S. (in press-a). Privileging identity positions and multimodal communication in textual practices. Intersectionality and the (re)negotiation of boundaries. In A. Pitkänen-Huhta & L. Holm (Eds.), *Literacy practices in transition: Perspectives from the Nordic countries.* Multilingual Matters.

Bagga-Gupta, S. (in press-b). The boundary-turn. Relocating *language, identity* and *culture* through the epistemological lenses of *time, space* and *social interactions.* In I. Hasnain, S. Bagga-Gupta, & S. Mohan (Eds.), *Language, culture and identity: Cross cultural perspectives.* England: Cambridge Scholars Publishing.

Bagga-Gupta, S., Vonen, A. M., & Hansen, A. L. (2011). Visual orientation and chaining: Communicative practices in deaf and hearing settings. Presentation at the ISB8, International Symposium on Bilingualism. Oslo, Norway, 15-18 June 2011.

Carlsson, R., & Bagga-Gupta, S. (2006). 'Verktyg och lådor'. En studie om språkfokuserade aktiviteter för minoriteter på förskolearenor ['Tools and Boxes'. A study of language focused activities for minorities in pre-school arenas]. *Nordic Educational Researcher, 26*(3), 193-211 [in Swedish].

Cromdal, J. (2000). Code-switching for all practical purposes. Bilingual organisation of children's play. Linköping, Sweden: Linköping Studies in Arts and Science 223. Doctoral Dissertation. Linköping University.

Dahlgren, G. M., & Bagga-Gupta, S. (submitted). Communication in the virtual classroom in higher education: Languaging beyond the boundaries of time and space. *Language, Culture and Social Interaction.*

Erting, C. (1999). Two languages at home and at school: Early literacy in ASL/English contexts. Föredrag vid European Days of Deaf Education Conference: Bilingual Education with a Focus on Reading and Writing. Örebro, Sweden, internal document.

Erting, C., J., Thumann-Prezioso, C., & Benedict, B., S., (2000). Bilingualism in a deaf family. Fingerspelling in early childhood. In P. E. Spencer, C. J. Erting, & M. Marschark (Eds.), *The deaf child in the family and at school. Essays in honor of Kathryn P. Meadow-Orlans.* Mahwah, NJ: Lawrence Erlbaum Associates.

Garcia, O. (2009). *Bilingual education in the 21st century. A global perspective.* UK: Wiley-Blackwell.

Grosjean, F. (1996). Living with two languages and two cultures. In I. Parasnis (Ed.), *Cultural and language diversity and the deaf experience.* New York: Cambridge University Press.

Gynne, A. & Bagga-Gupta, S. (2011). Young people's language usage and identity positioning inside and ourside a Swedish Finnish bilingual educational setting. Explorations from a pilot study. Paper presented at the 39th Congress of the Nordic Educational Research Association, Rights and Education, Jyväskylä, Finland, 10-12 March 2011.

Hansen, A. (2005). Kommunikative praksiser i visuell orienterte klassrom. En studie av et tilrettelagt opplegg for døve laerestudenter [Communicative practices in visually oriented classrooms. A study of an adapted education for teacher-students; in Norwegian]. Trondheim: The Norwegian Technological-Natural Sciences University, Doctoral dissertation. NTNU 2005:132.

Heath, S., B. (1983). *Ways with words. Language, life and work in communities and classrooms.* Cambridge: Cambridge University Press.

Hornberger, N. H. (Ed.) (2003). *Continua of bi-literacy. An ecological framework for educational policy, research and practice in multilingual settings.* Clevedon: Multilingual Matters.

Hornberger, N. H. (2002). Multilingual language policies and the continua of bi-literacy. An ecological approach. *Language Policy, 1,* 27-51.

Hult, F. M. (2004). Planning for multilingualism and minority language rights in Sweden. *Language Policy, 3,* 181-201.

Knobel, M. (1999). *Everyday literacies. Students, discourse and social practice.* New York: Peter Lang.

Lave, J., & Wenger, E. (1991). *Situated learning. Legitimate peripheral participation.* Cambridge: Cambridge University Press.

Myndigheten för skolutveckling. (2004). Kartläggning av svenska som andraspråk [Overview of Swedish as a second language]. Dnr 2003:757. Stockholm: The Swedish National Agency for School Improvement.

Rogoff, B. (1990). *Apprenticeship in thinking.* New York: Oxford University Press.

Rosén, J., & Bagga-Gupta, S. (2011). Languaging and identities in the construction and organization of 'Swedish for immigrants'. Paper presented at the 14th Biennial Conference of EARLI, European Association for Research on Learning and Instruction, Education for a Global Networked Society in Exeter, UK, 30 August-3 September 2011.

Säljö, R. (2000). *Lärande i praktiken – Ett sociokulturellt perspektiv* [Learning in practice – A sociocultural perspective]. Stockholm: Prisma.

Scribner, S., & Cole, M. (1981). *The psychology of literacy.* Boston: Harvard University Press.

Skolverket (2000). *Nationella kvalitetsgranskningar. Läs- och skrivprocessen som ett led i undervisningen* [National quality evaluations. Reading and writing processes as an aspect of instruction]. Stockholm: Liber.

Street, B. (1984). *Literacy in theory and practice.* Cambridge: Cambridge University Press.

Teruggi, L. A. (Ed.) (2003). *Una scuola, due lingue. L'esperienza di bilinguismo della scuola dell'Infanzia ed Elementare di Cossato* [One school, two languages. Experiences of bilingualism at the preschool and school in Cossato]. Milano: FrancoAngeli.

Vasquez, O. A., Pease-Alvarez, L., & Shannon, S. M. (1994). *Pushing boundaries. Language and culture in a Mexican community.* Cambridge: Cambridge University Press.

Wenger, E. (1998). *Communities of practice. Learning, meaning, and identity.* Series: Learning in Doing: Social, Cognitive, and Computational Perspectives. Cambridge: Cambridge University Press.

Wertsch, J. (1998). *Mind as social action.* Cambridge MA: Cambridge University Press.

Wikan, U. (2002). *Generous betrayal. Politics of culture in the New Europe.* Chicago: University of Chicago Press.

Wikan, U. (1999). Culture: A new concept of race. Debate. Culture in the nation and public opinion: a Norwegian case. *Social Anthropology, 7*(1), 57-64.

Sangeeta Bagga-Gupta
School HumES, Humanities, Education and Social Sciences
Örebro University

EVELINE WUTTKE

8. SILENCE IS SILVER, TALK IS GOLD?
ANALYSIS OF CLASSROOM TALK IN A LEARNER CENTRED SETTING

INTRODUCTION

In one of our studies we asked students about the nature of their classroom communication. Amongst others we got the following answer (and some very similar versions of it): "… Oh well, what can I say. It's always the same. We sit around in our classroom. And the teacher talks non-stop. And we try not to fall asleep. Sometimes we do, though … The only chance we get to say something is, when teachers ask questions and we are supposed to answer them. And then it has to be exactly the answer our teachers expect. Otherwise they won't accept it."

This comment reflects a way of communicating in classrooms that still seems to be fairly typical. Students are - of course - not happy with it but seem to accept it as part of everyday life at school. Nevertheless: various studies indicate that there are more efficient kinds of classroom talk and that it can be important that students get the chance to participate actively in communication processes.

We know that classrooms are environments that are highly dependent on communication. By talking with each other teachers and students give, accept, and exchange information. Mostly this is done with the intention to help students to acquire knowledge. Other important functions of communication are the circulation of interaction rules and the organization of social relationships. All things considered there are hardly any pedagogically relevant activities in classrooms that can be realized without communication (Wuttke, 2005). Mostly, communication follows quite standardized patterns and is structured by socially accepted ways in which knowledge is presented (Kleine-Staarman, 2009). Classroom talk can be symmetric or asymmetric (Hofer, 1981). Symmetric means that all participants have – at least theoretically – the same chance and the same right to participate in communication and to initiate it. In classrooms this is hardly ever the case. Students have the (quite understandable) feeling that there is a hierarchy – teachers have more power, they are more knowledgeable, they evaluate work and grade it, they punish and/or praise. And because of this hierarchy teachers are the ones who are "allowed" to initiate communication (Hofer, 1981; Becker-Mrotzek & Vogt, 2001; Spychiger, Oser, Hascher & Mahler, 1999). If we look closely at patterns of classroom talk, we find that everyday classroom communication still follows this tacit assumption that teachers are the ones to

E. Hjörne et al. (eds.), Learning, Social Interaction and Diversity – Exploring Identities in School Practices, 103–117.

initiate, structure, and organize interaction. Therefore, the most common pattern still is the classical IRF-Structure (Mehan, 1979: invitation by the teacher, response by the student, feedback by the teacher). And the teacher-student speech-ratio seems to be largely unchanged as well. Bellack, Kliebard, Hyman and Smith (1974) report that teachers talk about three times as much as students do – and this means all students in one class! More recent studies show that nothing much has changed. Teachers produce about 60% of all sentences spoken in classrooms. Again the remaining 40% are distributed among all students in a class (Sumfleth & Pitton, 1998; Wuttke, 2005; Seifried, 2010; Wuttke & Seifried, 2010). This must lead to the conclusion that there cannot be enough room for students' questions or discussions, even if that might prove helpful in acquiring knowledge.

As a consequence of these typical communication patterns, instruments to analyse classroom talk are mostly adapted to a leading communicative role of teachers (e.g. in the tradition of Sinclair and Coulthard, 1975: 17 categories to analyse teacher talk, 3 to analyse students' talk). We therefore know a lot about the way teachers talk in classrooms and not enough about students' talk and its effects. In the following chapters we will concentrate on three research questions:

– In case students are given the chance to actively participate in classroom talk: to what extent do they seize their chance?
– Of which quality is their talk?
– What are the effects of students talk?

STUDENTS' PARTICIPATION IN CLASSROOM TALK: EFFECTS OF VERBALISATION ON KNOWLEDGE BUILDING

General Considerations

Already in 1973 Spanhel discussed various functions of students' talk. His considerations were mainly focused on standard classroom interaction, meaning that teachers initiated and regulated communication. Advantages of students' talk were seen for *classmates* (fostering their learning process through repetition of learning contents) and *teachers* (by providing information about what students know and by giving the chance to correct wrong assumptions and to give feedback; Fischer, Bruhn, Gräsel & Mandl, 2002), and not so much for the speakers themselves. Nevertheless, Spanhel argued that talking might "force" students to clarify their ideas and therefore foster the development of thinking, memory and language skills. But the benefit for teachers was seen as foremost. Nowadays, though, the focus is shifting. Advantages of students' talk are mostly discussed as being useful for the speakers themselves and for the co-learners.

In summary students' talk can fulfill the following useful functions:

– Articulation of ideas can help to *create new concepts* and to *test available concepts*. By speaking, people kind of "stand apart" from their own knowledge, they listen to what they say and can therefore test if their knowledge, their assumptions are correct (e.g. Chinn, O'Donnell & Jinks, 2000; Fischer et al., 2002; O'Keefe, 1995).

– When learners have to articulate their ideas they have to *organise* them. Even without feedback, learners very often notice inconsistencies and mistakes. Positive effects are expected especially in group processes of questioning, testing and hypothesizing. In such processes *new ideas should arise* and *assumptions can be tested*. This is expected to be useful for knowledge building of all participants, not just the speakers. Traditional forms of answering teachers' questions have proven to have different effects. Even if learners speak and articulate their knowledge they are expected to present a "perfect" and correct form of it, not to test and hypothesize. And very often answers should be a repetition of teachers' previous presentations. The development of own ideas is usually not requested (Brown & Palinscar, 1989; Fox, 1995; Renkl, 1997; Webb, 1989).

– If learners are given the chance to discuss their solutions and ideas *cyclic discussions* might emerge. In this form of discussion thoughts are presented, picked up by co-learners, and reformulated. Ideas and different solutions are thus developed and distributed which can enable every learner to tie in with his or her individual pre-knowledge (Brown, Metz & Campione, 1996; Brown & Renshaw, 2000).

Generally, advantages through students' talk are seen in connection with Vygotskys (1962) idea of the zone of proximal development. When all learners – not only teachers – externalize their knowledge and their ideas, there is not only one expert who can generate such a zone, but many. Through internalization processes strategies that are communicated in the group will become part of individual thinking and knowledge (Brown et al, 1996; Brown & Renshaw, 2000). If we follow Vygotsky (1962) that talk cumulates in cognitive change, it can be expected that active verbal interaction will help learners to find out inconsistencies in their body of knowledge, to build new concepts and to link new information with previous knowledge. This should result in an increasing amount of understanding instead of just learning by rote. Furthermore, learners should be able to transfer knowledge and to use it in new situations. In addition, argumentation sequences can trigger cognitive conflicts (Piaget, 1989) because they can demonstrate knowledge deficits to learners. According to Piaget this should lead to uncertainty and curiosity and later on to critical reflection and revision of one's own knowledge (see also Cazden, 1988; Kumpulainen & Mutanen, 2000; Straub, 2001).

Even if these considerations seem to be plausible, some critical remarks are necessary. First of all it is not really clear yet if speaking is helpful in knowledge building, especially if it is *more* helpful than other forms of learning. There are some studies that indicate that learners who articulate their ideas during the learning process increase their knowledge. Nevertheless it is not possible to say whether they would have learned the same amount had they experienced the same material in a more traditional teacher centered setting without much verbalization of their own (Stables, 1995). Furthermore it is problematic that analyses of classroom talk are quite often methodologically flawed. Results are presented narratively and backed up with carefully selected parts of transcripts that seem to prove positive effects. Very often the ratio of teachers' and students' talk, numbers of questions, or the participation in discussions is counted without linking these verbalizations to measures of successful learning, e.g. knowledge. And some of the results that seem to prove the building of common knowledge might only show the tendency of students to agree with the opinion of their classmates. It follows that it is not clear whether an individual has learned something and what this something is. This might show in transfer tests but very often students are not tested (Stables, 1995; Fischer et al., 2002). To sum it up we can follow Westgate and Hughes who state that:

> More firmly reliable criteria are required by which rational judgements can be made concerning pupil-pupil as well as teacher-pupil talk, and about teaching and learning processes which may be ‚visible' in and through such talk. (Westgate & Hughes, 1977, 129)

It is not just by any kind of talking that a positive effect on learning can be achieved. Instead we have to focus on the *quality* of teacher and student talk (Chinn et al., 2000; Fisher, 1993; Kawanaka & Stigler, 1999; Mercer, 1996; Webb, Troper & Fall, 1995). The following paragraphs will leave general considerations about the usefulness of talk, and will concentrate on potential effects of *questions* and *argumentation*.

Effects of Questioning

As argued before, students' questions are expected to have positive effects on learning. Research on questions began in 1912, when Stevens stated that questions are the most common form of communication in classrooms (West & Pearson, 1994). This has not changed much in the meantime: questions are still a substantial part of classroom talk. For a long time research interests concentrated on teachers' questions. This might be due to the fact that – at least in more traditionally oriented classroom settings – teachers are the ones asking questions, students are supposed to answer them. Teachers' questions account for about 20% of communication in classrooms, whereas students' questions (all students in one class!) are only about 13%. The quality of especially students' questions is rather low, usually they are short and aimed at organizational clarification (what?, say again?, who, me?, Dillon, 1990; Sumfleth & Pitton, 1998; Wuttke, 2005). Furthermore, teachers ask so many questions in a short time that students do not get a chance to reflect and to really think about answers. And the quality of teachers' questions is not convincing as well. Most of them aim at superficial answers and don't initiate critical thinking. Quite frequently students are just requested to reproduce bits of knowledge they have learned by rote (Niegemann, 2004).

West and Pearson (1994) have identified common patterns of questioning: Students mainly ask for *classroom procedures* (e.g. "Will this be in the test?"; see as well Sumfleth & Pitton, 1998). Furthermore, they want to have *general information* concerning learning matters ("How do you calculate this again?") and try to *clarify matters that should have been learned already*. These three categories comprise about 70% of students' questions. Classical combinations are still the ones mentioned by Mehan (1979).

While students mainly ask for information, teachers control interaction with the help of questions. Generally teachers have specific "right" answers in their mind which they wish to hear. If such an answer is given, teachers praise the student who produced it. What students do learn from such forms of interaction is, that they have to use exactly the "right" terminology, and they do not have to demonstrate, whether they have actually understood what they are talking about (Cazden, 1988; Edwards & Mercer, 1987; Edwards & Westgate, 1994; Sumfleth & Pitton, 1998). This is nicely illustrated by the following example Gopnick (2001, p. 62) describes:

> At one point I asked my six-year-old if he knew why the moon changed its shape. He replied with a surprisingly polished recital of the scientific story, only to add at the end: Actually, I don't know why it changes at all; this is just what my big brother told me.

It is still open if and how common interactional patterns are helpful at all in the process of knowledge building. Studies show mixed results. Where questions are concerned, especially so-called *higher-order questions* are said to foster learning and help with knowledge building. Higher order questions are those that are asked in a way that answers should be well-founded and provide thorough explanations. Lower-order questions aim at short answers like "yes" or "no" or at short definitions. They are said to be without much effect on understanding (Dillon, 1990). There are various effects that are discussed in connection with higher order questions, the most prominent being that answers that follow higher order questions (explanations, well-founded reasoning) help to detect knowledge deficits and identify mistakes and wrong concepts. Unfortunately, classroom research shows that the first problem is that students' do not really have a chance to ask questions (see above, the ratio of student/teacher questions). The second problem is that – when they do ask questions – their quality is rather low.

When we analyze why students rarely ask questions and especially why the quality of their questions is low we find the following potential reasons (O'Keefe, 1995; Scardamalia & Bereiter, 1992):

– Teachers do not wait long enough after asking a question. Students get the impression that they have to answer fast, not think thoroughly.
– Mostly teachers' questions aim for knowledge reproduction not for reflection and critical thinking.
– Teachers are not good role models as the quality of their own questions is rather low. Furthermore, there is no scaffolding involved in questioning (teaching students to ask better questions).
– Students need a certain amount of pre-knowledge to ask good questions, so sometimes they probably just cannot do so because they do not know enough about a topic (Miyake & Norman, 1979).

Effects of Argumentation

Quality and effects of argumentation have been central in many studies dealing with classroom talk (e.g. Cazden, 1988; Fisher, 1993; Sweigart, 1991; Wegerif & Mercer, 2000; Wegerif, 2002b). In this context Mercer (1995, 1996) identified three kinds of argumentation that have been in the centre of attention of many classroom studies (disputational talk, cumulative talk, and exploratory talk). The general idea goes back to Habermas' (1981) theory of communication. On the basis of this theory the authors tried to identify successful communication (see Edwards & Mercer, 1987). Exploratory talk is considered a mode of communication that should foster learning and the generation of knowledge. All three types and their respective effects can be described as shown in Table 1 (Mercer, 2000).

Table 1. Modes of classroom talk and attributed effects

Modes	Description	Attributed Effects
Disputational talk	Short exchanges, consisting of assertions and counter-assertions Disagreement, individualized decision making Little constructive criticism Few well-founded justifications	Negative atmosphere Fighting instead of learning (from each other)
Cumulative talk	Repetitions and confirmations Speakers build positively but uncritically on what others have said	Mistakes and wrong solutions cannot be detected due to hasty agreement Hardly any learning from each other
Exploratory talk	All relevant information is shared All members of the group are invited to contribute to the discourse All opinions and ideas are respected and considered Challenges and counter-challenges may exist, but they have to be justified Alternative hypothesis are offered Critical but constructive engagement with each other's ideas Statements and suggestions offered for joint consideration	Knowledge is made publicly accountable Reasoning is visible in the talk Various suggestions and solutions from various points of view allow connection of new information with individual previous knowledge Learning from each other Creation of well-linked knowledge basis

As Table 1 shows, positive effects of exploratory talk may be expected because students are supposed to support each other in the process of reaching the zone of proximal development and therefore to enlarge their overall body of knowledge.

This can be done with the help of critical questions, feedback and explanations that are so-called "linguistic scaffolding tools" (Fernandez, Wegerif, Mercer, Rojas-Drummond, 2001). The metaphor of scaffolding was introduced by Wood, Bruner and Ross (1976) who described what happens when a teacher works with learners attempting a task that is slightly beyond their ability. Originally the idea of scaffolding (Bruner 1985) only considered experts as helpful, but Fernandez et al. (2001) showed that peers can play such a role as well, and that linguistic scaffolding works. This can be due to the fact that classrooms where students' talk is allowed can provide a more symmetrical environment for the co-construction of knowledge because power and status differences between expert and novice are less likely to apply (Mercer, 2000). However, exploratory talk is seldom used spontaneously by learners (Fisher, 1993; Rojas-Drummond & Tapia, 2007). It seems to be essential that in the beginning students are made familiar with a set of so-called ground rules (Wegerif & Mercer, 2000). These rules are: (1) share all relevant information, (2) the group will try to reach agreement, (3) the group is responsible for their decisions (up to this the rules are applicable for cumulative talk as well), (4) justifications are expected, (5) challenges are acceptable and (6) alternatives have to be discussed before reaching a decision.

If there is an explanation and training of ground rules before the actual work in collaborative groups starts, positive results can be shown. Compared with groups without ground rules preparation these groups are more often engaged in exploratory talk. And tests show that this has a positive effect on individual problem solving that again goes back to Vygotsky's assumption that thinking is at first social and cognitive abilities are fostered through socialization and discussion processes (Vygotsky, 1962). Many authors therefore conclude that training in argumentation is helpful and that exploratory talk can be taught (Wegerif, Mercer & Dawes, 1999; Wegerif & Mercer, 2000; Wegerif, 2002a). And this seems to be true for students with varying levels of cognitive abilities. In transfer tasks those prepared in using ground rules use more elaborations and show better metacognitive competence. This is especially true when tasks are complex. There is no advantage when "easy" tasks have to be solved. The reason might be that it is sufficient to use knowledge learned by rote when solving non-complex problems and that this can be done without the help of critical and reflective group discussions (Sweigart, 1991).

In our study we analyzed classroom interaction with the focus on teachers' and learners' questions and the quality of argumentation in two groups of learners. Furthermore it was of interest whether there was a connection between classroom talk (questions and argumentation) and learning outcome.

METHODOLOGY

Participants and location

We analyzed classroom talk in a student centred learning environment in a German vocational school. Students who attend this kind of vocational school in the so-called German dual system are at school for an average of 1 ½ days per week. The rest of their working time is spent in their respective companies, learning, working and being trained on the job. The students were in training to be business management assistants. A learner centred setting had to be chosen because traditional teacher centred settings are not suitable to analyze students' talk. As described before there is hardly any student communication in these environments, and as a consequence there is nothing to analyse.

Students worked and learned in groups of 4 or 5 members and had to solve complex problems relevant for their professional life. Two groups were selected for the analysis, one having five, the other one four participants. 16 classrooms hours were videotaped (4 adjoining weeks, 4 lessons per week) and transcribed for communication analysis. In the beginning a coder training was done and texts from 4 classroom hours were coded by two people. Intercoder reliability was satisfactory (Cohens Kappa = .75).

Communication analysis

As described before, questions and high quality argumentation should support learning and knowledge building. This was coded as follows:
a) The quality of students' questions according to the cognitive demands necessary to answer the question is listed in Table 2.
b) The quality of argumentation (disputational talk, cumulative talk or exploratory talk) was analysed according to the categories and descriptions mentioned before (see Table 1).

Table 2. Categories, qualities and examples of students' questions

Category	Quality	Expected answers	Example for question
F1	Lower order question (1)	Short answers, mainly yes or no	Is value added tax 19%?
F2	Lower order question (2)	Short descriptions, short definitions, one-word sentences	What exactly is a "limited liability company"?
F3	Higher order questions	Longer explanations, elaborate reasoning	How can I find out if it is better to produce the parts of the furniture or to buy them?

Knowledge Test

To find out whether there is any connection between high quality communication and knowledge building students were tested at the end of the study. There were two tests: A teacher-made test, measuring declarative knowledge, and a test measuring how well-linked students' knowledge was (Sembill, 1992; Wuttke, 1999).

RESULTS

Students' Questions and Their Effects

Results are shown in Table 3. F1 stands for lower order questions 1, F2 for lower order questions 2, and F3 for higher order questions. 16 lessons were analysed. Table 3 largely reveal that students ask more questions than they do in traditional teacher centred settings.

Table 3. Quality and number of questions asked by students and their teacher

Categories	Students				Teacher
	Min.	Max.	Mean	Sum	
F1	13	40	28,8	223	5
F2	9	68	29,3	264	58
F3	1	10	4,9	44	25
Total	531				88

Students asked all in all 531 questions. With nine students this means an average of 59 questions per student. In the same time the teacher asked 88 question. We know from studies in traditional settings that the ratio is often about 20 teacher-questions to one student question. The results in Table 3 show that students play an almost equal role.

Nevertheless, there is still a problem. The quality of the questions is low: students mainly ask lower order questions (223 of Type F1 and 264 of Type F2). Only a small amount of students' questions is of Type F3 (44) that supposedly fosters learning. The quality of the teacher's questions is better but even with them we find many lower order questions (5 of Type F1 and 58 of Type F2 compared to 25 higher order questions of Type F3).

The correlations in Figure 1 reveal a substantial interrelation between questions and knowledge.

The findings in Figure 1 show that questions should be at least of the second level (F2), if they are to influence knowledge building. There is no connection between F1-questions and knowledge. On the other hand, not only highest quality level questions (F3) are helpful to foster knowledge acquisition. Short answer questions (F2) can do this as well.

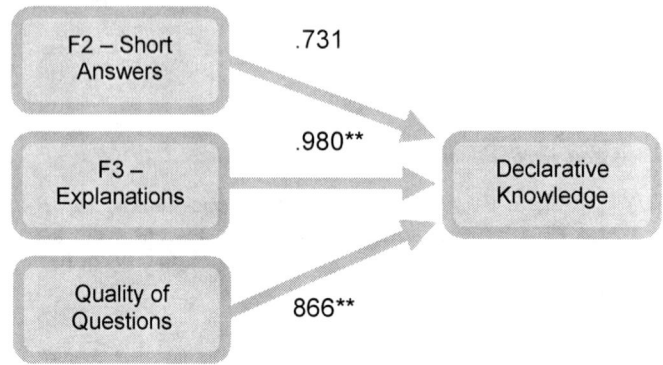

*Figure 1. Interrelation between the quality of questions and declarative knowledge. "Quality of questions" stands for an average question quality generated from individual measures in the three categories F1 to F3. * = p < .05; ** = p < .01.*

Argumentation Sequences and Their Effects

In both groups classroom talk is governed by argumentation that is uncritical and tends toward agreement without much reflection (cumulative talk). In total we identified 262 argumentation sequences, of those 159 are cumulative. They are not completely negative – at least they are good for the general group climate. But – as argued before – they do not foster knowledge building and they use time that could be spent in a more effective way. Exploratory talk is expected to be effective concerning learning and knowledge building. We found 48 sequences that we classified as exploratory talk. 55 sequences (20 %) were classified as disputational: This seems substantial if we keep in mind that this kind of classroom talk is expected to be counterproductive for knowledge building.

When we compared the two groups we found that most of the disputational talk happens in group 1 (51 sequences). The students hardly had talk that adds to learning and to building knowledge. In group 2 communication is characterized by a high amount of cumulative talk as well (107 sequences) but with hardly any disputational talk (4 sequences) and some sequences of exploratory talk (45).

We found a clear result concerning the interrelation of argumentation and knowledge building. Exploratory talk and the quality of argumentation in general (a variable that was generated for every learner and reflects his or her overall quality of argumentation) are closely (and significantly) connected with knowledge: the more high-quality argumentation there is, the better learners are able to link new contents to their pre-knowledge and to other content areas. Disputational talk shows a close interrelation with knowledge as well, but it is negative: the more learners are engaged in disputational talk, the less they are able to generate (declarative) knowledge. Figure 2 shows the interrelations.

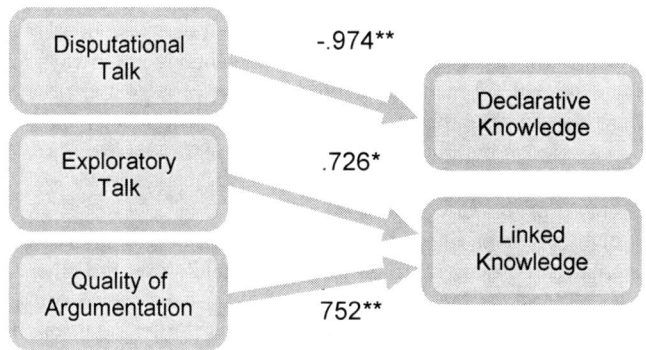

Figure 2. Interrelation of argumentation and knowledge
* = p < .05; ** = p < .01

CONCLUSIONS AND DISCUSSION: ALL THAT GLITTERS IS NOT GOLD

To sum up the results it can be concluded that students do participate actively in classroom talk if they are given the chance. But not everything is "perfect". Coming back to the research questions previously presented, the following can be stated:

Ad 1) If students are given the chance to actively participate in classroom talk: to what extend to they seize their chance?
Our data show that students talk a lot more when they got a chance to do so. Most of their talk is centred on learning tasks. Only about 17-18% is „private" talk (Wuttke, 2005). Even if there is a certain amount of private talk this is probably quite useful because it fulfills a function in socializing and is therefore helpful for relations in the group and for reduction of tension (O'Keefe, 1995). In addition it seems to work against the so-called sucker-effect in groups: some members work, the others benefit from it (Renkl, Gruber & Mandl, 1997). But this is only part of the message: Talking in itself does not lead to better learning outcomes. Only if students ask high quality questions and engage in exploratory talk can we expect an effect on their learning.

Ad 2) What is the quality of students' talk (questions and argumentation)?
As we have seen in our data the quality of talk is moderate and varies significantly between groups. All in all there are not enough higher order questions and not every student is apparently able to participate in high quality discussions (exploratory talk). One explanation could be that in groups where all learners are new to the topic in question, talk is difficult and stretches of high quality discourse may not happen. Furthermore: learners are not teachers and may not understand

113

why their talk should be of a quality that helps other students to develop their thinking (Dawes, 2004). The results are not really surprising if we take a closer look at the quality of teachers' talk. They seem to be rather poor 'role models': the data show that the quality of their questions and argumentation is not always better than the talk of their students. Teachers therefore do not provide the necessary linguistic scaffolding. Given that there should be a connection between higher order questions and knowledge building this result is quite alarming.

Ad 3) What are the effects of students' talk?
The findings show that there is an interrelation between high quality questions and high quality argumentation on one side and knowledge building on the other side. Questions should be at least of the second level (F2), if they are to influence knowledge building. There is no connection between lower order questions (F1) and knowledge. On the other hand highest quality level questions (F3) do not appear essential. This is good news because a lot of students might not be able to produce higher quality questions, especially if they are novices in the respective domain. As mentioned above, a certain amount of expertise is necessary to ask sophisticated questions (Miyake & Norman, 1979).

The conclusion we draw from our data is that talk *can be* gold, but unfortunately, very often it is not. Various consequences could be considered. One possibility is to train students to ask better questions and to engage more often in exploratory talk. From several studies we know that this approach is a realistic possibility: the quality of questioning as well as the quality of argumentation can be enhanced (e.g. Mercer, 2008; Renkl, 1997; Wegerif & Mercer, 2000). Maybe, though, training should not start with students but with teachers. It is quite apparent from our data that teachers themselves are not very good in higher quality classroom talk. So before we train students we should probably train teachers and then we can rely on them to be better role models in the future.

REFERENCES

Becker-Mrotzek, M., & Vogt, R. (2001). *Unterrichtskommunikation. Linguistische Analysemethoden und Forschungsergebnisse* [Classroom communication. Linguistic analysis methods and research results]. Tübingen: Max Niemeyer Verlag.

Bellack, A.A., Kliebard, H.M., Hyman, R.T., & Smith, F.L. (1974). *Die Sprache im Klassenzimmer* [Classroom language]. Düsseldorf: Pädagogischer Verlag.

Brown, A.L., Metz, K.E., & Campione, J.C. (1996). Social interaction and individual understanding in a community of learners: The influence of Piaget and Vygotsky. In A. Tryphon, & J. Vonèche (Eds.), *Piaget – Vygotsky. The social Genesis of thought* (pp. 145-170). East Sussex: Psychology Press.

Brown, A.L., & Palinscar, A.S. (1989): Guided, cooperative learning and individual knowledge acquistion. In L.B. Resnick (Ed.), *Knowing, learning, and instruction* (pp. 393-451). Hillsdale, NJ: Erlbaum.

Brown, R.A.J., & Renshaw, P.D. (2000): Collective argumentation: A sociocultural approach to reframing classroom teaching and learning. In H. Cowie, & G. van der Aalsvoort (Eds.), *Social interaction in learning and instruction. The meaning of discourse for the construction of knowledge* (pp. 52-66). Oxford: Elsevier.

Bruner, J. (1985). Vygotsky: A historical and conceptual perspective. In J.V. Wertsch (Ed.), *Culture, communication, and cognition: Vygotskian perspectives* (pp. 21-34). Cambridge: Cambridge University Press.

Cazden, C.B. (1988). *Classroom discourse. The language of teaching and learning.* Portsmouth, NH: Heinemann.

Chinn, C.A., O'Donnell, A.M., & Jinks, Th. S. (2000). The structure of discourse in collaborative learning. *The Journal of Experimental Education, 69*(1), 77-97.

Dawes, L. (2004). Talk and learning in classroom science. *International Journal of Science Education, 26*(6), 677-695.

Dillon, J.T. (1990). *The practice of questioning.* London: Routledge.

Edwards, A.D., & Mercer, N. (1987). *Common knowledge: The development of understanding in the classroom.* London: Methuen.

Edwards, A.D., & Westgate, D.P.G. (1994). *Investigating classroom talk.* (2nd Ed, fully rev. and extended). London: Routledge Falmer.

Fernandez, M., Wegerif, R., Mercer, N., & Rojas-Drummond, S. (2001). Re-conceptualising "scaffolding" and the Zone of Proximal Development in the context of symmetrical collaborative learning. *Journal of Classroom Interaction, 36*(3), 54-63.

Fischer, F., Bruhn, J., Gräsel, C., & Mandl, H. (2002). Fostering collaborative knowledge construction with visualization tools. *Learning and Instruction, 12*, 213-232.

Fisher, E. (1993). Distinctive features of pupil-pupil classroom talk and their relationship to learning: How discursive exploration might be encouraged. *Language and Education, 7*(4), 239-257.

Fox, R. (1995). Teaching through Discussion. In Ch. Desforges (Ed.), *An introduction to teaching. Psychological perspectives* (pp. 132-149). Oxford, UK; Blackwell Publishers.

Gopnick, A. (2001). Theories, language, and culture: Whorf without wincing. In M. Bowerman, & S.C. Levinson (Eds.), *Language acquisition and conceptual development* (pp. 45-69). Cambridge: Cambridge University Press.

Habermas, J. (1981): *Theorie des kommunikativen Handelns* [Theory of communicative action]. Frankfurt: Suhrkamp.

Hofer, M. (1981). Lehrer-Schüler-Interaktion [Teacher-Student-Interaction]. In H. Schiefele, & A. Krapp (Hrsg.). *Handlexikon zur Pädagogischen Psychologie* [Handbook of pedagogic psychology] (pp. 218-222). München: Ehrenwirth.

Kawanaka, T., & Stigler, J. (1999). Teachers' use of questions in eighth-grade mathematics classrooms in Germany, Japan, and the United States. *Mathematical Thinking and Learning, 1*(4), 255-278.

Kleine-Staarmann, J. (2009). The joint negotiation of ground rules. Establishing a shared collaborative practice with new educational technology. *Language and Education, 23*(1), 79-95.

Kumpulainen, K., & Mutanen, M. (2000). Mapping the dynamics of peer group interaction: A method of analysis of socially shared learning processes. In H. Cowie, & G. van der Aalsvoort (Eds.), *Social interaction in learning and instruction. The meaning of discourse for the construction of knowledge* (pp. 144-160). Oxford: Elsevier.

Mehan, H. (1979). *Learning lessons.* Cambridge, MA: Harvard University Press.

Mercer, N. (1995). *The guided construction of knowledge: Talk amongst teachers and learners.* Clevendon: Multilingual Matters.

Mercer, N. (1996). The quality of talk in children's collaborative activity in the classroom. *Learning and Instruction, 6*(4), 359-377.

Mercer N. (2000). *Words and minds. How we use language to think together.* London: Routledge.

Mercer, N. (2008). Talk and the development of reasoning and understanding. *Human Development, 51*, 90-100.

Miyake, N., & Norman, D. A. (1979). To ask a question, one must know enough to know what is not known. *Journal of Verbal Learning and Verbal Behavior, 18*, 357-364.

Niegemann, H. (2004): Lernen und Fragen: Bilanz und Perspektiven der Forschung [Learning and questions: Research results and perspectives]. *Unterrichtswissenschaft, 4*(33), 345-356.

O' Keefe, V. (1995). *Speaking to think /thinking to speak: the importance of talk in the learning process.* Portsmouth, NH: Boynton/Cook Publishers Inc.

Piaget, J. (1989). *Das Erwachen der Intelligenz beim Kinde* [The awakening of childrens' intelligence]. Stuttgart: Klett-Cotta.

Renkl, A. (1997). Lernen durch Erklären: Was, wenn Rückfragen gestellt werden [Learning through explanations: What if queries occur]? *Zeitschrift für Pädagogische Psychologie, 11*(1), 41-51.

Renkl, A., Gruber, H., & Mandl, H. (1997). Kooperatives problemorientiertes Lernen in der Hochschule [Cooperative and problem-orientied learning at university]. In J. Lompscher, & H. Mandl (Hrsg.): *Lehr- und Lernprobleme im Studium* [Problems in teaching and learning at university] (pp. 131-147). Bern: Huber.

Rojas-Drummond, S., & Tapia, A.A. (2007). Oracy, literacy, conceptual maps and ICT as mediators of the social construction of knowledge among peers. *Reflecting Education, 3*(1), 98-115.

Scardamalia, M., & Bereiter, C. (1992). Text-Based and knowledge-based questioning by children. *Cognition and Instruction, 9*(3), 177-199.

Seifried, J. (2010). Unterrichtliche Kommunikation von Lehrkräften an kaufmännischen Schulen [Teachers' communication in the classroom at vocational school]. *Zeitschrift für Berufs- und Wirtschaftspädagogik, 3*, 379-398.

Sembill, D. (1992). *Problemlösefähigkeit, Handlungskompetenz und Emotionale Befindlichkeit* [Problem-solving skills, action competence and emotions]. Göttingen: Hogrefe.

Sinclair A., & Coulthard, R.M. (1975). *Towards an analysis of discourse. The English used by teachers and pupils.* Oxford: Oxford University Press.

Spanhel, D. (1973). Schülersprache und Lernprozesse [Pupils talk and learning processes]. In W. Loch & G. Priesemann (Hrsg.). *Sprache und Lernen. Internationale Studien zur pädagogischen Anthropologie* [Language and learning. International proceedings on Pedagogic Anthropology]. Düsseldorf.

Spychiger, M., Oser, F., Hascher, T., & Mahler, F. (1999). Entwicklung einer Fehlerkultur in der Schule [The development of an error culture at school]. In W. Althof (Hrsg.). *Fehlerwelten. Vom Fehlermachen und Lernen aus Fehler* [World of Errors: About making errors and learning from errors] (pp. 43-70). Opladen: Leske + Budrich.

Stables, A. (1995). Learning through talk and learning through talking: Sound and silence in the classroom. *Language and Education, 9*(1), 61-68.

Stevens, R. (1912): *The question as a measure of efficiency in instruction: A critical study of classroom practise.* Teachers College Contributions to Education, 48.

Straub, D. (2001). *Ein kommunikationspsychologisches Modell kooperativen Lernens. Studien zu Interaktion und Wissenserwerb in computergestützten Lerngruppen* [A communication psychological model of cooperative learning. Studies on interaction and knowledge acquistion in computer-supported groups of learners. Berlin: dissertation.de - Verlag im Internet.

Sumfleth, E., & Pitton, A. (1998). Sprachliche Kommunikation im Chemieunterricht – Schülervorstellungen und ihre Bedeutung im Unterrichtsalltag [Classroom talk in chemistry – Expectations of pupils and their significance for everyday school life]. *Zeitschrift für Didaktik der Naturwissenschaften, 4*(2), 4-20.

Sweigart, W. (1991). Classroom talk, knowledge development and writing. *Research in the Teaching of English, 25*(4), 469-496.

Vygotski, L.S. (1962). *Thought and language.* Cambridge, MA: The MIT Press.

Webb, N.M. (1989). Peer interaction and learning in small cooperative groups. *International Journal of Educational Research, 13*, 21-39.

Webb, N.M., Troper, J.D., & Fall, R. (1995). Constructive activity and learning in collaborative small groups. *Journal of Educational Psychology, 87*(3), 406-423.

Wegerif, R. (2002a). Walking or Dancing? Images of thinking and learning to think in the classroom. *Journal of Interactive Learning Research, 13*(1/2), 51-70.

Wegerif, R., & Mercer, N. (2000). Language for thinking: A study of children solving reasoning test problems together. In H. Cowie, & G. van der Aalsvoort (Eds.), *Social interaction in learning and instruction. The meaning of discourse for the construction of knowledge* (pp. 179-192). Oxford: Elsevier.

Wegerif, R., Mercer, N., & Dawes L. (1999). From social interaction to individual reasoning: an empirical investigation of a possible socio-cultural model of cognitive development. *Learning and Instruction 9*, 493-516.

West, R., & Pearson, J. C. (1994). Antecedent and consequent conditions of student questioning: An analysis of classroom discourse across the university. *Communication Education, 43*, 299-311.

Westgate, D., & Hughes, M. (1997). Identifying 'quality' in classroom talk: An enduring research task. *Language and Education, 11*(2), 125-139.

Wood, D.J., Bruner, J.S., & Ross, G. (1976). The role of tutoring in problem solving. *Journal of Psychology and Psychiatry, 17*(2), 89-100.

Wuttke, E. (1999). *Motivation und Lernstrategien in einer selbstorganisationsoffenen Lernumgebung. Eine empirische Untersuchung bei angehenden Industriekaufleuten* [Motivation and learning strategies in a self-organized learning environment. A study on prospective business management assistants]. Frankfurt: Peter Lang.

Wuttke, E. (2005). *Unterrichtskommunikation und Wissenserwerb. Zum Einfluss von Kommunikation auf den Prozess der Wissensgenerierung* [Classroom communication and knowledge acquisition. The effect of communication on the process of knowledge generation]. Frankfurt: Peter Lang.

Wuttke, E., & Seifried, J. (2010): Unterrichtliche Kommunikation in schülerzentrierten Lehr-Lern-Arrangements [Classroom communication in student-centred learning environments]. In R. Nickolaus, G. Pätzold, H. Reinisch & T. Tramm (Hrsg). *Handbuch Berufs- und Wirtschaftspädagogik* (pp. 118-122). Bad Heilbrunn: Julius Klinkhardt.

Eveline Wuttke
Professor für Wirtschaftspädagogik, insbes. empirische Lehr-Lern-Forschung
Goethe Universität Frankfurt

ANN-CARITA EVALDSSON AND YVONNE KARLSSON

9. SHAPING MARGINALIZED IDENTITIES AND INDEXING DEFICIENT BEHAVIOURS IN A SPECIAL NEEDS UNIT

In this chapter, we are concerned with the local social process through which a group of boys in a special needs practice are identified and described as deviating from the local norms of school conduct (cf. Hester & Francis, 2000). More specifically we will demonstrate how a more permanent (and deviant) identity is talked into being during a remedial activity organized in the special educational needs unit. In the context of such an activity, individual boys' are attributed a set of emotional, social and behavioural deficiencies, which are made a daily topic of inquiry, in order to remedy the problem behaviours in question.

As has been noted elsewhere, boys are more likely than girls to be found in special education classes for pupils considered to have emotional, social and behavioural deficiencies (Daniels, Hey, Leonard & Smith, 1999; Emanuelsson & Persson, 2002; Giota & Lundborg, 2007; Reed, 1999; Riddell, 1996; Soles, Bloom, Heath, & Karagiannakis, 2008). As Reed (1999, p. 37) notes, the increasing identification of psychological and physiological syndromes attributed to boys in far greater numbers than girls may partially account for the predominance of boys in special educational needs units. So far however, the highly gendered and social dynamics of special educational needs practices have received little attention (Daniels et al., 1999). Building on the assumption that the school may in fact be an important player in portraying particular boys as deficient, we were interested in how deviant identities were constructed and attributed to boys in the context of a special education needs unit. More specifically, we explore how a group of pupils, who all are boys, in and through their everyday participation in special educational activities, came to be identified and associated with the psychologically based category of boys with Social, Emotional and Behavioural Difficulties (labelled as SEBD in Britain, see Cooper & Whitebread, 2002; Rutherford, Quinn & Mathur, 2004).

RESEARCH ON CHILDREN WITH SOCIAL, EMOTIONAL AND BEHAVIOURAL DIFFICULTIES

Thus far, most studies on children considered to be in need of special educational support have been largely restricted to identifying the Social, Emotional and Behavioural Difficulties (labelled as SEBD in Britain) of individual children

E. Hjörne et al. (eds.), Learning, Social Interaction and Diversity – Exploring Identities in School Practices, 119–137.

(Cooper & Whitebread, 2002; Rutherford, Quinn & Mathur, 2004). Researchers in the fields of psychology and education have concentrated on individual children's level of SEBD to effectively assess and provide intervention for boys who are referred to special education (Binnie & Allen, 2008; Humphrey & Brooks, 2006). Levels of SEBD have been assessed using standardized measures such as Achenbach's 'Child Behaviour Checklist' (Achenbach, 1991), Rutter's 'Child Behaviour Rating Scale' (Rutter, 1967) and the Goodman 'Strengths and Difficulties Questionnaire' (SDQ) (Goodman, 1999). As has been noted, there is an increasing tendency in the fields of psychology and education towards identification of certain psychological and physiological syndromes that in turn predominantly affect boys as a group. Still, there is no standard definition of, for example, what constitutes SEBD. The various behaviour-screening questionnaires share characteristics such as: "behaviour that goes to an extreme; behaviours or emotions that are outside societal norms; behaviours or emotions that negatively affect a child's educational functioning" (Soles, et al., 2008, p. 276). From the ethnomethodological perspective taken in this chapter, a fundamental problem remains with the ways in which these questionnaires predetermine the descriptive categories of children's problem behaviours in terms of underlying problems with psychological and physiological states. In this way, the problem behaviours are abstracted from everyday practices in which the teachers and the boys themselves make sense of these descriptive categories (see Hester, 2000).

In addition, the essentialist explanations dominating the fields of psychology and education have emphasized the dual nature of children's behavioural disorder by recognizing the existence of internalizing as well as externalizing measurable gender-contrary components. While boys have been rated more severely on externalizing behaviours (aggressive and delinquent behaviours), academic difficulties and social skills deficits, girls have been rated more severely on internalizing domains (withdrawal, somatic complaints and anxiety/depression) (see Achenbach, 1991; Keenan, Shaw, Delliquadri, Giovannelli, & Walsh, 1998; Lloyd, Kauffman, Landrum, & Roe, 1991). The psychological findings that acting-out behaviours are more common among boys while girls more often are referred for internalizing disorders can be said to support a form of gender dualism that (over)emphasizes gender differences and reinforces gender stereotypes (for a critique, see Daniels, et al., 1999; Reed, 1999; Riddell, 1996). Much of this research is underpinned by an essentialist treatment of gender as a set of fixed components that reside in individuals. However, such a narrow focus on measurable gender-contrary category components does not manage to capture the social process through which psychologically based categories such as SEBD are attributed to boys as a group in everyday special educational practices. In general relatively little sociological analytical attention has been paid to the intricate ways in which 'problem behaviours' are made sense of and treated as the grounds for various kinds of special needs practices (see Hester, 2000; Hjörne, 2004; Mehan, 1993; Mehan, Hertweck, & Meihls, 1986).

SOME METHODOLOGICAL CONSIDERATIONS

Thus far, most research on children considered to have emotional, social and behavioural deficiencies has been based on self-report methodology (i.e., questionnaires, surveys, laboratory methods). As a result of the quantitative research tradition, we know a good deal about the prevalence and main types of behavioural deficiencies, the number and characteristics of its participants, and the correlates of behavioural deficiencies with individuals' psychological and mental states. However, we know very little about the interactional processes through which categories such as 'boys with acting out behaviours' are invoked, recognized and negotiated in everyday educational activities. By means of a naturalistic case study, we explore how a categorization process, taking place in a special educational unit during the unfolding of a reoccurring remedial activity in which a more permanent deviant identity is talked into being and attributed to individual boys.

The present study combines ethnography with ethnomethodological work on members' understanding of social categories in talk-in-interaction (cf. Antaki & Widdicombe, 1998; Hester & Eglin, 1997; Hester & Francis, 2000). The approach taken provides a way of exploring the constitutive role of talk in local identity work and how issues associated with the wider social and educational framework can be located, observed and described within situated action. Membership categorization analysis, as Hester and Eglin (1997, p. 3) note, directs attention to the locally used, invoked and organized 'presumed common-sense knowledge of social structures' to which members orient when conducting their everyday affairs. Categories, such as 'children with social, emotional and behavioural deficiencies' and 'boys with acting out behaviours', and the inferred activities, are in this view treated from an anti-mentalist view "as topics under investigation (participants' resources for doing descriptions and explanations)" (Edwards, 1998, p. 13) rather than as "an explanatory resource that we as analysts haul with us to a scene" (Antaki & Widdicombe, 1998, p. 2). As Sacks (1972) noted in his early work on membership categorizations, people make use of categories – and the actions (category-bound activities) or characteristics (natural predicates) they imply – to conduct their daily business. Not only is the conventional connection between categories and activities a sense-making device in that it makes inferences about other people, but the activity itself may be used as a way of implicitly describing and categorizing people (Watson 1983, p. 40). For example, the classification of the particular boys as having 'emotional, social and behavioural deficiencies' is as we will demonstrate occasioned by the particular local (remedial) activity, in which the teachers describe and evaluate the boys' behaviours in order to remedy their difficulties. Thus the specific remedial activity in focus can be seen to offer a particularly interesting site, as actions and attributes associated with membership in the psychologically based category are invoked and negotiated.

In order to prove that the problem behaviours referred to, involving, for example, 'controlling anger', 'not listening', 'exaggerating', etc., are linked to the psychological category of 'boys with social, emotional and behavioural deficiencies' we, as analysts, have also made "an inference about what membership category is relevant" (see Antaki & Widdicombe, 1998, p. 10). In doing so, we have drawn upon knowledge of how the categorizations are conventionally used in the psychological literature and in the educational setting in particular. In addition, we are interested in how gendered dimensions are made invisible through the essentialist and psychologically based explanations that are mobilized within the specific sequential context of talk in the remedial activity (Stokoe & Smithson, 2001). In this process, we consider ethnographic analyses of the educational setting, including spatial and gendered arrangements, as crucial to understanding how the categorizations attributed to the boys are contextually embedded in the institutional practice (see Mehan, Hertweck, & Meihls, 1986; West & Zimmerman, 2009).

Thus, before continuing with our detailed analysis of how the categorization process is accomplished within the particular remedial activity, ethnographic analyses of the social organization of the specific special educational needs setting and its participants are required.

SPATIAL, SOCIAL AND GENDERED ARRANGEMENTS WITHIN THE SPECIAL EDUCATIONAL NEEDS SETTING

The present study draws on ethnography combined with AV recordings in a special educational needs unit for a period of one year (2002-2003); made by the second author (Karlsson, 2007). The special educational needs unit in focus was integrated into a comprehensive school with 600 students, of mixed socioeconomic status, in a middle-sized town in Sweden. Five preadolescent boys between 7 and 12 years of age attended the unit. The boys had been excluded from their ordinary classes and regular school activities with other students. They participated in separate educational and social activities in a building located on the periphery of the school area. The boys' marginal and subordinated position in everyday school life was manifested by the fact that there was no official information (i.e., webpage, catalogues, schedules, etc.) about the special educational needs unit at the school.

Four female teachers with different professional backgrounds (special needs education teacher, leisure-time pedagogue, youth recreation leader, child minder) were responsible for the boys' educational activities. The boys' placement in the unit varied from eight months to three years. The official explanation given by the school authorities was that the boys had 'behavioural, emotional and social difficulties'. The descriptions of the boys as 'having behavioural, emotional and social difficulties' marked them out not only as different, but also as being 'in need of remedial help'. As Hester (1998, p. 142) notes, the category 'remedial' implies various predicates, including being in 'need of help', 'being behind', etc., that ascribe incompetence to the individuals referred to. The school's categorization of individual boys as 'in need of remedial help' was made sense of and recognized in everyday school activities over a long period of time (Hester & Francis, 2000; Mehan, 1991). Through the ethnographic work, it became evident that troubling classroom behaviours had been the starting point for a series of meetings, leading up to *ad hoc* interpretations of the boys' problems behaviours as individualistic in nature rather than as situated in social practice (Hester, 2000, p. 220).

Although the school did not refer to gendered behaviours as a reason for excluding the boys, the fact that all the pupils in the special educational unit were boys who were more or less excluded for causing trouble in class creates a highly gendered dynamic to the special educational needs practice (cf. Daniels, et al. 1999). The fact that the boys were portrayed as troubling demonstrates the teachers' (and the school authorities') background knowledge of the gendered nature of the referred problem behaviours. 'Common-sense' and 'cultural' knowledge about the link between masculinity and 'troubling classroom activities' as a gendered activity (see, for example, Connell, 2000; Mac an Ghaill, 1994; Frosh, Phoenix & Pattman, 2002) is therefore as we will show even made invisible in everyday practices within the remedial activity in focus. Of importance in the analysis of the categorization practice is that the teachers in the special needs practice do not explicitly orientate to the boys problem behaviours as a gendered activity and that we can problematize this (cf. Stokoe & Smithson, 2001).

Seating Arrangements during the Remedial Activity

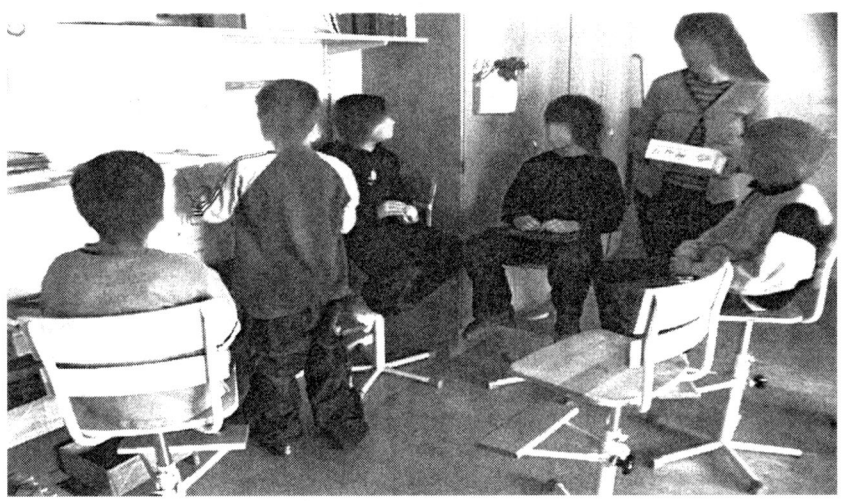

Figure 1 (Seating arrangements during the remedial activity)

The key activity for discussions of remedial intervention in the boys' problematic school behaviours was a scheduled activity called "smiley". In general, daily efforts were more likely to focus on social care and controlling the boys' behavioural, social and emotional difficulties than on teaching school subjects (Karlsson, 2007). The remedial activity in focus took place at the end of each school day in a separate room and lasted for around 25 minutes. During the activity, the five children were seated in a half circle while the two teachers in charge stood behind them.

The seating arrangement, with the five boys facing the wall positions the boys as subordinate to the female teachers, who take on a powerful position. From their position behind the boys' backs, the teachers are able to monitor and evaluate the individual boys one at a time, without the boys really knowing 'whose turn is next?'. Only when an individual has managed to remedy his emotional, behavioural and social deficiencies will he be rewarded with a smiley sticker. The five maps hanging on the wall in front of the boys demonstrate how many smiley stickers each of the boys has managed to attain. In this way, the deficiencies attributed to each one of the individual boys as well as their individual efforts to remedy their problem behaviours becomes visually manifested and a matter of public interest to the whole group of boys.

Record Keeping as a Categorization Practice

As will be further shown in the analysis of talk-in-interaction during the remedial activity, the individualistic character of the boys' problem behaviours is also manifested in and through the teacher's use of the written record through which the teacher builds and manages the individual cases of remedial intervention. Hall, Slembrouck and Sarangi (2006, p. 90) note, in regard to work on social welfare that records on clients "are institutional requirements and a professional resource" in many institutional settings. In addition, "incompleteness and incoherence is intrinsic to case records, because by definition they are selective for the purpose of day-to-day management" (ibid. p. 91, see also Garfinkel, 1967, pp. 186-207). If we consider the original construction of the written record used within the remedial activity in focus, it had been worked out during a former teacher-parent conference.

As illustrated in Example 1, the written record gives no information about what was discussed during the teachers' previous meetings with the parents. Instead we are presented with incoherent and incomplete written information, including an informal checklist with the names of each of the five boys, and a list of problem behaviours assessed in terms of individual characteristics and anticipated behaviours. As will be further demonstrated in our analysis of the remedial activity, the selective linguistic, rhetorical and thematic form of the informal checklist resonates with the future purpose of this written record. The checklist on the written record refers primarily to teachers' daily management of and remedial interventions of the individual boys' disorderly behaviours.

Example 1 (written record)

To get a "Smiley" sticker you have to:

Anton
* Control your anger.
* Don't say "no".
* No exaggerating.
* Don't make mistakes even if your friends are doing things that are wrong.

Jesper
* Did you do your homework?
* Finish your school tasks.
* Listen to adults and obey.
* Don't make bad faces.

Marcus
* Talk nicely
* No dirty words.
* No complaining.
* Confess when you make mistakes.
* Do not tease

Oskar
* Don't correct anyone else.
* Don't say dirty words.
* Do not exaggerate
* Tell and explain what you want.
* Leave the room when told to do so.

Tom
* Leave the room when you get disturbed.
* Don't say "what".
* No unpleasant tone.
* Take off your outdoor clothes before you enter the room
* Be attentive to the social situation.
* Eat up the food you have put on your plate.

As can be seen from the written record, the individual boys' problem behaviours are formulated as imperatives such as "Don't say 'no'", "Don't correct anyone else", "Don't say dirty words", "Do not exaggerate", etc. The directives clearly prescribe the specific course of action that is expected from each of the individual boys. For the teachers who have formulated the written record, such bald imperatives position the teacher, in relation to the boys, as an authority who has the right to control and remedy the boys' disorderly behaviour without offering deference (cf. Goodwin, 2006).

In addition, the anticipated behaviours on the check-list construct each of the individual boys as a particular moral and social actor, who has not managed to demonstrate the levels of social, emotional and behavioural competencies that are normally expected from pupils in school and children at that age. In this way, the individual boys are marked as different and categorized as both incompetent and as deviant by virtue of their failure to display the kinds of activities that are normally bound to the category of 'children' in general and of 'pupil' in particular (Hester, 1998, p. 138). In addition, the individual characteristics of the written record can be read as making relevant classificatory items such as 'hyperactivity', 'aggressive behaviour', 'conduct problems', 'peer problems' and 'prosocial behaviour', all of which are associated with the psychologically based category of 'boys with externalizing behaviours'.

As will be shown in our detailed analysis of talk-in-interaction during the remedial activity, the written record provides a point of entry or procedural basis for the teachers as well as the boys to evaluate and remedy a set of decontextualized individual properties that are animated by the category of 'boys with externalizing disorders'. Our argument is that the written list of the individual boys' social, emotional and behavioural difficulties, which are invoked in teachers' evaluations during the remedial activity, function to solidify negative characteristics of individuals. In what follows, we will demonstrate how a deviant identity is accomplished and solidified in talk-in-interaction during the activity through the participants' use of different but overlapping rhetorical and interactional resources such as a) contrastive identity work, b) intensified category work and c) cumulative identity work (cf. Hall, Slembrouck & Sarangi, 2006).

Invoking a Contrastive Deviant Identity

We will now continue to investigate how a deviant identity as 'boys with externalizing behaviours' is talked into being as the boys' emotional, behavioural and social deficiencies are made a daily topic of inquiry during the remedial activity. As will be shown, the written record plays a central role both in the organization of the activity and in the categorization of the boys.

In the following example, one of the female teachers addresses the first boy on the written record, Anton (see Example 2, line 1). The teacher's use of first names such as 'Anton', 'Jesper', 'Oskar', etc., identifies the boys personally and indicates that the boys' personal life and identities, and not the teacher's, are open to detailed examination (Edwards, 1998: 22). As will be shown, the naming also offers opportunities for the teacher to make the individual boy accountable for his emotional, social and behavioural deficiencies.

Example 2 (video recording 1842002 12)

1	KARIN:	Anto::n
2	Anton:	((lean backwards and looks at Karin)) (2s)
3	KARIN:	have you managed to control your anger? ((reads in the
4		written record)) (4s)
5	Anton:	I have not had any anger ((looks at Karin))
6	KARIN:	((nods yes)) (6s)

7	KARIN:	and not said <u>no</u>? ((reads from the written record)) (2s)
8	Anton:	I have <u>not</u> said that ((looks at Karin))
9	KARIN:	((nods yes)) (2s)
10	KARIN:	not made any mistakes (.) even if your friends have
11		done something wrong? ((looks at Anton))
12	Anton:	I have not <u>do</u>ne that ((looks at Karin))
13	KARIN:	((nods))
14	KARIN:	not exaggerated? ((looks at Anton)) (2s)
15	Anton:	°not done° ((looks at Karin))
16	KARIN:	((nods and cuts out a smiley sticker)) (4s)
17	Oskar:	then it's my turn (.) after Anton
18	LENA:	°you got a sticker° ((looks at Anton))
19	KARIN:	[great (.) Anton] ((cuts out a smiley sticker))
20	KARIN:	[he's worth that] (.) will you give it to him

As shown in example 2 the boys' behaviours are constructed as deficient through a series of contrasts that infer what constitutes normal ways of acting. A contrast between, for example, 'managing to control your anger' and 'not being able to control your anger' is implicitly inferred through the teacher's request, "have you managed to control your anger?" (line 3). As Hester (1998, p. 136) notes, contrast structures are a key device for "describing deviance in that they are constructed for the local situation at hand to make just this point" (see also Hall, Slembrouck, & Sarangi, 2006, p. 56). Thus, given the logic that students in general and boys in particular should manage to 'control their anger' (line 3), 'not make any mistakes even if friends do' (line 10-11) and 'not exaggerate' (line 14), the inferred contrasts implicitly support a negative category depiction of Anton as a 'boy with acting out behaviours'.

Furthermore, we can observe how this category contrast is collaboratively produced. As can be seen, the teacher's request occasions an answer from the boy in focus (lines 5, 8, 12, 15), which is then followed by another request from the teacher. The teacher morally evaluates the boy's response work, such that compliance with the requested behaviours warrants a degrading of the inferred negative descriptions (Freebody & Freiburg, 2000). Throughout the sequence, Anton manages to conform to the required response practice by producing a preferred second next turn to the teacher's questions: "I haven't had any anger", "I have not said that", "I have not done that" and "°not done that°" (line 5, 8, 12, 15). His minimal responses align with and reuse the format of the teacher's talk, thus confirming her right to confirm or disconfirm his behavioural displays.

At the end of the sequence, the two female teachers morally evaluate Anton's displayed behaviour, one after the other, in a positive fashion (lines 19-20). The teachers' moral evaluations temporarily occasion an identity for Anton as a 'good student', who performs routine-like classroom activities. The positive identity is inferred by way of contrast with the negative category of 'boys with externalizing behaviours' and the category-bound activities this implies of 'not controlling your anger', 'saying no' and 'exaggerating', etc. The contrastive positive occasion-specific identity of 'good student' is further confirmed as Anton finally receives the smiley sticker as additional evidence of his compliance with the positive category-bound activities referred to (lines 18-20). In this process, the individual boy is positioned as an agent who is assigned full moral responsibility for his deviant actions. Thus, only when Anton publicly shows his willingness to comply with the contrastive (positive) behaviours do the teachers decide that he has managed to control the negative behaviours in question.

Intensified Category Work

As will be further shown, the outcome of the remedial intervention associated with the boys' negative category-bound behaviours is intricately interwoven with the ways in which the targeted boy manages to comply with the identity descriptions formulated by the female teacher during the remedial activity. For the boys, this involves discovering what counts as proper ways of acting in the teacher-student interaction as well as recovering the consequences of the teachers' descriptions of their deficiencies.

The next example will demonstrate how the targeted boys' noncompliance with the teachers' identity descriptions warrants an upgrading of the inferred negative identity descriptions. In what follows, the teachers' remedial actions are noticeably absent, while the negative identity descriptions are intensified, casting the individual boy as accountable for the fact that his problem behaviours have worsened (as you can see in turns 5, 6, 8 and 9).

Example 3 (video recording F5 2542002 -12:09:44)

1	LENA:	ah (.) Jesper K
2	Jesper:	hm (4s)
3	LENA:	homework (.) did you not do it today
4	Jesper:	NO
5	LENA:	school tasks, listen to adults and obey (2s) ONE THING
6		(.) I've begun to think of that concerns you Jesper
7	Jesper:	hm
8	LENA:	which irritates me (.) it's that you say "no, no, no, no"
9		(2s) when we tell you to do certain things
10	Tom:	that was tough

11	LENA:	you have argued against us several times (.) instead of
12		listening (.) if you think that something is wrong (.) then
13		<u>tel</u>l us (.) instead of just saying no
14	Boy?:	no
15	Anton:	no
16	Oskar:	no, no
17	Marcus:	I thought he was going to say no again
18	Oskar:	no
19	KARIN:	he said okay (.) he listened very well now

As can be seen from example 3, Jesper responds quite strongly with a negation (line 4) to the teacher's requested actions regarding his homework. Jesper's oppositional move may have come from the teacher's prior turn, in which he is indirectly expected to not have done his homework. Jesper's noncompliance with the requested action of 'doing homework' implicitly casts the teacher as someone who has the obligation to take the boy's oppositional stance into account.

In what follows, the teacher makes available the list, i.e. "school tasks", "listen to adults" "obey" (line 5), from which the boy's deviant identity can be implicitly inferred. Following this, the teacher initiates what can be heard as an account of two of the attributes, "obey" and "listen to adults", which have just been reported, namely that Jesper "says "no, no, no, no" (2s) when we tell you to do certain things" (lines 8-9). As shown, the boy's noncompliance with the prescribed category-bound activities occasions an upshot from the teacher, who in a high-pitch voice explicitly states her emotional stance after a lengthy pause, which occasions trouble (Freebody & Freiburg, 2000, p. 156). At the end of her detailed account, she elaborates on Jesper's moral character by employing an extreme case formulation "you have argued against us several times", thereby describing his deviant behaviour as long-standing and consistent (line 11). As Pomeranz (1986) notes, 'extreme case formulation' is a practice that may be used to legitimize claims in adversarial situations. By portraying the boy as having extreme behavioural problems, the teacher not only manages to undermine Jesper's oppositional stance, but also to account for the seriousness of his behavioural problems, for which he is made personally accountable (lines 11-13).

The teacher's extended account of Jesper's negative demeanour of 'not obeying' and the detailing of how he says "no no no no" that this signifies are made a public concern for the whole group of boys. The teacher's talk is designed to attract the other boys' attention, as well as the other teachers', to Jesper's transgressions as a serious violation worthy of a public reprimand. Thus, the teacher's talk lays the foundations for the other boys, one after the other, aligning with her portrayal of Jesper. As can be noted in line 17, one of the boys even ratifies the teacher's negative description of Jesper, thereby mutually confirming with the teacher that the negative category depiction is of public and shared interest to the whole group of boys (Freebody & Freiburg, 2000). Interestingly enough, the collection of boys' negative commentaries enables the teacher to invoke a contrastive description at the end of the sequence and to evaluate Jesper in a more positive fashion: "he said okay (.) he listened very well now" (line 18). In this way, the boys as a collective can paradoxically be seen as the instigator of a more positive identity ascription of the targeted boy, instantiating it as the whole "group's reasoned intervention" (Freebody & Frieberg, 2000, p. 160).

Removing and Adding Negative Category Affiliation

Thus far, our analysis has demonstrated how the teachers use talk to identify and evaluate the individual boys' deficient emotional and social behaviours while subordinating the targeted boy's own identity descriptions. As will be shown, the targeted boy may use the same strategy to remove negative category affiliation and gain positive category affiliation. In this process, the destiny of the particular boy is placed in the hands of the teachers, who can either support or disqualify the boy's version of his behavioural and emotional displays.

In the next example, Marcus makes a contribution in which he tries to remove one of the listed negative category descriptions, "I think we can remove complaining" (in line 13), attributed to him as a person on the written record.

Example 4 (video recording F6 252002 -12:02:47)

1	KARIN:	now it's best that you are quiet (.) if we're gonna do it
2		fast like someone requested (5s)
3	LENA:	Marcus
4	Marcus:	no (.) yes
5	LENA:	has it been a good day?
6	Marcus:	yes
7	LENA:	((reads in the written record)) (7s)
8	Marcus:	tell <u>those</u> things <u>then</u>
9	LENA:	((reads in the written record)) (5s) what? (2s) yes (.)
10		talk nicely, and no dirty words, no complaining, and
11		admit when you've done something wrong
12	Marcus:	I think we can remove complaining
13	LENA:	do you think so?
14	Marcus:	no- (.)yes
15	LENA:	I <u>don't</u> <u>think</u> so (4s) however (.) I think we will add teasing

As shown, Marcus' attempts to control the teacher's actions engender further counter-moves providing the teacher with an opportunity to instead take on an oppositional stance and produce an upgraded negative category affiliation, "I don't think so (4s.) however (.) I think we will add teasing" (lines 15). Like in the previous example, it is the teacher's reaction to some emergent properties of the targeted boy's talk to the teacher that is crucial to understanding the significance and the function of the intensified negative category depiction. The question is, however, why the teacher disqualifies Marcus' contribution and instead says "I think we will add teasing"? In the case of Marcus, whose warrants for launching the directives in line 8 and 12 may come from the other teacher's previous turn in lines 1, where she proposes that they need to speed up the activity, he is nonetheless made accountable and attributed a negative category-bound activity of "teasing". In this way, the agentive way in which Marcus directs the teacher's actions and opposes the negative category depictions ascribed to him are disqualified and treated as non-serious.

The above sequence demonstrates that the process of categorizing the boys is not only tied to the teachers' descriptions of the boys' emotional and social behaviour as deviant. Categorizations are also mobilized as part of the interactional work between the teacher and the targeted boy. The teacher's right to disqualify and even undercut the boys' accounts indicates that an asymmetrical category relation between the teachers and the boys is invoked in the teacher-student interaction. By taking the initiative to alter the identity descriptions and not comply with the teacher's version of appropriate behaviour, the targeted boy takes the risk of intensifying the deviant identity ascribed to him, and the subordinated position that the boys are delegated as a group, in the teacher-student interaction.

Appropriating a Cumulative Identity

In this last section, it will be further demonstrated how the boys' habitual experiences of participating in the remedial activity are consequential to their appropriation of a more permanent deviant identity and marginal position. The habitual marginal position and deviant identity constructed for the targeted boys in the remedial activity illustrate what Antaki, Condor and Levine (1996) note in relation to identity work: "The speakers are doing three things at once: invoking social identities, negotiating what the features or boundaries of those identities are, and accumulating a record of having those identities" (p. 488). Thus, once an individual boy's negative category affiliation has been assumed in the conversational display of identities within the remedial activity, there is always the potential that the targeted boy's actions will be understood solely based on what is expected according to his interactional history (Evaldsson, 2002).

As will be shown in our last example, it is not only the teachers who ascribe negative characteristics to the boys, but the boys themselves may also take the initiative to invoke the accumulated record of negative identity descriptions, appropriating them and making them their own.

Example 5 (video recording 2542002 12:07:10)

1	LENA:	<u>Oska</u>::r ((reads in the written record and looks at Oskar)) (2s)
2	Oskar:	I'm not <u>wo::</u>rth anything ((looks at Lena)) (2s)
3	LENA:	you're not worth anything? (.) what do you mean?
4		((looks at Oskar)) (2s)
5	Oskar:	I've been exaggerating ((looks at Lena)) (2s)
6	LENA:	when? (2s)
7	Oskar:	at lunch (6s)
8	LENA:	but do you know-↑ ((the other children talk)) (18s)
9	LENA:	<u>yo::</u>u
10	Oskar:	°hm° ((looks at Lena))
11	LENA:	to<u>day-</u>
12	Oskar:	hm
13	LENA:	it was different (2s) we thought that (2s) Karin and I
14		(5s) you <u>sta:::rted</u> to <u>exa::g</u>gerate (5s) and then we
15		told you (2s) that you should think it over (.) and be
16		<u>qui</u>et (2s)
17	Oskar:	hm (3s)
18	LENA:	and you <u>di::</u>d that today (5s) and we <u>rea::</u>lly want to say
19		that you did very well
20	Oskar:	the- (.) is it blame or?
21	LENA:	what did you say?
22	Oskar:	is it blame or? (2s)
23	LENA:	blame?
24	KARIN:	no it's praise
25	LENA:	that was very well done (.) that you did <u>not</u>-
26	Oskar:	praise (.) then I'll get- ((looks at Karin and Lena
27		referring to a smiley sticker))
28	LENA:	get so angry::: (2s)
29	Oskar	hm

As shown in example 5, the targeted boy Oskar takes the initiative in doing his own membership: "I'm not worth anything" (line 2). By employing an extreme case formulation such as "not worth anything", he actively contributes to constructing himself not only as a 'boy in need of remedial intervention' but also as an 'incompetent person'. He then initiates what can be heard as an account of the activities that this self-identification signifies, namely that "I've been exaggerating" (line 5). The negative self-identity is assessed in relation to shared attributes referring to the formulations made by the teachers in the written record. The fact that Oscar gives voice to and re-assesses himself using a genre associated with school authorities points out the cumulative process whereby the boys establish their marginal positions over time by building on the negative assessments of others (i.e., mainly teachers) (Hall, Slembrouck & Sarangi, 2006, p. 65). Interestingly enough, the response work of the teacher in lines 13-16 and 18-19 warrants a contrastive oppositional account, including a more positive category depiction of Oskar's character, which is now outlined in a series of positive assessments including attributes such as "think it over", "be quiet" and "very well done". The kind of inferences that these attributes make available downplays Oskar's self-imposed negative self-identification. In addition, the teacher makes use of the inclusive personal pronoun 'we' to establish the shared nature and the collective view of Oskar's positive category affiliation. In this way, the negative identity ascription earlier attributed to Oskar is paradoxically being challenged, by the teacher.

There are several interesting features in the above exchange between the teacher and the targeted boy that provide an understanding of the targeted boy's negative identity ascription in the first sequence. One is that the asymmetry between the teacher and the targeted boy is a noticeable feature. In the subsequent turns, both the targeted boy and the teacher provide an account in which they address the problem of categorizing the boy as an 'incompetent person'. Their accounts display sensitivity to the asymmetrical relation between the boys and the teachers, and simultaneously attend to the risk of displaying repeated, extended and appropriated negative category assessments of the boys' conduct. Another feature is seen when Oskar presents himself using the personal pronoun *I* (line 2), thereby disassociating himself from the talk (Goffman, 1981, p. 147). This format introduces some distance between the displayed negative character and the serious self, allowing the targeted boy to invoke and comment on the meaning structure of the evaluation process imposed by the teacher (lines 20-29). In this agentive way, Oskar paradoxically manages to temporarily resist a more permanent deviant identity and instead positions himself as fulfilling the category-bound obligations of a 'good pupil' who performs routine-like classroom activities.

DISCUSSION

In this chapter, we have shown how psychologically based categorizations provide teachers with methods for locating and remedying individual boys' thought to have emotional, social and behavioural deficiencies. In this process, person references and activity descriptions are selected in classroom talk-in-interaction, such that individuals are ascribed and attributed a emotional ("angry", "exaggerating", etc.), behavioural ("using dirty words", "saying no", etc.) and social ("teasing others", "impolite", etc.) deficiencies. The negative attributes invoked in the teachers' talk can be read as making relevant psychologically based classificatory items such as hyperactivity, aggressive behaviour, conduct problems, peer problems and prosocial behaviour, all of which are associated with the psychologically based category of 'boys with externalizing behaviours' (see, for example, Lloyd et al., 1991; Soles, et al., 2008). As can be seen, there is a 'noticeable absence' of all forms of social categories such as gender, social class, ethnicity and age in the remedial activity at hand. Nevertheless, it can be argued that the negative activities attributed to the boys implicitly invoke references to gendered activities (such as troubling school behaviours, aggression, etc.), and as we could see in the context of the wider school setting, references to troubling classroom behaviours as gendered activities were part of explanations and reasons for remedial interventions. However, focussing on individual characteristics, and calling into play psychologically based categories, rather than on contextually embedded practices, tend to mystify these interconnections (cf. Arnot, 2006; Hjörne, 2004; Riddell, 1996).

What becomes evident in our analysis is that invocation of individual characteristics is a method for the remedial intervention, in which the individual boy is assigned full responsibility for the problem behaviours (cf. Hall, Slembrouck, & Sarangi, 2006). In the intervention process, the teachers repeat, intensify and appropriate the increasingly negative assessments of the boys' emotional and social behaviours, building assessments on top of one another. The negative identity ascriptions invoked in the remedial activity are built on earlier contributions made frequently in other kinds of meetings and written records, but also through the recurrent remedial interventions and contacts with the boys. The effect of the accumulating characterizations made in the remedial activity is that they point out the boys' deficiencies in a more pervasive and persistent fashion, which in turn functions to solidify negative characteristics of individuals and more permanent deviant identities over time. Thus, the repeated emphasis on highly individualistic identity ascriptions, invoking negative properties of persons, partly accounts for the solidification of the boys' deviant identities and their marginal position in school.

One noticeable feature of the remedial talk is the absence of any explicit explanations for the boys' deviant behaviours; it is obviously enough to simply indicate and point out the boys' deficiencies (Hester, 1998, p. 149). As our examples demonstrate, the teachers systematically attribute a set of individually based deficiencies and incompetencies to the boys and recurrently set up a remedial activity that is tailored to display these same incompetencies (Freibody & Frieburg, 2000). Similarly, based on what has been found in prior research in Britain on teachers' perceptions and expectations of boys with Social, Emotional and Behavioural Difficulties, these are often negative and stereotypic (Hannah & Pilner, 1983; Soles et al., 2008). The particular group of boys is constantly described as 'aggressive', 'anxious', 'affectionless', 'unmotivated' or 'hostile' (Marlowe, Maycock, Palmer & Morrison, 1997). It can thus be argued that remedial interventions tend to increase social, emotional or behavioural problems instead of helping the boys change their behaviours and to put these boys at even greater risk of academic failure (cf. Cooper, 2006). As demonstrated, the outcome of the remedial intervention is intricately interwoven with the ways in which the targeted boys comply with the negative identity descriptions formulated by the female teachers. In this process, the boys themselves reinforce and distance themselves in different ways from the descriptions and assume different types of alignments and footings with respect to the teachers' talk. Some boys, by means of comments on their own and others' conduct even assist the teachers in indexing and solidifying negative behaviours. Thus, the boys themselves may in fact appropriate interactional patterns that cast them as agents in the formations of more permanent deviant and marginalized identities, a topic that must be addressed in further analyses. All in all, our study indicates that everyday special educational activities are important players in the shaping of marginal and deviant identities and that further investigations of everyday special educational and interactional practices are needed if we are to understand the subtle processes of negative identity formations in special needs practices.

REFERENCES

Achenbach, T.M. (1991). *Manual for the child-behavior checklist/4-18 and 1991 profile*. Burlington, VT: University of Vermont, Department of Psychiatry.

Arnot, M. (2006). Gender voices in the classroom. In C. Skelton, B. Francis & L. Smulyan (Eds.), *Handbook of gender and education* (pp. 407-422). London: Sage publication.

Antaki, C., Condor, S. & Levine, M. (1996). Social identities in talk: Speakers' own orientations. *British Journal of Social Psychology, 35*, 473-492.

Antaki, C. & Widdicombe, S. (1998). Identity as an achievement and as a tool. In C. Antaki & S. Widdicombe (Eds.), *Identities in talk* (pp. 1-14). London: Sage Publications.

Binnie, H. L. & Allen, K. (2008). Whole school support for vulnerable children: The evaluation of a part-time nurture group. *Emotional and Behavioural Difficulties, 13*(3), 201-216.

Connell, R.W. (1989). Cool guys, swots and wimps: The interplay of masculinity and education. *Oxford Review of Education, 15*(3), 291-303.

Cooper, P. & Whitebread, D. (2002). *The effectiveness of Nurture Groups*. Leicester: University of Leicester.

Cooper, P. 2006. Awareness, understanding and the promotion of educational engagement. *Emotional and Behavioral Difficulties, 11*(3), 151-153.

Daniels, H., Hey, V., Leonard, D., & Smith, M. (1999). Issues of equity in special needs education from a gender perspective. *British Journal of Special Education, 26*(4), 189-195.

Edwards, D. (1998). The relevant thing about her. Social identity categories in use. In C. Antaki & S. Widdicombe (Eds.), *Identities in talk* (pp. 15-34). London: Sage Publications.

Emanuelsson, I. & Persson, B. (2002). Differentiering, specialpedagogik och likvärdighet. En longitudinell studie av skolkarriärer bland elever i svårigheter. *Pedagogisk forskning i Sverige, 7*(3), 183-199.

Evaldsson, A-C. (2002) 'Boys' gossip telling: Staging identities and indexing (non-acceptable) masculine behaviour, *Text, 22*(2), 1-27.

Freebody, P. & Freiberg, J. (2000). Public and pedagogic morality. The local orders of institutional and regulatory talk in classrooms. In S. Hester & D. Francis (Eds.), *Local educational order. Ethnomethodological studies of knowledge in action* (pp. 141-162).

Frosch, S., Phoenix, A., & Pattman R. (2002). *Young masculinities: Understanding boys in contemporary society*. Basingstoke: Palgrave Macmillan.

Garfinkel H. (1967). *Studies in ethnomethodology*. Cambridge: Polity press.

Giota, J. & Lundborg, O. (2007). Specialpedagogiskt stöd i grundskolan. Omfattning, former och konsekvenser. IPD-rapport 2007:03.

Goodman, R. (1999). The extended version of the strengths and difficulties of questionnaire as a guide to child psychiatric cases and consequent burden. *Journal of Child Psychology and Psychiatry, 40*(5), 791-800.

Goodwin, M.H. (2006). Participation, affect, and trajectory in family directive/response sequences. *Text and Talk, 26*(4/5), 513-542.

Goffman, E. (1981). *Forms of talk.* Philadelphia: University of Pennsylvania Press.

Hall, C., Slembrouck, S., & Sarangi, S. (2006). *Language practices in social work. Categorizations and accountability in child welfare.* London: Routledge.

Hannah, M.E. & Pilner, S. (1983). Teacher attitudes toward handicapped children: A review and synthesis. *School Psychology Review, 12*, 12-25.

Hester, S. (1998). Describing deviance in school: Recognizable educational psychological problems. In C. Antaki and S. Widdicombe (Eds.), *Identities in talk* (pp. 133-150). London: Sage Publications.

Hester, S. (2000). The local order of deviance in school. Membership categorization, motives and morality in referral talk. In S. Hester and D. Francis (Eds.), *Local educational order. Ethnomethodological studies of knowledge in action* (pp. 197-222). Philadelphia: John Benjamins Publishing Co.

Hester, S. & Francis, D. (2000). Ethnomethodology and local educational order. In S. Hester & D. Francis (Eds.), *Local educational order. Ethnomethodological studies of knowledge in action* (pp. 197-222). Philadelphia: John Benjamins Publishing Co.

Hester, S. & Eglin, P. (Eds.). (1997). *Culture in action. Studies in membership categorization analysis.* Lanham, MD: University Press of America.

Hjörne, E. (2004). Excluding for inclusion? Negotiating school careers and identities in pupil welfare settings in the Swedish school. PhD Thesis. Gothenburg: University of Gothenburg.

Humphrey, N. & Brooks, G. (2006). An evaluation of a short cognitive-behavioural anger management intervention for pupils at risk of exclusion. *Emotional and Behavioural Difficulties, 11*(1), 5-23.

Karlsson, Y. (2007). Att inte vilja vara ett problem. Social organisering och utvärdering av elever i en särskild undervisningsgrupp. PhD Thesis. Linköping Studies in Pedagogic Practices No 6. Linköping University.

Keenan, K., Shaw, D., Delliquadri, E., Giovannelli, J., & Walsh, B. (1998). Evidence for the continuity of early problem behaviors: Application of a developmental model. *Journal of Abnormal Psychology, 26*(6), 441-452.

Lloyd, J. W., Kauffman, J.M., Landrum, T.J., & Roe, D.J. (1991). Why do teachers refer pupils for special education? An analysis of referral records. *Exceptionality, 2*(3), 115-126.

Mac an Ghaill, M. (1994). *The making of men: Masculinities, sexualities and schooling.* Buckingham: Open University Press.

Marlowe, M., Maycock, G.A. Palmer, L.F., & Morrison W.F. (1997). Utilizing literary texts in teacher education to promote positive attitudes toward children with emotional and behavioural disorders. *Behavioral Disorders, 22*(3), 152-159.

Mehan, H. (1991). The schools' work of sorting students. In D. Zimmerman & D. Boden (Eds.), *Talk and social structure.* Cambridge: Polity Press.

Mehan, H. (1993). Beneath the skin and between the ears: A case study in the politics of representation. In: S. Chaiklin & J. Lave (Eds.), *Understanding practice. Perspectives on activity and context* (pp. 241-268). Cambridge, MA: Cambridge University Press.

Mehan, H., Hertweck, A., & Meihls, J.L. (1986). *Handicapping the handicapped. Decision making in students educational careers.* Stanford, CA: Stanford University Press.

Pomeranz, A. (1986). Extreme case formulations: A way of legitimizing claims. *Human Studies, 9*, 219-229.

Reed, R. (1999). Troubling boys and disturbing discourses on masculinity and schooling: A feminist exploration of current debates and interventions concerning boys' in school. *Gender and Education. 11*(1), 93-110.

Riddell, S. (1996). Gender and special educational needs. In G. Lloyd (Ed.), *Knitting progress unsatisfactory: Gender and special issues in education*. Edinburg: Moray House of Education.

Rutherford, R.B., Quinn, M.M., & Mathur, S.R. (2004). *Handbook of research in emotional and behavioural disorders*. New York: Guilford Press.

Rutter, M. (1967). A children's behaviour questionnaire for completion by teachers: Preliminary findings. *Journal of Child Psychology and Psychiatry, 8*, 1-11.

Sacks, H. (1972). On the analyzability of stories by children. In J. Gumperz & D. Hymes (Eds.), *Directions in sociolinguistics: The ethnography of communication* (pp. 325-345). New York: Rinehart & Winston.

Sacks, H. (1992). *Lectures on conversation. Volume I*. Oxford: Blackwell Publishers.

Soles, T., Bloom, E.L., Heath, N.L., & Karagiannakis, A. (2008). An exploration of teachers' current perceptions of children with emotional and behavioural difficulties. *Emotional and Behavioural Difficulties, 13*(4), 275-290.

Stokoe, E. & Smithson, J. (2001). Making gender relevant: Conversation analysis and gender categories in interaction. *Discourse & Society, 12*, 217-244.

Watson, R. (1983). The presentation of victim and motive in discourse: The case of police interrogations and interviews. *Victimology, 8*, 31-52.

West, C. & Zimmerman D. (2009). Accounting for doing gender. *Gender & Society, 23*(1), 112-122.

Ann-Carita Evaldsson
Department of Education
Uppsala University

Yvonne Karlsson
Department of Education and Special Education
University of Gothenburg

EVA HJÖRNE AND PERNILLA LARSSON

10. BEYOND TEACHING AND LEARNING –
DISCIPLINING BOYS IN REMEDIAL CLASSES
DURING THE 1960s IN SWEDEN

INTRODUCTION

Traditionally, school and schooling as an activity has always had two main goals –
to explain curricular content, instruct, monitor and evaluate children in traditional
school subjects, for example, how to read and write, but also to keep order in the
classroom and foster the children socially concerning correct and desirable
behaviour in order to raise proper citizens in our democratic society (Walkerdine,
1988). Thus, the role of teacher implies mediating knowledge, but also training and
fostering the pupils in order to prepare them for life (Freebody & Freiberg, 2000).

These days, alarm reports appear on a regular basis claiming that children do not
behave correctly in schools. For example, they wear caps, listen to MP3 players,
use their cell-phones in the classroom, though they are not allowed to, they play
truant, are violent towards teachers and peers, tease and bully, etc. As a
consequence, there are growing demands for more disciplining strategies in school,
more decisive and authoritarian teachers, more specialists in special needs and
demands to reintroduce marks in order and conduct (Verkuyten, 2002; Persson,
2008).

From a historical point of view, it is interesting to note that demands concerning
socially fostering and caring for children in school are not a new phenomenon. On
the contrary, different strategies have been used through the years in order to
handle this task. For instance, when establishing the modern welfare state in
Sweden in the late 19th and the 20th century, there were special programs in schools
providing poor children with milk, free lunches, school baths and medical attention
(cf. SOU 1947:11; Börjesson, 1997). Furthermore, before the introduction of the
nine-year comprehensive school (grundskola) in 1962, there were different school
systems in Sweden where different strategies were developed. For example, in
junior secondary school,[1] and secondary grammar school[2] physical punishment
was not allowed, but in elementary school[3] (attended by the lower class pupils)

---

[1] Realskola.
[2] Läroverk.
[3] Folkskola.

E. Hjörne et al. (eds.), Learning, Social Interaction and Diversity – Exploring Identities
in School Practices, 139–154.

corporal punishment was sanctioned in order to discipline the pupils (Hjörne, Larsson, & Säljö, 2010).

Thus, fostering pupils and correcting unwanted behaviour in school are considered to be an important task in schools at any historical point. One way of regulating 'misbehaviour' has been, and still is, to place pupils in different segregated classes. In fact, not since the 1970s have we witnessed such an increase in special schools and classes, especially organised for children assumed to have behavioural problems (Hallam, Ireson, & Davies, 2004; Wendelborg & Tossebro, 2008). At present, special teaching groups are organised on a regular basis in Sweden for children diagnosed with, for example, Aspergers or AD/HD, with behavioural modifications of the pupils as an explicit focus (DuPaul & Stoner, 2003; Kos, Richdale, & Hay, 2006; Hjörne, 2006; Ljusberg, 2009). However, not many studies have been conducted through the years with the aim of shedding light on how this work is performed in practice. This chapter is a historical review and the main concern is to explore and make visible the classroom practices from the past assumed to suit children classified as having learning difficulties, i.e. children who were categorised as being intellectually disabled and having "irrelevant pupil behaviour". More specifically, what happened in the so-called remedial classes in the 1960s in Sweden? How were pupils fostered and what strategies were used by the teachers when correcting "wrong" pupil behaviour? Thus, the aim of this chapter is to shed light on the interaction between teacher and pupil when learning and instructing about how to behave in a proper way in the classroom organised for children categorised as being intellectually disabled.

A SCHOOL FOR ALL AND PUPILS IN NEED OF SPECIAL SUPPORT

In Sweden, the political idea of having one school for all is as old as school itself and is now a catchphrase. This implies having an inclusive school system where every child "irrespective of gender, geographical residence and social and economical conditions" should "have equal access to education in the compulsory school" (Lgr 80, p. 14, our translation). Thus, schools are obliged to meet the needs of all individuals and provide a suitable and democratically organised education of high quality in order to create responsible citizens. However, some pupils have difficulties in adapting to life in school, and the number of these children has increased lately to approximately 20% (Skolverket, 2000; Egelund, Haug, & Persson, 2006), and schools continuously have to handle dilemmas of this kind.This implies that schools have to develop certain institutional practices in response to such problems in order to handle various concrete dilemmas and prevent school failure.

From a historical point of view, ever since there have been schools there have been students who have had trouble adjusting to them. Throughout history, schools have adopted various techniques to deal with these students. Such students have been labelled in a variety of ways depending upon the discourse prevailing at the time (Mehan, 1993; Mehan, Mercer, & Rueda, 2002). Children have, for example, been classified as being 'vagrant' or 'idiot' when a moral, religious discourse was dominant in the 19th century and, as 'weak', 'slow learners', 'imbecile', when a psychometric discourse became dominant in the early 20th century. The consequences of these categorising practices were that children became marginalised in school by being offered a very short period of schooling, repeated a year, or were placed in special schools or classes, for example, a school for 'idiots', 'feeble-minded' or 'slow learners' (Hjörne & Säljö, 2010). In 1962, Sweden started a comprehensive school for all, but still eight different special classes were considered necessary and legitimate, and these should be adapted to the shortcomings of the children. This is also clearly articulated in the first national curriculum (Lgr 62), which is of some interest here since the data presented here are generated from two of these classes; the remedial class and the remedial reading class:

- *Remedial class* was intended for intellectually retarded pupils, who were incapable of successfully participating in regular teaching. The teaching recommended should be characterised by "simplicity and clarity" (p. 64). Tools for selection of pupils for this type of class were different kinds of tests, e.g. intelligence tests.
- *Remedial reading class* was intended for children of normal intelligence who had pronounced difficulties in reading and writing. The task of the teaching was to "remedy the individuals' reading and writing difficulties" (p. 67). The curriculum described these children in the following manner: they "often display nervous symptoms, are anxious and lack in concentration" (p. 67). When selecting pupils for these classes, tests of reading and writing skills as well as intelligence tests were used (Lgr 62, pp. 64-67).

Thus, the idea of a comprehensive school for all children was not seen as conflicting with strategies that implied differentiation on pedagogical grounds. At present, especially with the development of 'scientific" methods of measurement, such students have been identified as having a wide variety of disabilities and terms such as hyperactive, attention deficit disorder, Aspergers, dyscalculia, learning disability, mentally retarded prevail. Children were/are placed in special classes, for example, a remedial class in the 1960s (see above), or into today's special teaching groups, for example an AD/HD group or Aspergers group, in order to compensate for shortcomings (Haug, 1998) so that they can return to their regular class.

In the very few studies of this kind conducted in the classroom, the results unanimously show that the main focus during the lessons concerns correcting unacceptable pupil behaviour (Hjörne, 2006; Karlsson, 2007). Accordingly, we want to highlight how this was performed in the past. What behaviour was unacceptable in the segregated classroom in the 1960s and how was this corrected by the teacher?

CORRECTIONS AND TEACHER – PUPIL INTERACTIONS IN CLASSROOM

From a socialcultural perspective, teaching and learning are understood as interactionally constructed practices *in situ*. Studies show that the interaction between teacher and pupil in the classroom often follows a traditional question-answer pattern. This interaction is called I-R-E (see for example Mehan, 1979) – Interaction, Response, Evaluation, which means that the teacher asks a question (I), a pupil gives a response (R) and finally the teacher evaluates and decides whether the answer is correct or not (E). This form of communication is not very common anywhere else in society. Usually, you do not have to raise your hand when you wish to speak, and our interaction very seldom follows the I-R-E pattern. This implies that how pupils and teachers act in school is a special practice closely connected with the school's activity. As pupils and teachers, you have to decode and then stick to the expected agenda. For example, the agenda could be *when* you as pupil can talk, *what* you can talk about and *how* (Larsson, 2008). This is an activity all pupils have to learn.

Thus, as a pupil you have to learn regular school activities such as how to read, write and count, but also how to act and behave in school. There are some ways of acting and organizing the activity that is established and as a pupil you have to learn this. These patterns can be called "teacher talk" and "student talk" (Austin, Dwyer & Freebody, 2003). During a lesson, there are, of course, pupils who initiate talk themselves, but more often "student talk" is initiated by the teacher asking something (I-R-E) and pupils answering accordingly. Thus, "[T]he teacher governs the ownership, scope and breadth of knowledge production through the question – answer – response pattern" (Austin et al., 2003, p. 26).

Corrections are part of all social interaction in everyday life. We correct our children, our parents, workmates, etc. in order to maintain social rules and standards (Evaldsson, 2005; Jackson, Boostrom & Hansen, 1993). The task of society is also to reprimand or punish us for doing things that are prohibited. An example of this is speed checks by the police. These work as a deterrent, for the drivers who are speeding and actually get caught by the police, but they are also preventive since there is a chance that other drivers will reduce their speed. Corrections and reprimands function in the same way since even if you are not the subject of the reprimand it still serves the purpose of preventing it from happening (Evaldsson, 2005).

In school, corrections are important tools for maintaining social order in the classroom. This includes using different methods and strategies, for example, by means of gestures and body language, by using the pupil's name, by raising one's voice etc. (Evaldsson, 2005). Thus, it is part of the teacher's assignment to correct bad behaviour in order to maintain order in the classroom, but it is also a way of fostering the pupils so that they contribute to the democratic order, as already mentioned. In doing this, the notion of consequences is effective, which implies that very inappropriate behaviour has negative consequences and the opposite. Negative consequences could, for instance, be a verbal – or non-verbal response, a frown, additional work, being sent to another classroom or even another school, etc. The practices of these consequences produce what is meant by being a "good" and a "bad" pupil, respectively.

PREVIOUS RESEARCH

There are only a few studies (see below) concerning education in special teaching groups. However, there is a unique historical film-recorded body of material, which we have access to, aiming at showing how teaching was carried out in some remedial classes in Sweden in the 1960s. This project is called the DPA (Didactic Process Analysis) project and this chapter is based on some of the findings in this study and will be presented later on in the text.

Recent research on learning and teaching in special teaching groups (which can be compared with the special classes in the 1960s), for example in AD/HD classroom, show that the activity in the classroom mainly concerns maintaining the social order and teaching the pupil acceptable classroom behaviour (Hjörne, 2006, 2011; Karlsson, 2007). This is mainly done by means of reprimands and remarks about the pupils' problems and symptoms connected to the diagnosis of AD/HD.

In a classical study of classroom interaction, the results show that it can be difficult for pupils to behave in accordance with the school's agenda and to understand what behaviour is accepted by the institution (Jackson et al., 1993). The study describes, for example, how one pupil during a lesson gets a reprimand when jumping in the classroom. The jumping is seen as disturbing and therefore corrected by the teacher, although the same behaviour would have been accepted during a lesson in gymnastics or during the break. Thus, it is the situation, not the action *per se* that is the problem. Behaviour accepted in one situation might be unacceptable in another. Sometimes it is difficult for the pupil to see the difference. It is the teachers' responsibility to guide pupils and help them understand this complex activity.

In a microethnographic study by Evaldsson (2005), the moral activity in a first grade classroom is studied. The results show that the classroom is not only a room where pupils acquire knowledge in a traditional way, by learning how to read and write for example, but also a room where the pupils learn certain standards and rules about how to behave (the so-called hidden curriculum). Hence, the pupils have to "understand the meaning of the teachers reprimands, admonitions, gazes, vocal pitches, the use of names, accusations, etc." (our translation, Evaldsson, 2005, p. 57) to be able to become "the good pupil".

DATA CORPUS

As pointed out before, this study is a historical review of classroom practices in the context of special needs education. More specifically, the focus here will be on how 'slow learners' were educated and fostered in remedial classes during the 1960s. This interactive study is possible thanks to the data collected in classrooms in 1968. The data analysed here consist of video and audio recordings from twenty 6th grade classes (sixteen of of which were remedial classes and four remedial reading classes). This data were collected from ten lessons in each class in 1968. Additionally, there were also video-recorded lessons from sixty "normal" classrooms, but these are not included in our analysis. One interesting finding from the study at the time was that there was nothing unique about the teaching in these special classes (Gustafsson & and Stigebrandt, 1972; Larsson, 2008). Strategies for teaching were similar to teaching in a regular class, which can be seen as striking since the activity in the special classes was supposed to be adapted and connected to the pupils' own knowledge and experience. According to the curriculum, Lgr 62, the teaching should be simple and clear and the tasks should suit every pupil's own talent, development and working pace (Larsson, 2008).

Yet another finding from the study was that the teachers in the remedial classes more often corrected behaviour and disciplined the pupils since they were claimed to have "irrelevant behaviour" (Gustafsson & and Stigebrandt, 1972). We decided to explore this further. How was this done and what strategies were employed by the teachers?

ANALYSIS

During the 1960s, it was quite common for schools (i.e. the teachers) to be more responsible compared with today when it came to morally and socially fostering children (Backlund, 2007; Qvarsebo, 2006). For instance, it was prescribed in the curriculum that fostering and disciplining children were part of educating them (Lgr 62). This paragraph focuses on the remedial classes and how the teacher used different strategies for disciplining the pupils (mostly boys). We found that teachers used different techniques or strategies to reprimand the pupils. We have divided these strategies into three groups – explicit, admonitory and personal reprimands of an insulting nature. Using explicit reprimands as a strategy refers to the teacher using names, a loud voice etc. With admonitory or implicit reprimands, we mean instructions where the teacher is telling the pupils how to behave in a situation in order to prevent what is referred to as bad behaviour. Personal reprimands of an insulting nature refer to teacher talk about what is intricate or delicate issues for the pupil in front of his/her peers.

An example of an explicit reprimand, where the teacher demands the pupils' attention is presented below.

Explicit reprimands

Excerpt 1

1. Teacher: Listen up please (.) when you're ready, you won't be ready
2.   at the same time, you should start thinking about the meaning
3.   of the different words (.) we'll see if we get the time to
4.   look at that this lesson otherwise we'll do it in next Swedish
6.   lesson
7. Mats: ((asks something))

144

8. Teacher: I'M TALKING NOW (!) MATS, YOU SHOULDN'T
9.   INTERRUPT ME (.) I SHOULDN'T HAVE TO SAY THAT
10.   FIVE TO SIX TIMES A DAY TO YOU, IS THAT
11.   UNDERSTOOD (?) WE'LL NEVER BE ABLE TO
12.   START THIS LESSON IF I CANNOT FINISH MY
13.   EXPLANATION
14.   ((the teacher writes on the blackboard))
15. Pupils: ((some pupils talk to each other))
16. Teacher: Mats Karlsson, do not interfere with what Lars- Erik is doing,
17.   if you mind your own business everything will
18.   work so much better
19.   ((the pupils continue working))

At the beginning of this excerpt, the class is asked to: "Listen up". The teacher wants the children to listen as she is explaining the task. After a while, one pupil (Mats) asks something and the teacher immediately corrects him by telling him in a loud voice "I'M TALKING NOW, MATS, YOU SHOULDN'T INTERRUPT ME". The inappropriate behaviour is corrected by explicitly pointing out what the teacher is doing ("I'M TALKING NOW MATS") and what the pupil is doing wrongly "YOU SHOULDN'T INTERRUPT ME". Thus, the expected pupil behaviour in this situation is that the pupil should be quiet while the teacher is speaking. Telling him this is a way of fostering the pupil and a well-known teacher strategy from every classroom. When doing this, the roles of the teacher and the pupil are made clear.

Indexing names and talking in a loud voice are strategies commonly used when correcting someone (Evaldsson, 2005), not only at school. In this excerpt, a pupil (Mats) is pointed out as someone who does not act according to the expectations of the institution. Moreover, he gets singled out as one who repeatedly does not pay attention ("I shouldn't have to say that five to six times a day to you …"). In this sense, the teacher is constructing not only a bad example of pupils' actions, but also the opposite; i.e. the teacher constructs a "good pupil" as a pupil who listens to the teacher.

Another strategy when correcting behaviour is to point at a certain pupil and threaten him with negative consequences if he does not act in the expected way, see the next excerpt.

Excerpt 2

1. Teacher: and then of course, Carl is not keeping up with us as usual (..)
               you:: (.) strictly speaking, you ought to have to stand up so you
               learn properly to keep up with the rest of the class

This teacher reinforces her choice of words by emphasizing that Carl does not keep up with the rest of the class. She explicitly indexes his name when correcting his behaviour and uses this strategy to specifically point at a certain pupil (Evaldsson, 2005). With utterances like "of course" and "as usual" her statement is reinforced still further. This is an example of Extreme Case Formulations (Pomerantz, 1986), which means that the teacher uses intensifiers as a strategy to further elucidate that this is a common behaviour by this pupil. By this strategy she is reinforcing her correction. She also uses her teacher role (Austin et al., 2003) and "threatens" the pupil with some sort of sanction "You ought to have to stand up so you learn properly to keep up with the rest of the class". The form of this reprimand can be seen as an explicit correction, but it is also a personal reprimand that could be insulting since the teacher is pointing at one specific boy's shortcomings "Carl is not keeping up with us as usual". This negative description of the boy as someone who usually does not do what is expected of him as a pupil, in this case to keep up with the class (having in mind that the boy is categorised as being a "slow learner"), might influence pupils' self-image in a negative way and, above all, this also implies a risk of pupils being stigmatized (Goffman, 1963). Both the pupil himself as well as his classmates might see the boy as a boy having huge problems and in this case, this could be stigmatizing for the pupil.

The following two excerpts take place during a lesson when the class is watching a filmstrip called "ABC in conduct". The agenda for the lesson is to discuss acceptable and unacceptable behaviour. It is obvious that the pupils are supposed to learn properly how to behave and by this "bad" behaviour is prevented.

Admonitory reprimands

During the lesson in "ABC in conduct" the pupils watch different short film sequences showing everyday situations, for example, meals and how one should handle school books, but also specific situations that are in some sense problematic, for example, when children are fighting. During the lesson, the teachers ask questions about the film sequences and the pupils are expected to answer. Afterwards the teacher assesses the pupil's answer (cf. I-R-E situations, Mehan, 1979).

Excerpt 3

(Shows a short film sequence where two pupils are fighting in front of a door. One is blocking the door while the other one is trying to open it).

1. Teacher:	Do you have any practical example, which illustrates
2.	that its wrong doing like this (?) Could you give a practical
3.	example of this (.) has this happened to anyone in our class (?)
4. Pupils:	hums
5. Teacher:	yes (e::)
6. Pupil:	((giggles))
7. Teacher:	We have a brilliant example (.) I'm not talking bout when

8.	Anita was locked in the toilet'cause that's what you're
9.	giggling about, I think
10. Pupil:	No:
11. Teacher:	No: (.) but Lars-Erik gave me thirteen kronor today, do you
12.	remember (?)
13. Pupils:	m::
14. Teacher:	to pay for a broken window, why was that window broken ?
15. Pupil:	[says something, inaudible]
16. Teacher:	Yes it was Lars-Erik and Mats who broke that window, Sten
17.	do you remember what happened (?).
18. Sten:	Yeh, Mats was standing outside, no Lars-Erik was outside
19.	and Mats was blocking the door, then Lars-Erik put his foot
20.	on the window [inaudible)
21. Teacher:	Yes, it was Mats who had his foot on the window, yes
22.	that's right, that's a brilliant example

The I-R-E pattern is quite distinct in this excerpt when the teacher asks the class: "Do you have any practical example, which illustrates that its wrong doing like this (?)". Some pupils respond to her question only by saying "m::". The teacher assesses this by first saying yes and then she develops the response by adding: "we have a brilliant example". By this expression the teacher reinforces her reprimand by assessing it as a "brilliant" example.

This excerpt once again shows that the teacher is constructing both good and bad examples of how to be as a pupil. In this case, this is done by referring to an authentic incident from the class in relation to a short film sequence. Once more, the teacher does this by pointing at certain pupils who have been acting in a "wrong" way. With this strategy, these pupils are constructed as bad examples. In excerpt 3, the teacher also uses a third boy, who not has been involved in the incident, to tell the other pupils about what has happened. In this sense, this pupil is constructed as a good pupil who is aware of what is right and wrong when it comes to behaviour in school. Furthermore, this example could be regarded as an implicit, admonitory reprimand made beforehand, by giving examples of how you not should act in school. Thus, this is a way of correcting not only the boys who were fighting at the door, but the whole class. This example also shows that the institution has a fostering assignment since one of the boys in the excerpt has paid for the broken window. In other words, pupils' actions have material consequences and here this is made explicit.

The following excerpt shows not only an admonitory reprimand but gives an example of how reprimands construct masculinity (cf. Connell, 2000).

Excerpt 4

1. Teacher:	What is happening here, then (?)
2. Ingemar:	One boy is kicking another boy in the stomach
3. Teacher:	Yes (..) that boys are fighting that's not at all strange

147

4.		that they do that, but in this way (..) you don't fight like
5.		this, do you (?) Then it's not natural any longer, one boy
6.		is holding another boy down on the ground and then, as
7.		Ingemar says, the other boy is kicking him, what's wrong
8.		with this way of fighting (?)
9.	A pupil:	Two against one
10.	Teacher:	Two against one, that's cowardly and then I think the
11.		one on the ground seems to be smaller and then about the
12.		kick, that's not according to the rules (..) is it(?) is there
13.		anything else that's not according to the rules (?) What else is
14.		very nasty if you insist on fighting and so on (?)

In this excerpt, the class is learning about acceptable behaviour when fighting. They also learn that "boys are fighting that's not strange that they do that". When commenting on it in this way, the teacher also constructs a masculine identity where it is normal that boys fight (Connell, 2000). In addition, the class is asked to say what is right and wrong when it comes to fighting. When adding "but in this way", the teacher constructs a good/bad example of how to fight. For example, the teacher asks "what's wrong with this way of fighting" and one pupil answers "two against one". Immediately, the teacher assesses this answer by repeating "two against one, that's cowardly". The pupils learn that it is OK to fight as long as it not is two against one. Finally, the teacher says "I think the one on the ground looks smaller" to further show what is wrong in this situation. When fighting, you are supposed to stick to what the teacher refers to as "the rules" and the pupils are, by using examples, shown what the rules are. In the case here, the teacher is referring to rules regarding when someone is on the ground or younger than yourself. One more rule is that you should not fight two against one. Thus, the teacher and the school take a moral responsibility for the pupils' way of acting (cf. Jacksons et al., 1993; Evaldsson, 2005).

Thus, we have shown some examples of explicit reprimands but also admonitory reprimands accomplished mainly to prevent unacceptable behaviour in school. The last category of reprimands found in our material are more of an insulting nature.

PERSONAL REPRIMANDS OF AN INSULTING NATURE

The corrections made by the teachers are sometimes directed towards a single pupil and could be of more of a personal nature. As a consequence, this could be interpreted as insulting to the pupil.

Excerpt 5

This conversation takes place just after a lesson when some of the pupils have left, but some are still in the classroom.

1. Teacher:	Ingemar about washing yourself there has to be a change
2.	it's almost unbearable to be around you.
3. Ingemar:	hums
4. Teacher:	Please, for your own sake (.) It can't be fun when people avoid
5.	coming close 'cause you don't smell that good
6. Ingemar:	hums.
7. Teacher:	Take the chance to have a bath, Ingemar, scrub yourself.

This is an example of how a reprimand can be very personal and also insulting to the pupil. The teacher's way of acting may appear controversial today, but at this time it was more common for teachers to be more responsible and caring for pupils' personal hygiene (Backlund, 2007). With this in mind, one can see this as the teacher's way of showing her concern for Ingemar and his wellbeing. However, the pupil's response (or lack of one) can be interpreted as his way of showing that he is not really comfortable with discussing this in front of his classmates. So, when the teacher says "It's almost unbearable to be around you" Ingemar only responds with "hums". The teacher continues by asking him "Please, for your own sake it can't be fun when people avoid coming close to you" and thereby makes him accountable for his hygiene. Once again Ingemar answers only with "hums:". We don't know anything about Ingemar except that he is a sixth grader in Sweden during the 1960s. This implies we do not know anything about his home conditions. He could be a child with parents who do not care about his hygiene, for example. Maybe the teacher knows and maybe this is why she brings this topic up and also tells him "for your own sake". However, there is a risk that this reprimand can be insulting to Ingemar, but also important, to bear in mind that this example is probably more shocking today than it was at the time.

Excerpt 6

1. Teacher:	Dan ((it is his turn to read from the book))
2. Pupil:	I don't know where we are.
3. Teacher:	No, you never know that Dan(.) you have to learn to keep up
4.	Dan [.] How many times have I told you that you learn
5.	by keeping up (.) you have to keep up all the time
6. Pupil:	hums
7. Teacher:	Now you haven't kept up so you can't read

((Dan has huge difficulties reading))

In this excerpt, the pupils are supposed to follow the text when someone in the class is reading aloud (högläsning). The teacher points out that Dan never can keep up when they read aloud "No you never know that Dan", she reinforces this by then saying "How many times have I told you that you learn by keeping up". The teacher clearly thinks that Dan is not coping with the assignment in a satisfactory way. When the teacher points out that Dan never knows where they are in the text, she uses Extreme Case Formulations (Pomerantz, 1986) when she says "You

149

never know that Dan". By using this strategy the teacher reinforces her reprimand. The question is in what way this statement influences the pupil and if it motivates him henceforth. Once again, the pupil's name is indexed and used as a strategy, which can also be seen as a reinforcement of the reprimand. In this case, it is Dan's role as a pupil and his inability to keep up that is defined as "wrong". He has to learn to keep up, which is expected pupil behaviour. When analysing the tape recording of this lesson, it is obvious that Dan has huge difficulties reading, which can be the reason why he cannot follow the text when the other pupils read. Considering that he is attending a special class, this might not be very sensational. Most likely he has been placed in this special environment because of his reading problems. It is interesting to note that it seems to be difficult for this pupil to adapt to the educational form chosen by the teacher in the special class.

SOME CONCLUSIONS

The results in our study of teaching and learning practices in special classes in 1968, show that the interaction between teacher and pupils is characterised by fostering pupils towards an acceptable school behaviour. This is mostly done by disciplining and correcting unwanted school behaviour and different strategies for accomplishing this have emerged. Three kinds of reprimands appeared in our material:

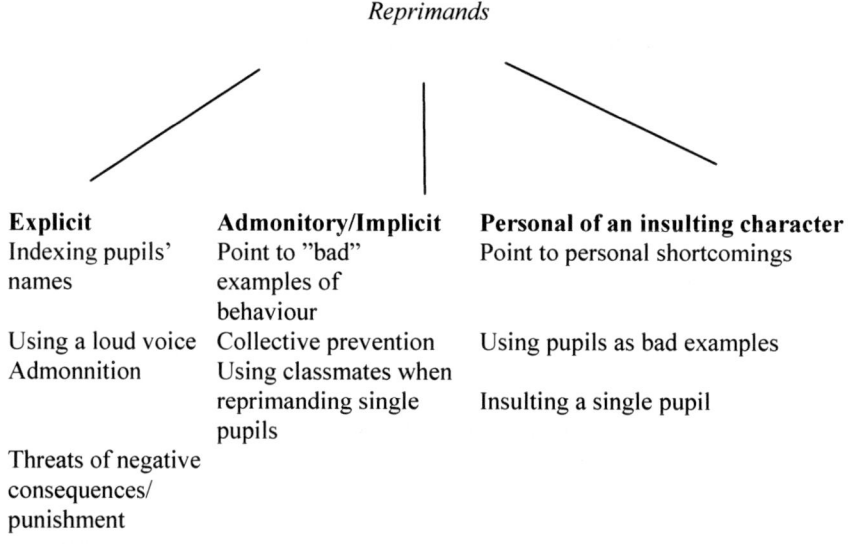

Reprimands

Explicit	**Admonitory/Implicit**	**Personal of an insulting character**
Indexing pupils' names	Point to "bad" examples of behaviour	Point to personal shortcomings
Using a loud voice Admonnition	Collective prevention Using classmates when reprimanding single pupils	Using pupils as bad examples Insulting a single pupil
Threats of negative consequences/ punishment		

Fig 1. Teacher strategies for disciplining pupils

– *Explicit reprimands*
These reprimands are characterized by strategies like indexing a pupil's name and in this way explicitly point to one specific pupil and reinforcing the correction.

Teachers sometimes also use some sort of negative consequences as a "threat". By varying vocal pitch, a teacher can use his/her voice to reinforce a reprimand.

– Admonitory reprimands
A common strategy in our data is to collectively foster pupils as a group by using 'bad' or 'good' examples from the class (see e.g. excerpts 3 and 4) in order to teach the pupils about a "good" pupil behaviour and thus prevent "bad" pupil behaviour. Usually, this takes the form of short personal reprimands directed to a single pupil, who is used as an example of what is meant by being a "bad" or a "good" pupil (Freebody & Freiberg, 2000). Teachers can also use threats to force the pupils to change their behaviour (see excerpts 3 and 4).

– Personal reprimands that could be insulting to the pupil
Another strategy employed in these examples is using reprimands that concern personal qualities as 'bad' examples of how not to be or talk. Sometimes, the teachers even talk about sensitive matters concerning a specific pupil in front of his/her peers. This strategy is of an insulting nature, where the pupils are at risk of losing face in public (cf. Goffman, 1963).

It is interesting to note that life in the special classroom seldom is about adapting instructions, lessons or tasks in a way that the pupil can profit from them. The form of schooling and the fostering assignment seem to be the main concern rather than considering what students learn in terms of skills such as reading, writing, etc. Having in mind that the pupils are categorised as being intellectually disabled and placed in a special class organised for children with these difficulties it is notable.

The pupils in the special class are labelled as being intellectually disabled and in need of special support. In addition, they are also segregated from their regular class and sent to a special class or school. Furthermore, they are seen as having an "irrelevant pupil behaviour", according to the teachers, which has to be disciplined or corrected (Persson, 2008; Hjörne, 2006; Mehan, 1992). This implies that pupils who are already stigmatised by segregation in school become even more stigmatised. Considering the results we found in this historical review and the strategies used by the teachers when disciplining the pupils it could be claimed that these strategies contributes to the development of shaping an identity of a deviant pupil. This could be compared to what Austin et al. (2003) call the non-disadvantage classrooms and the disadvantage classrooms, where pupils' actions in the classroom were valued differently by the teachers depending on what classroom the pupils belonged to. One conclusion is that pupils who belonged to the "disadvantage classroom" were less able to influence their school situation than pupils in the "non-disadvantage classroom".

The question is what opportunities for participating on equal terms do pupils in the "disadvantage classroom" (cf. the special class) have? Considering that several strategies are similar to what happens in today's segregated groups (cf. Evaldsson & Karlsson in this book; Hjörne, 2006; Karlsson, 2007), it seems obvious that certain pupil identities have been and still are constructed in school. In the case here, the identity of a deviant pupil is constructed. This has implications for the pupil's future career in school and in life. Thus, adapting to learning and diversity in school are important issues and a challenge for a modern society in the future.

REFERENCES

Austin, H., Dywer, B., & Freebody, P. (2003). *Schooling the child* (chapters 2-4). New York: RoutledgerFalmer.

Backlund, Å. (2007). *Elevvård i grundskolan – Resurser, organisering och praktik* [Pupil care in the compulsury school – Resources, organization and practise]. Report in social work nr. 121. Stockholm: University of Stockholm, Institution for Social Work.

Börjesson, M. (1997). *Om skolbarns olikheter: Diskurser kring "särskilda behov" i skolan - med historiska jämförelsepunkter* [On differences between children: Discourses about "special needs" in the school – with historical comparisons]. Stockholm: Liber.

Connell, R.W. (2000). *The men and the boys.* Cambridge: Polity.

DuPaul G. J., & Stoner, G. (2003). *ADHD in the schools. Assessment and intervention strategies.* New York: The Guilford Press.

Edwards, D. (1991). Categories are for talking. On the cognitive and discursive bases of categorization. *Theory & Psychology, 1*(4), 515-542.

Egelund, Haug & Persson (2006). *Inkluderande pedagogik i skandinaviskt perspektiv* [Inclusive education from a Scandinavian perspective]. Stockholm: Liber.

Evaldsson, A-C. (2005). Vardaglig moralisk verksamhet i första klass [Moral everyday activity in a first grade class]. In I. Carlgren, I. Josefson, C. Liberg, J. Anward, M. Alexandersson, A-C. Evaldsson, F. Marton, G. Molloy, G. Malmgren & C. Pehrson (Eds.), *Forskning av denna världen II – om teorins roll i praxisnära forskning* [Research in this world II – The role of theory in research close to praxis] (pp. 39-62). Stockholm: Vetenskapsrådet.

Freebody, P., & Freiberg, J. (2000). Public and pedagogic morality. The local orders of instructional and regulatory talk in classrooms. In S. Hester (Ed.), *Local education order. Ethnomethodological studies of knowledge in action* (pp. 141-162). Philadelphia, PA: John Benjamins Publishing Company.

Goffman, E. (1963). *Stigma. Notes on the management of spoiled identity.* London: Prentice-Hall.

Gustafsson, B., & Stigebrandt, E. (1972). *Vad kännetecknar undervisning i hjälpklass. En jämförelse mellan undervisningsprocesser i hjälpklass och vanlig klass. DPA-projekt 3.* [What characterizes education in remedial class. A comparison between the educational process in remedial class and regular class. DPA-project 3]. (Rapport 29). Göteborg: Lärarhögskolan i Göteborg, Pedagogiska institutionen.

Hall, C., Sarangi, S., & Slembrouck, S. (1997). Moral construction in social work discourse. In B. Gunnarsson, P. Linell, & B. Nordberg (Eds.), *The construction of professional discourse* (pp. 265-291). London: Longman.

Hallam, S., Ireson, J., & Davies, J. (2004). Primary pupils' experiences of different types of grouping in school. *Educational Research Journal, 30*(4), 516-533.

Haug, P. (1998). *Pedagogiskt dilemma: Specialpedagogik* [Pedagogical dilemma: Special education]. Stockholm: Skolverket.

Hjörne, E. (2004). *Excluding for inclusion? Negotiating school careers and identities in pupil welfare settings in the Swedish school.* Göteborg: Göteborgs Universitet.

Hjörne, E. (2006). Pedagogy in the AD/HD-classroom: an exploratory study of the Little Group. In G. Lloyd, D. Cohen, & J. Stead (Eds.), *Critical new perspectives on Attention Deficit/Hyperactivity disorder* (pp. 176-197). Oxon: RoutledgeFalmer.

Hjörne, E., & Säljö, R. (2010). *Att platsa in en skola för alla. Elevhälsa och förhandling om normalitet i den svenska skolan Med samtalsguide* [To fit into a school for all. Pupil health and the negotiation of normality in the Swedish school]. Stockholm: Norstedts.

Hjörne, E., Larsson, P., & Säljö, R. (2010). From instructing pupils to coaching children: Social change and the broadening of responsibilities for the teacher profession. I V. Ellis, A. Edwards, & P. Smagorinsky, *Cultural-Historical Perspectives on Teacher Education and Development : Learning Teaching* (pp 153-182). Oxford: Routledge/Taylor & Francis.

Jackson, P., Boostrom, R., & Hansen, D. (1993). *Moral life in schools*. San Fransisco: Jossey-Bass.

Karlsson, Y. (2007). *Att inte vilja vara problem – social organisering och utvärdering av elever i en särskild undervisningsgrupp* [Resisting problem talk - social organization and evaluation practices in a special teaching group]. Diss. Linköping: Linköping University.

Kos, J.M., Richdale, A.L., & Hay, D (2006). Children with Attention Deficit Hyperactivity Disorder and their teachers: A review of the literature. *International Journal of Disability, Development and Education, 53*(2), 147-160.

Larsson, P. (2008). *Vi får nog göra så att vi skärper oss nu! En studie av tillrättavisningar i 1960-talets hjälpklassundervisning* [We have to wake up! A study of corrections in 1960s special classes]. Masteruppsats, Göteborg: Göteborgs Universitet.

Lgr 62. (1962). *Läroplan för grundskolan* [Curriculum for the compulsory school 1962]. Stockholm: Kungliga Skolöverstyrelsen.

Lgr 80. (1980). *Läroplan för grundskolan,* [Curriculum for the compulsory school 1980]. Stockholm: Liber.

Ljusberg, A. (2009). *Pupils in remedial classes*. Diss. Stockholm: Stockholm University.

Mehan, H. (1979). *Learning lessons: Social organization in the classroom*. Cambridge, MA: Harvard.

Mehan, H. (1992). Understanding inequality in schools: the contribution of interpretive studies. *Sociology of Education, 65,* 1-20.

Mehan, H. (1993). Beneath the skin and between the ears: A case study in the politics of representation. In J. Lave, & S. Chaiklin (Eds.), *Understanding practice. Perspectives on activity and context* (pp. 241-268). Cambridge, MA: Cambridge University Press.

Mehan, H., Mercer, J.R., & Rueda, R. (2002). Special education. In D.L. Levinson, P.W. Cookson Jr., & A.R. Sadovnik (Eds.), *Education and sociology* (pp. 619-624). New York, NY: RoutledgeFalmer.

Persson, B. (2008). On other people's terms: Schools' encounters with disabled students. *European Journal of Special Needs Education, 23*(4), 337-347.

Pomerantz, A. (1986). Extreme case formulations: A way of legitimizing claims. *Human Studies, 9,* 219-229.

Qvarsebo, J. (2006). *Skolbarnets fostran. Enhetsskolan, agan och politiken om barnet 1946-1962* [The training of the schoolchild. The comprehensive school, corporal punishment and the politics of the child.] Linköping:Linköping Universitet.

Skolverket [The Swedish Board of Education]. (2000). *Hur särskild får man vara* [How special can you be?]. Retrieved October 2, 2003, from http://www.skolverket.se/pdf/regeringsuppdrag/sarskola/pdf.

SOU 1947. *Utredning och förslag rörande vissa socialpedagogiska anordningar inom skolväsendet. Statens offentliga utredningar* [Investigation and suggestions concerning social-pedagogical arrangements within school. The official investigations of the government]. Stockholm: Esselte.

Walkerdine, V. (1988). *The mastery of reason: Cognitive development and the production of rationality*. London: Routledge.

Wendelborg, C., & Tossebro, J. (2008). School placement and classroom participation among children with disabilities in primary school in Norway: A longitudinal study. *European Journal of Special Needs Education, 23*(4), 305-319.

Verkuyten, M. (2002). Making teachers accountable for students' disruptive classroom behaviour. *British Journal of Sociology of Education, 23*(1), 107-122.

Eva Hjörne
Department of Education and Special Education
University of Gothenburg

Pernilla Larsson
Department of Education and Special Education
University of Gothenburg

ADINA SHAMIR AND RENAT FELLAH

11. THE EFFECT OF AN EDUCATIONAL ELECTRONIC BOOK ON THE EMERGENT LITERACY OF PRESCHOOL CHILDREN AT RISK FOR LEARNING DISABILITIES

INTRODUCTION

Early childhood education is currently finding itself at an important juncture in its development as technological innovations meet policy change. The major innovation we are referring to is the entry of computers into the classroom, especially the kindergarten, at an age preceding the formal learning of reading and writing. With respect to policy, the significant change lies in the field of education for children with diverse needs, including children with learning disabilities (hereinafter LD). Inclusion of these children in regular classes is now driving the search for new and more flexible educational tools. In our attempt to respond to the challenges, this chapter contains a description of a study conducted to explore whether computer technology in the form of an electronic book can help children with LD expand their vocabulary and increase their phonological awareness. As the study was conducted in Israel, any adaptations of English-language tools to the needs of Hebrew speakers are noted.

The chapter begins with a short survey of the literature on the use of computer technology for the promotion of emergent literacy. We then discuss the special needs of children at risk of LD and the possibilities that specially programmed e-books may open up for them. After we report the findings of the research, which aimed at evaluating the effectiveness of an educational e-book developed by the authors for promoting emergent literacy among preschool children at risk for learning disabilities, we close with a short discussion of the implications of the research.

COMPUTERS AND EMERGENT LITERACY

Emergent literacy – the child's development of skills requisite for facility in print and oral language – is generally acquired before formal schooling begins (Teale & Sulzby, 1986; Whitehurst & Lonigan, 2001). This conclusion appears to apply world-wide (Hutinger, Bell, Daytner, & Johanson, 2005; Shatil, Share, & Levin, 2001). Children's early acquisition of the fundamentals of emergent literacy, such

E. Hjörne et al. (eds.), Learning, Social Interaction and Diversity – Exploring Identities in School Practices, 155–168.

as new vocabulary acquisition and phonological awareness while still in kindergarten, has also been found to be directly related to a child's later academic achievement in reading and writing (Aram & Levin, 2002; Sénéchal & LeFevre, 2002).

For children growing up in modern society, emergent literacy is supported by a combination of traditional literacy tools (e.g., printed books, paper, pencils, and magnetic letters), established technologies (radio and television) as well as new technologies (e.g., all types of computers, TV-connected console games, cellular phones). Children tend to use these tools in the company of others (family members, educators or peers), in group environments or when working individually (Marsh, Brooks, Hughes, Ritchie, Roberts, & Wright, 2005). Yet, despite the recent acceptance of computers as standard equipment in preschool learning environments, as well as the available array of learning contexts and tools, research began to focus on exactly how exposure to this new technology affects the acquisition of emergent literacy among young children only of late (Snyder, 2002; Turbill, 2001; Yelland, Hull & Mulhearn, 2006).

Wachob (1993) claimed that because children have begun to regard computer technology as a natural part of their lives, educators can take advantage of computers in order to promote literacy skills among children with diverse academic needs. Later research has confirmed Wachob's claim (e.g., Underwood & Underwood, 1998). Other studies, focusing on phonological awareness, have also shown improvement among young subjects trained in this basic skill with the help of computer games and dedicated computer programs (Mioduser, Tur-Kaspa, & Leitner, 2000; Segers & Verhoeven, 2004). Segers and Verhoeven (2004), for example, attributed the positive outcomes of their research among young children to the computer program's advantages over the teacher, especially its ability to allow innumerable repetitions, provide immediate feedback and maintain a neutral stance with respect to error (children do not feel that they are being judged when working with computers). When testing the effect of a reading skills acquisition program among kindergartners prior to their exposure to regular reading exercises, Van Daal and Reitsma (2000) found that children who completed the program exhibited greater improvements in word recognition and comprehension (i.e., they learned to read) than did the group exposed only to the regular reading program. According to Van Daal and Reitsma, the computer program's main advantage rested in the possibility of adjusting the program's level of difficulty to the child's individual needs.

COMPUTER-ASSISTED LEARNING FOR ENHANCING EMERGENT LITERACY AMONG CHILDREN AT RISK FOR LEARNING DISABILITIES

Estimates of the percentage of the general population exhibiting some type of learning disability range between 5% and 20% (Gadbow & Du Bois, 1998; Gerber & Reiff, 1994; DSM IV TR, 2000). Israel's Ministry of Education reports a rate of 10% (Margalit, 2000) although a recent study estimates the figure to be 17% (Brook & Boaz, 2005). The incidence of learning disabilities in Israel, the site of the study reported here, therefore lies within the internationally reported range. Irrespective of the size and variety of the affected population, children with learning disabilities – that is, children evidencing developmental difficulties in perception, language, memory or motor abilities – are increasingly being taught in heterogeneous classrooms.

For educators, the appearance of computer software for educational purposes has motivated the search and construction of new tools to help young children at risk for LD who find it especially difficult to acquire fundamental reading and writing skills in both the special and heterogeneous classroom. For children in school, one approach introduced to meet this goal is the application of tools aimed at enhancing new vocabulary retention at the word-meaning level. Improvement in vocabulary retention is considered necessary before improvement in text comprehension can take place (Bryant, Goodwin, Bryant, & Higgins, 2003).

The question before us was whether computer technology could be applied with preschoolers at risk of LD within an educational regime aimed at improving two selected emergent literacy skills. Children at risk of LD are so classified due to the neurological origins of their learning difficulties (Breznitz, 2008; NJCLD, 2006). Their young age and the wish to avoid labelling apparently impede reaching accurate diagnoses of the learning disability involved (Costenbader, Rohrer, & DiFonzo, 2000). Israel's Ministry of Education, similar to education authorities in many countries worldwide, therefore delays classifying children as having learning disabilities until first grade. In the Israeli case, young children with developmental delays are considered to be "at risk for learning disabilities", a term that avoids specifying the particular disability as well as much of the attendant stigmatization (Margalit, 2000).

The study described here focused on this very issue by examining whether *electronic storybooks* ("e-books", "living books" or "CD-ROM storybooks") can help children at risk for learning disabilities acquire two cornerstones of emergent literacy – vocabulary acquisition and phonological awareness – in a more effective way. The e-book used was an educational e-book designed to take into account the limited educational qualities characterizing software available in the market together with the encouraging results of research using this tool for enhancing literacy (e.g., Chera & Wood, 2003; de Jong & Bus, 2002; Segers & Verhoeven, 2002; Wood, 2005). The specific features of the e-book that demonstrate its educational orientation are described later in the chapter.

Children with LD and other special needs can be considered good audiences for e-book instruction. Research has shown that computerized technologies can promote improvement in emergent literacy and writing among these children because the technology can be more accurately adjusted to reflect their experiences and language (Howell, Erickson, Stanger & Wheaton, 2000; Hutinger et al. 1998; Van Daal & Reitsma, 2000). Hutinger et al. (1998), in the course of a three-year project, examined the effect of a computerized emergent literacy teaching program among kindergarten-aged children (3-5) exhibiting mild learning difficulties. Among other features, the technology included a commercially available e-book.

Our own research on the learning and teaching of reading has likewise led us to believe that any technique embedded in a child's authentic experience can motivate learning more effectively than straightforward drills and skills practice. Supporting this claim are that studies indicating that children with low reading motivation and considerable insecurity regarding their learning capacities displayed more positive behaviour during computer-based practice sessions (correct spelling) than during regular classroom learning (Van Daal & Reitsma, 2000). The findings suggested that the more-structured nature of computer-based instruction, the possibilities for immediate feedback as well as the fact that the children were able to remain task-focused for a greater period of time contributed to the e-book's effectiveness.

The research conducted by Lonigan et al. (2003) on computer-assisted training for phonological sensitivity among kindergarten children at risk for reading difficulties also provides evidence for the accuracy of these claims. The children exposed to the intervention program exhibited considerable improvement in their rhyming and word recognition skills in comparison to the control group, which was not exposed to the program.

READING E-BOOKS AS AN EMERGENT LITERACY EXPERIENCE

Young children are generally introduced to the world of written and oral literacy during joint adult-child reading of books (Bus, van Ijzendoorn & Pellegrini, 1995; Ninio, 1980). E-books are, in effect, technically enhanced digital versions of children's books generally obtainable in print format; they, too, can be read alone, without an adult's direct presence. E-books tend to include text and illustrations identical to their print versions although many also integrate multimedia features such as animation, music, sound effects, illuminated text and text narration (de Jong & Bus, 2003; Labbo & Kuhn, 2000; Reinking, 1997). By synchronizing the highlighting with the narrator's reading, e-books can help children keep track of the written text, behaviour that appears to promote better understanding of the link between print and reading. Many e-books include optional user-activated (hidden) hot-spots that, with their activation, help children improve language and story comprehension by adding information excluded from the original text (Shamir & Korat, 2007). Educators and researchers are therefore of the opinion that the e-book's attractive features can be employed to support young children's emergent literacy (de Jong & Bus, 2003; Labbo & Kuhn, 2000; Lefever-Davis & Pearman, 2005; Shamir & Korat, 2006; Shamir, 2009). Put simply, through e-books, young children are given the opportunity to develop the habit of "reading" – or, perhaps more correctly, "listening" – to books via the computer, a context geared to independent (as opposed to shared) learning activity.

Yet, some research does indicate that the use of e-books has not diminished the importance of adults reading to children, an activity that we, as early childhood researchers and educators, continue to view as the paramount learning experience (Bus et al., 1995). Inconsistent results have been obtained in studies comparing improvements in emergent literacy after a child's independent reading of an e-book with those measured following an adult's reading a printed book to the child.

Whereas some studies have shown that e-book reading makes a greater contribution (de Jong & Bus, 2002; Segers, Takke, & Verhoeven, 2004), others showed similar results for both methods (de Jong & Bus, 2004; Korat & Shamir, 2007; Wood, 2005). According to Wood, the software's interactive features appeared to influence reading strategies among children aged 5-6 more effectively than did adult support. In other studies, e-books were also found to advance children's oral language (Shamir & Korat, 2007; Korat & Shamir, 2008; Segers & Verhoeven, 2003, 2004) and phonological awareness (Chera & Wood, 2003; Shamir, 2009; Wise et al., 1989).

From an educational perspective, e-book features are not uniformly positive. Two recent content analyses of commercial e-books for young children, one carried out in Holland with Dutch e-storybooks (de Jong & Bus, 2003) and the other in Israel with Hebrew e-books (Korat & Shamir, 2004), indicated that the multimedia effects (colours, sounds, and graphics) did not uniformly support emergent literacy (de Jong & Bus, 2003; Korat & Shamir, 2004; Shamir & Korat, 2006). Importantly, because these effects were often distractive, they interfered with the educational advantages the e-books might otherwise offer.

To overcome – or at least partially control – these inconsistencies, we designed an e-book based on clear educational purposes for use in an examination of the technologies potential for enhancing the emergent literacy of young children. For example, we purposefully excluded features reported to be distractive, such as the possibility of activating hotspots extraneous to the learning task, or in the midst of reading activities; that is, we programmed the hotspots to appear only after the narrator had completed his reading of the page's text. In keeping with the literature, we included three different modes that the children could activate separately: "Read story only," "Read story with dictionary," and "Read story and play." These modes were developed to foster early language and literacy development by integrating principles of amusement with educational goals while focusing on vocabulary acquisition, phonological awareness and text tracking.

While taking the educational e-book's features and the related literature into account, the skills targeted were vocabulary and phonological awareness because children with LD often have problems in acquiring these skills (Bryant et al., 2003; Hutinger et al., 2005; Most, Al-Yagon, Tur-Kaspa, & Margalit, 2000). The dictionary, read and play modes were thought to be potentially supportive of phonological awareness due to the possibility they offered of multiple activations together with the linking of oral explanations of difficult words to visual explanations, tools that increase learning through the multisensory exposure to words. In consideration of these factors, our study focused on comparing the results of children's activity with the e-book, those obtained after being read the book's print version and results obtained from a control group that participated in the regular kindergarten program, We consequently planned our research in order to obtain answers to the following research questions: (1) Does e-book activity foster the improvement of emergent literacy among preschoolers at risk for LD? (2) Which areas of emergent literacy – vocabulary or phonological awareness – will show greater improvement following the e-book activity? (3) Will literacy improvements vary as a function of the media to which the children are exposed (e-book activity vs. reading a print version)?

EVALUATION OF AN EDUCATIONAL E-BOOK

Before the experiment began, all the participants were assessed with a comprehensive psycho-educational assessment test and identified by Israeli educational psychological services as being at risk for learning disabilities. Children with other potential causes of learning problems, such as low general intelligence, lack of opportunity to learn, and sensory or emotional impairment, were excluded from the study. A total of 110 kindergarteners aged 5-7 were selected to participate in the study. The children were randomly assigned to three groups: children in the first intervention group activated the e-book; in the second group the children heard the print version of the e-book as read by an adult; in the third group, the control group, children participated in the regular kindergarten program, which generally excludes structured reading sessions even though children are frequently read to and voluntarily browse through books. We would like to note that preschool programs generally allow taking part in games involving syllabic segmentation and rhyming, aimed at promoting phonemic awareness. Teachers are free to encourage spelling and grapho-phonemic awareness although little time is devoted to alphabet recitation or letter naming. Work sheets for visual discrimination training (including letter discrimination) and letter copying are available (Shatil et al., 2001) but their use is subject to the teacher's discretion. Despite the varying level of targeted activity, children in this age group usually recognize their written names and are able to write them independently. Most kindergarten classes also have one or two computers. Hence, children soon become exposed to computers, different types of software, and sometimes e-books as part of the standard curriculum. This situation made it possible to recruit participants for the study who had already been exposed to computers.

In order to select a sufficiently uniform sample of study participants, an intelligence test was administered to all the children. Cognitive level (verbal and non verbal) was assessed using two subtests – analogies and antonyms – from the Kaufman Assessment Battery for Children (KABC) of the Kaufman Intelligence Inventory (Kaufman & Kaufman, 1983). Children who earned scores less than two standard deviations from the mean in one of the two subtests were excluded from the study. The children's emergent literacy skills (vocabulary and phonological awareness) were assessed before and after the e-book activity.

The e-book used in this study was an electronic version of a popular children's book, *Yuval Hamebulbal* (*Confused Yuval*) by Miriam Roth (2000), adapted to our educational criteria (Shamir & Korat, 2006; de Jong & Bus, 2003). To maintain the similarity between the electronic and the print versions, we scanned the pages from the printed book when producing the e-book. The story's protagonist, Yuval, is a young boy with a tendency for confusion and forgetfulness until his grandmother makes him a special memory-improving hat. On each of the book's 15 pages, a large coloured drawing appears, covering more than half of the page; in addition, 3

160

to 5 written sentences, totalling about 40 words, also appear. The written text is printed in pointed letters (*nekudot* in Hebrew, indicating vowels), to facilitate reading (the points are eliminated at higher levels of reading and writing). The story's simple structure and narrative elements – setting, characters, goals, initiating event, problem, and resolution/ending (Mandler & Johnson, 1977) – are geared toward kindergarten-aged children.

The e-book features include an animated figure that explains the different options for activating the story in the electronic version of the book. The children are offered four modes or options: (1) Read story only, (2) Read story with dictionary, (3) Read story and play (programmed for phonological awareness activities) and (4) Print. Each activation mode includes a recorded oral reading of the printed text. The e-book also provides automatic dynamic visuals to dramatize story details, fragments, and scenes; extra music and film effects help transform the e-book into a "living" book. To stimulate the children's orientation towards reading, the e-book includes a forward button (a coloured arrow pointing to the right) and a backward button (an arrow pointing to the left) on each screen to allow repetition of previous screens or continuation onto the next screen. Another function enables children to re-read/re-listen to the text. Written phrases are highlighted as the text is read aloud to help children focus on the relationship between text and oral reading, an exercise thought to support word recognition in addition to reading (de Jong & Bus, 2002).

The "Read story only" mode includes an oral reading of the printed text as well as automatic dynamic visuals that dramatize the story. The "Read story with dictionary" mode provides an identical oral reading of the text with added explanations for difficult words, which appear automatically on the screen after the entire page is read by the narrator (children can reactivate these words). As each difficult word appears on the screen, it is pronounced clearly by the narrator while pictures supporting it's meaning appear on the screen. The "Read story and play" mode is designed to enhance the children's story understanding and phonological awareness. By clicking on hidden hotspots as they appear on (a) characters or objects and (b) on words appearing in the text, children can activate the various learning-oriented electronic features associated with the story. To avoid the distraction that interactivity can cause, the hotspots are programmed to be activated only after the children have read/listened to the text, by page. Activation enriches story comprehension by initiating a discourse between the main characters and the voice and sound effects. The hotspots associated with the words promote children's phonological awareness of syllables and sub-syllables.

THE EXPERIMENT

The vocabulary measure (word meaning) administered prior to the e-book activity included ten words taken from the book's text that also appeared in the e-book's dictionary mode. The ten words were judged to be relatively difficult for children of this age as well as the most difficult words in the book. In consideration of the children's age, the vocabulary test required them to point to the picture that best illustrated the word's meaning, chosen out of a set of four pictures. Three easy words, representing a preliminary phase, were presented to the children first so as to allow them to understand the task as well as give them a feeling of success. Each of the ten additional words was orally presented to the children, who were then asked to repeat the picture-selection procedure.

Phonological awareness was measured using 12 two-syllable words that did not appear in the e-book. The words were orally presented one at a time, with the children being asked to repeat them first in a syllabic (breaking them into two parts, e.g., *Yu-val*) and then in a sub-syllabic format (breaking them into three parts, e.g., *Yu-va-l*).

During the intervention phase, the e-book group (i.e., the children working in the group assigned to reading the e-book) took part in six activity sessions, during which they could experience the two modes selected for their group, "Read story with Dictionary" and "Read the story and Play." Each session lasted about 30 minutes (range: 20-35 minutes).

Children belonging to the print version group (where experimenters read the print version of the e-book) participated in six activity sessions as well. The experimenters were two third-year undergraduate students in the School of Education. Reading sessions were conducted in a strictly prescribed manner. In order to design a reading protocol that was also ecologically valid, that is, one that reflected how adults might read the book to their own children, a questionnaire was administered to 20 kindergarten teachers, A list of instructions on how the student teachers were to read the book to the children was then created on the basis of the responses. The list included four comments that the readers were required to make, as well as five words and five questions the readers were expected to introduce at designated places during the reading (see de Jong & Bus, 2004, for a similar method). Two of the four comments were made before the book reading began, two of the five questions were asked after the story had been read, with the remaining questions, comments and word meanings inserted at set points throughout the story's reading.

The reading activity progressed as follows. Prior to reading the story, the experimenter presented the book to the children (the cover with the book's title, the author's name and a picture). In the first reading, the story was read straight through; during the second to sixth readings, the experimenter asked questions, made comments and provided explanations for the selected vocabulary words at set points throughout the story. Throughout the activity, the experimenter and the children sat with the book facing all of them, which made it possible to see all the text and illustrations. Each session involved small groups of 3-5 children. The experimenter was instructed to answer all the questions in brief to ensure similar treatment for all the children as well as a consistent delivery of the reading protocol.

After exposure to the e-book activity as well as the adult reading sessions, all the children were reassessed with the same emergent literacy measures, given in the same order as during the pre-intervention phase. In accordance with the study's goals, the results are presented here in the following order: (a) the effect of e-book activity on vocabulary and (b) the effect of e-book activity on phonological awareness.

To test for the effects of the e-book activity on vocabulary acquisition, we used a 3x2 repeated measures MANOVA of *group* (e-book activation/printed book/control) x *time* (pre- and post-intervention), with time employed as a repeated-measures variable. Kindergarteners' pre-intervention *vocabulary* scores showed no significant group differences (e-book activation/printed book/control). There was a significant main effect for time ($F_{(1,107)}$=300. 34, p<.001, η^2=.74), indicating that children's post-intervention vocabulary scores (M=8.26, SD=1.27) were higher than their pre-intervention scores (M=4.71, SD=1.59). There was also a significant interaction between *group* and *time* ($F_{(2,107)}$=42.08, p<.001, η^2=.44), indicating that the pre- to post-intervention differences in improved vocabulary varied among the three comparison groups.

Simple effects analyses for dependent samples, carried out for each group separately, indicated that the size effect of the e-book group ($F_{(1,41)}$=262.99, p<.001, η^2=.87), was higher than that of the printed book group ($F_{(1,33)}$=89.23, p<.001, η^2=.30); both effects were higher than that of the control group ($F_{(1,33)}$=15.35, p<.001, η^2=.32). Further analysis showed significant differences between the e-book and control groups ($F_{(1,74)}$=98.94, p<.001, η^2=.57) and between the printed book and control groups ($F_{(1,66)}$=34.85, p<.001, η^2=.35). In addition, significant differences were found between the e-book and the printed book groups ($F_{(1,74)}$=7.68, p<.01, η^2=.09). Kindergarteners' pre-intervention *phonological awareness* scores showed no significant group differences (e-book activation/printed book/control). To test for the effects of the e-book activity on *phonological awareness*, we used a 3 x 2 repeated-measures MANOVA of *group* (e-book activation/printed book/control) x *time* (pre- and post-intervention), with the last variable employed as a repeated-measures variable. There was a significant main effect for time ($F_{(2,105)}$=22.75, p<.001, η^2=.30), indicating that children's post-intervention *phonological awareness* scores were higher than their pre-intervention scores in the two subtests (syllabic and sub-syllabic segmentations). There was also significant interaction between *group* x *time* ($F_{(4,212)}$=4.38, p<.01, η^2=.08), indicating that the pre- to post-intervention differences in phonological awareness improvement varied by group.

No significant group differences were found between the groups regarding pre- to post-intervention syllabic awareness ($F_{(2,106)}$=.98, p>.05). However, significant group differences were found in sub-syllabic segmentation ($F_{(2,106)}$=7.27, p<.01, η^2=.12). Simple effects analyses for dependent samples, carried out for each group separately, indicated that only the e-book group showed any significant improvement in sub-syllabic awareness from pre-intervention (M=40.51, SD=13.43) to post-intervention ($F_{(1,41)}$=22.80, p<.001, η^2=.36; M=49.71, SD=9.95). No such improvement was found in either the printed book group ($F_{(1,32)}$=.1.02, p>.05) or the control group ($F_{(1,33)}$=..75, p>.05). It is important to note that the syllabic awareness remained fairly constant even though the phonological activity enabled the children to work on syllabic and sub-syllabic segmentation. This finding probably resulted from the high scores gained in the pre-intervention phase (ceiling effect). Children at the age of those in our study (5-6 years old) usually obtain high scores on this task. Hence, repeated testing should not yield significant changes in their scores.

CAN E-BOOKS HELP CHILDREN AT RISK FOR LD?

Research has shown that young children with LD have problems developing emergent literacy skills such as vocabulary acquisition and phonological awareness (Bryant et al., 2003; Hutinger et al., 2005; Jenkins, Matlock, & Slocum, 1989; Most, Al-Yagon, Tur-Kaspa, & Margalit, 2000), the absence of which affects their learning of reading and writing in later stages of schooling (Lange & Thompson, 2006; Most et al., 2000; Stanovich, 1991). This same difficulty is thought to undermine their motivation to engage in activities that require reading (Van Daal & Reitsma, 2000). The outcomes of the present study imply that activity with specially designed educational e-books may be effective for inculcating basic vocabulary and phonological awareness skills among this group of children. Like previous findings obtained with preschoolers without LD (Shamir, 2009; Shamir, Korat & Barbi, 2008), the current study's findings show that even preschoolers at risk for LD, that is, children showing low levels of verbal ability, can learn the meaning of infrequently used and individually unknown words if provided with an appropriate dictionary option. These results are unique. To the best of our knowledge, no research such as that reported here has ever been conducted among children at risk for LD.

But why is the dictionary so effective? We suggest that the greater improvement in vocabulary acquisition by the group exposed to the e-book's modes may be explained by at least three factors, all of which relate to the interactivity – a technology-related characteristic – it offers. That is, computerization of texts provides children with an opportunity to interact with a story and its educational features in ways unavailable in printed books (Shepperd, Grace, & Koch, 2008).

We therefore argue that the "Read story with dictionary" mode is stronger in its effect than are the verbal explanations commonly given by teachers in the printed story setup. The e-book's dictionary provides automatic oral explanations combined with pictures supporting meaning presented in a lively (including music and sound effects) and immediately format that is fully integrated into reading/listening. However, it is also possible that because the children in the e-book group were able to repeatedly activate the dictionary mode whenever they wished – that is, when needed – the activations more effectively promoted memorization by combining reading with viewing of the same vocabulary word. Our findings thus comply with those reported by Bryant et al. (2003), who stated that interactive memory devices and graphic displays capable of attracting and retaining attention appear to be more effective for children with LD than are straightforward explanations.

Interactivity may also help students remain focused on reading while preventing

164

attention lapses (otherwise known as "zoning out", see Schooler, Reichle, & Halpern, 2005). We should note here that a dictionary option was found in only 4.3% of the commercially available Israeli and Dutch e-books evaluated by Korat and Shamir (2004) as well as by de Jong and Bus (2002). This implies that most commercially available e-books should not, as a rule, be considered vocabulary-enhancing tools either at home or in the school.

Regarding the second emergent literacy skill – phonological awareness – previous research with children of this age has shown that activity with computer software, including e-books, can promote phonological awareness (Chera & Wood, 2003; Littleton, Wood, & Chera, 2006; Olson & Wise, 1992; Shamir et al., 2008). For example, Olson and Wise (1992), who compared software based on phonological awareness with the whole-word approach to reading, found that while all children benefited from computer-assisted learning, those using the phonologically oriented software benefited most. Others have reported that exposing beginning readers (i.e., those already in a formal reading program) to e-books that include phonological awareness features at the level of onset and rime does promote reading acquisition (Littleton et al., 2006) as well as phonological awareness (Chera & Wood, 2003).

We should recall, however, that the current study focused on kindergarteners at risk for LD, a population that often demonstrates difficulties with phonological awareness skills (Fletcher, Reid, Fuchs, & Barnes, 2006; Swanson, Harris & Graham, 2003). Yet, as in vocabulary acquisition, our findings indicate that interactivity promotes phonological awareness as well. Interactivity provides an opportunity to practice the "intensity of training" that Byrne and Fielding-Barnsley (1995, p. 500) find so important for children with LD. Especially striking is the finding that greater improvement in the children's sub-syllabic phonological awareness – as opposed to syllabic awareness – was observed among those who activated the educational e-book. We should note that both phonological awareness skills (syllabic and sub-syllabic) were specifically targeted in the "Read story and play" mode that is unavailable in the book's print version. We ascribe these results to the fact that children in the age group studied (5-6 years old) usually gain high scores on this task. However, since we are speaking of children at risk for LD, the fact that they showed greater improvement in the more difficult of the two phonological skills demands further investigation.

In sum, although an adult reading a book out loud is one of the pivotal literacy events affecting all children in terms of language and literacy development (Bus et al., 1995; Sénéchal, 2006), activities with educational e-books may offer effective opportunities to meet the training and practice needs of young children at risk for LD, especially in the areas of vocabulary acquisition and phonological awareness (see Aram & Levin, 2002).

These hopeful findings should stimulate additional research, especially among this population of children. Further study is also needed to clarify how the process of learning with educational e-books occurs in regular heterogeneous as well as LD class settings. For instance, what features of software operation help children acquire other emergent literacy skills such as those explored here? How much does self-initiated activation – beyond the automatic vocabulary provided by the program – affect children's vocabulary skills? How often do children activate phonological hotspots in the "Read story and play" mode of their own accord and how does this affect their phonological awareness following the activity? Are these two behaviours related to independent, self-initiated reading? Research comparing print with electronic storybooks is also required to ascertain which format is more educationally appropriate for other emergent literacy skills (Matthew, 1996; Reinking, 1997). Finally, all these questions should be repeated in research aimed specifically at adapting the technology to help children at risk for LD learn more effectively.

REFERENCES

Aram, D., & Levin, I. (2002). Mother-child writing and storybook reading: Relations with literacy among low SES kindergartener. *Merrill-Palmer Quarterly, 48*(2), 202-224.

Breznitz, Z. (Ed.). (2008). *Brain research in language.* New York: Springer.

Brook, U., & Boaz, M. (2005). Attention deficit and learning disabilities (ADHD/LD) among high school pupils in Holon (Israel). *Patient Education and Counseling, 58*(2), 164-167.

Bryant, D.P., Goodwin, M., Bryant, B., & Higgins, K. (2003). Vocabulary instruction for students with disabilities: A review of the research. *Learning Disability Quarterly, 206,* 117-128.

Bus, A.G., van IJzendoorn, M.H., & Pellegrini, A.D. (1995). Joint book reading makes for success in learning to read: A meta-analysis on intergenerational transmission of literacy. *Review of Educational Research, 65,* 1-21.

Byrne, B., & Fielding-Barnsley, R. (1995). Evaluation of a program to teach phonological awareness to young children. *Journal of Educational Psychology, 87*(3), 488-503.

Chera, P., & Wood, C. (2003). Animated multimedia 'talking books' can promote phonological awareness in children beginning to read. *Learning and Instruction, 13,* 33-52.

de Jong, M.T., & Bus, A.G. (2002). Quality of book-reading matters for emergent readers: An experiment with the same book in a regular or electronic format. *Journal of Educational Psychology, 94,* 145-155.

de Jong, M.T., & Bus, A.G. (2003). How well suited are electronic books to supporting literacy? *Journal of Early Childhood Literacy, 3,* 147-164.

de Jong, M.T., & Bus, A.G. (2004). The efficacy of electronic books fostering kindergarten children's emergent story understanding. *Reading Research Quarterly, 39,* 378-393.

DSM IV TR. (2000).. *Diagnostic and statistical manual of mental disorders* (4th ed.). Retrieved October 1, 2004, http://www.dsmivtr.org.

Fletcher, J.M., Reid, G., Fuchs, L.S., & Barnes, M.A. (2006). *Learning disabilities, from identification to intervention.* New York: Guilford Press.

Gadbow, N.F., & DuBois, D.A. (1998). *Adult learners with special needs.* Malabar, FL: Krieger.

Gerber, P.J., & Reiff, H. (Eds.). (1994). *Learning disabilities in adulthood: Persisting problems and evolving issues.* Stoneham, MA: Butterworth-Heinemann.

Hutinger, P., Bell, C., Beard, M., Bond, J., Johanson, J., & Terry, C. (1998). *The early childhood emergent literacy technology research study. Final Report.* Washington, DC: Office of Special Education and Rehabilitation Services. (Eric Document Reproduction Service No. ED 418545)

Hutinger, P., Bell, C., Daytner, G., & Johanson, J. (2005). *Disseminating and replicating an effective emerging literacy. Technology Curriculum: A Final Report.* Washington, DC: Office of Special Education and Rehabilitation Services. (Eric Document Reproduction Service No. ED 489575)

Jenkins, J.R., Matlock, B., & Slocum, T.A. (1989). Two approaches to vocabulary instruction: The teaching of individual word meanings and practice in deriving word meaning from context. *Reading Research Quarterly, 24,* 215-235.

Kaufman, A.S., & Kaufman, N.L. (1983). *The Kaufman assessment battery for children*. Circle Pine, NM: American Guidance Service.

Korat, O., & Shamir, A. (2004). Do Hebrew electronic books differ from Dutch electronic books? A replication of a Dutch content analysis. *Journal of Computer Assisted Learning, 20*, 1-12.

Korat, O., & Shamir, A. (2007). Electronic books versus adult readers: Effects on children emergent literacy as a function of social class. *Journal of Computer Assistance Learning, 23*, 248-259.

Korat, O., & Shamir, A. (2008). The educational electronic book as a tool for supporting children's emergent literacy in low versus middle SES groups. *Computers and Education, 50*, 110-124.

Labbo, L.D., & Kuhn, M.R. (2000). Weaving chains of affect and cognition: A young child's understanding of CD-ROM talking books. *Journal of Literacy Research, 32*, 187-210.

Leferver-Davis, S. & Pearman, C. (2005). Early readers and electronic texts: CD-ROM storybook features that influence reading behaviors. *The Reading Teacher, 58*, 446-454.

Littleton, K., Wood, C., & Chera, P. (2006). Interactions with talking books: Phonological awareness affects boy's use of talking books. *Journal of Computer Assisted Learning, 22*, 382-390.

Lonigan, C.J., Driscoll, K., Phillips, B.M., Cantor, B.G., Anthony, J.L., & Goldstein, H. (2003). A computer-assisted instruction phonological sensitivity program for preschool children at-risk for reading problems. *Journal of Early Intervention, 25*, 248-262.

Mandler, J.M., & Johnson, N.S. (1977). Remembrance of things parsed: Story structure and recall. *Cognitive Psychology, 9*, 111-151.

Margalit, M. (2000). *Report of a committee for examination of implementation of the law for special education* (Margalit Report). Jerusalem: Ministry of Education [in Hebrew].

Marsh, J., Brooks, G., Hughes, J., Ritchie, L., Roberts, S., & Wright, K. (2005). *Digital beginnings: Young children's use of popular culture, media and new technologies*. University of Sheffield: Literacy Research Centre.

Matthew, K.I. (1996). The impact of CD-ROM storybooks on children's reading comprehension and reading attitude. *Journal of Educational Multimedia and Hypermedia, 5*, 379-394.

Mioduser, D., Tur-Kaspa, H., & Leitner, I. (2000). The learning value of computer-based instruction of early reading skills. *Journal of Computer Assisted Learning, 16*, 54-63.

Most, T., Al-Yagon, M., Tur-Kaspa, H., & Margalit, M. (2000). Phonological awareness, peer nomination and social competence among preschool children at risk for developing learning disabilities. *International Journal of Disability, Development & Education, 47*, 89-105.

National Joint Committee on Learning Disabilities (NJCLD). (2006). *Learning disabilities and young children: Identification and intervention*. Retrieved on 25 May 2009 from: http://www.ldonline.org/about/partners/njcld#reports.

Ninio, A. (1980). Picture-book reading in mother-infant dyads belonging to two subgroups in Israel. *Child Development, 51*, 587-590.

Olson, R.K., & Wise, B.W. (1992). Reading on the computer with orthographic and speech feedback: An overview of the Colorado Remedial Reading Project. *Reading and Writing: An Interdisciplinary Journal, 4*, 107-144.

Reinking, D. (1997). Me and my hypertext: A multiple digression analysis of technology and literacy (sic). *The Reading Teacher, 50*, 626-643.

Roth, M. (2000). *Yuval Hamebulbal* [Confused Yuval]. Tel Aviv: Poalim Publishing [in Hebrew].

Schooler, J.W., Reichle, E.D., & Halpern, D.V. (2005). Zoning-out during reading: Evidence for dissociation between experienced and meta-consciousness. In D.T. Levin (Ed.), *Thinking and seeing: Visual metacognition in adults and children*. Cambridge, MA: MIT Press.

Segers, E., Takke, L., & Verhoeven, L. (2004). Teacher-mediated versus computer mediated storybook reading to children in native and multicultural kindergarten classrooms. *School Effectiveness and School Improvement, 15*, 215-226.

Segers, E., & Verhoeven, L. (2002). Multimedia support of early literacy learning. *Computers & Education, 39*, 207-221.

Segers, E., & Verhoeven, L. (2003). Effects of vocabulary training by computer in kindergarten. *Journal of Computer Assisted Learning, 19*, 557-566.

Segers, E., & Verhoeven, L. (2004). Computer-supported phonological awareness intervention for kindergarten children with specific language impairment. *Language, Speech, and Hearing Services in Schools, 35*, 229-239.

Sénéchal, M. (2006). Testing the home literacy model: Parent involvement in kindergarten is differently related to grad 4 reading comprehension, fluency, spelling and reading for pleasure. *Scientific Studies of Reading, 10*, 59-87.

Sénéchal, M., & LeFevre, J. (2002). Parental involvement in the development of children's reading skill: A five-year longitudinal study. *Child Development, 73*, 445-460.

Shamir, A. (2009). Processes and outcomes of joint activity with e-books for promoting kindergarteners' emergent literacy. *Educational Media International, 46*(1), 81- 96.

Shamir, A., & Korat, O. (2006). How to select CD-ROM storybooks for young children: The teacher's role. *The Reading Teacher, 59*, 532-543.

Shamir, A., & Korat, O. (2007). Developing an educational e-book for fostering kindergarten children's emergent literacy. *Computers in the Schools, 24*, 125-145.

Shamir, A., Korat, O., & Barbi, N. (2008). The effects of CD-ROM storybook reading on low SES kindergarteners' emergent literacy as a function of learning context. *Computers & Education, 51*(1), 354-367.

Shatil, E., Share, D., & Levin, I. (2000). On the contribution of kindergarten writing to grade one literacy: A longitudinal study in Hebrew. *Applied Psycholinguistics, 21*, 1-21.

Shepperd, J.A., Grace, J.L., & Koch, E.J. (2008). Evaluating the electronic textbook: Is it time to dispense with the paper text? *Teaching of Psychology, 35*, 2-15.

Snyder, I. (Ed.). (2002). *Silicon literacies: Communication, innovation and education in the electronic age.* London: Routledge.

Stanovich, K. (1991). Discrepancy definitions of reading disability: Has intelligence led us astray? *Reading Research Quarterly, 26*(1), 7-29.

Swanson, H.L., Harris, K.R., & Graham, S. (Eds.). (2003). *Handbook of learning disabilities.* New York & London: Guilford.

Teale, W.H., & Sulzby, E. (1989). Emergent literacy: New perspectives. In D. Strickland, & L.M. Morrow (Eds.), *Emerging literacy: Young children learn to read and write* (pp. 1-15). Newark, NJ: International Reading Association.

Turbill, J. (2001). A researcher goes to school: Using technology in the kindergarten literacy curriculum. *Journal of Early Childhood Literacy, 1*, 255-279.

Underwood, G., & Underwood, J.D.M. (1998). Children's interactions and learning outcomes with interactive talking books. *Computers and Education, 30*, 95-102.

van Daal, V.H.P., & Reitsma, P. (2000). Computer assisted learning to read and spell: Results from two pilot studies. *Journal of Research in Reading, 23*, 181-193.

Wachob, R. (1993). Young minds soar with technology. *Computing Teacher, 20*, 53-55.

Whitehurst, G.J., & Lonigan, C.J. (2001). Emergent literacy: Development from pre-readers to readers. In S.B. Neuman, & D.K. Dickinson (Eds.), *Handbook of early literacy research* (pp.11-29). New York: Guilford.

Wood, C. (2005). Beginning readers' use of 'talking books' software can affect their reading strategies. *Journal of Research in Reading, 28*, 170-182.

Yelland, N.J., Hill, S. & Mulhearn, G. (2006). Children of the new millennium. *The Learning Journal, 11*, 1603 - 1617.

Adina Shamir & Renat Fellah
School of Education
Bar-Ilan University

KRISTIINA KUMPULAINEN, AULI TOOM AND MERJA SAALASTI

12. VIDEO AS A POTENTIAL RESOURCE FOR STUDENT TEACHERS' AGENCY WORK

INTRODUCTION

The importance of the social and cultural processes mediating teachers' professional identity formation has been increasingly recognised in the research literature (Beijaard, Meijer & Verloop, 2004; Davydov, Slobodchikov, Tsukerman, 2003; Edwards, 2005; Edwards & D' Arcy, 2004; Engle & Faux, 2006; Zuckerman, 2007; Lipponen & Kumpulainen, 2011). A central element of teacher professional identity is agency. The basic idea of agency is that people do not merely react to and repeat given practices. Instead, people should have the capacity for independent social action during which they intentionally transform and refine their social and material worlds and take control of their lives. Thus, agency can be defined as the capacity to initiate purposeful action that implies will, autonomy, freedom and choice (Bandura, 1989; Biesta & Tedder, 2007; Edwards & D'Arcy, 2004; Emirbayer & Mische, 1998; Engeström, 2005; Giddens, 1991; Greeno, 2006; Holland, Lachicotte, Skinner, & Cain, 1998).

If we want to educate agentic teachers who do not just deliver the curriculum, but also are able and willing to critically analyze and act upon teaching and learning situations, we must understand more deeply the processes of becoming an agentic teacher, and ways to support this development (Edwards & D'Arcy, 2004; Edwards & Protheroe, 2003). Any educational institution should cultivate learners' capacity for active and agentic learning. Yet, the cultures of many educational institutions fail to do this. In teacher education, student teachers are typically reported as learning to plan lessons and deliver the curriculum, but are not learning how to respond to increasingly complex readings of classroom situations (Edwards & D'Arcy, 2004; Edwards & Protheroe, 2003). Moreover, there is a growing need for teachers to work across professional boundaries, requiring the capacity to collaborate with other teachers and professions (Edwards, 2005, 2007; Edwards & D'Arcy, 2004).

In this chapter, we are interested to explore the ways in which the collaborative investigation of video cases embedded in a teacher education programme can afford opportunities for student teachers' agency work and support their professional identity formation. Via our sociocultural analyses of student teachers' agency work as reflected in their written essays, we highlight the ways in which teacher candidates start to view their developing experiences and knowledge(s) as

E. Hjörne et al. (eds.), Learning, Social Interaction and Diversity – Exploring Identities in School Practices, 169–187.

powerful resources to be learned from and acted upon, which constitute taking a reflective, inquiring stance into practice.

Teacher Identity Formation as Sociocultural and Situated Processes

In this study, teacher learning and professional identity formation are conceptualized as sociocultural and situated processes. From this perspective, the process of becoming a professional teacher does not simply involve the development of procedural skills and competences. Growing to become an active member of the professional teaching community is a complex, dynamic, culturally and socially constituted process that extends beyond knowledge re-production to the construction of a professional identity (Day & Gu, 2007; Korthagen, 2001; Zeichner, 1996).

The sociocultural and situated perspectives of professional learning and development challenge the traditional views based on cognitive psychology by considering thinking and learning as essentially connected with the physical and social context of cognitive action, i.e. participation (Brown, Collins, & Duguid, 1989; Greeno, 1997; Lave & Wenger, 1991). Learning is the process of enculturation, including adopting ways of thinking as well as the actions of a community (Lave & Wenger, 1991). The discourses of the teaching profession play an important role in defining the thinking and actions of teachers. This includes teachers' interpretations of their work and its practice (Gudmundsdottir, 1995; Putnam & Borko, 2000).

From the sociocultural perspective, a personal way of thinking and communicating develops according to in different formal and informal discourse communities (Wenger, 1998; Wertsch, 1991). The discourses provide and develop such tools as ideas, theories and concepts for constructing collaborative and personal meaning. It is also important to recognize that it is not just knowledge that is constructed. Humans, their identities, positions and agencies are constructions too; learning is, thus, a matter of personal and social transformation (Packer & Goicoechea, 2000).

Recent research has highlighted the importance of gaining an understanding of the interactional and relational processes within which teacher identities are constructed, negotiated and contested. In contemporary theorizing, identity is not viewed as an individual characteristic or a disposition. Rather, identity is conceptualized as an ongoing process of becoming that is contextually and historically situated, occasional, multi-faceted, relational and transitory (Moran & John-Steiner, 2003). Identity development is seen as a dynamic improvisational state that is constructed relationally in interaction within a community of practice. Identity formation involves ongoing transformations of both the community and the self (Wenger, 1998). It is via discourse that identities are constructed, contested, negotiated and re-negotiated.

In this study, student teachers' identity formation and agency work are viewed as complex entities that are mediated and shaped by unique circumstances, lives and experiences of individuals and the meanings in play within the wider social world. Identity and agency are not seen as fixed qualities or dispositions (Schwartz & Okita, 2009), not something people have. They are rather something that people do in social practice. Thinking of identity in terms of achievement makes it possible to understand why an individual can practice it in one situation but not in another (Biesta & Tedder, 2007). In this study, identity is seen as a negotiated experience evidencing community membership and learning trajectories between the local and the global (cf. Wenger, 1998; Ivanic, 1998). Wenger (1998) reminds us that talking about identity in social terms does not deny individuality. Rather individuality is defined as part of a community of practice. In other words, membership does not determine who we are in a simple way, but our experience and, for example, our 'professional image' of ourselves is shaped by belonging to a community with a unique identity. This view should be considered as one of the guiding principles in teacher education so as to provide students with opportunities for agency work.

Promoting Agency Work in Teacher Education

To steer student teachers towards active agency a new kind of learning culture is needed, a culture that mediates agency (Lipponen & Kumpulainen, 2011). One important aspect of developing agency is having the opportunity to participate and contribute in interaction where one is framed and positioned as the author of one's own learning, that is, to act as an accountable author. Acting as an accountable author is made possible by the creation of pedagogical spaces in which students are positioned as contributors whose inputs are recognized and credited. The students should also have the possibility to problematize and resolve noteworthy issues. Dialogic, inquiry-based learning cultures can provide students with cultural bridges to participate meaningfully and powerfully in rich and diverse professional learning spaces (Greeno, 2006; Boaler & Greeno, 2000; Brown & Renshaw, 2006; Engle & Faux, 2006),

The use of video cases has provided teacher education with extended landscapes to support the professional development of teachers (e.g. Dolk, den Hertog, & Gravemeijer, 2003; Kumpulainen, 2004; Lampert & Ball, 1998; Merseth, 1996). In particular, the potential of video cases has been recognized for their power to create social and discursive spaces for pre-service and in-service teachers to investigate and reflect upon teaching and learning practices in local and distant classrooms (Brophy, 2004; Fisher, Higgins, & Loveless, 2006; Kumpulainen, 2004; Lampert & Ball, 1998; Merseth, 1996). Moreover, the investigation of video cases in socially-shared learning situations has been shown to elicit tacit knowledge and beliefs that teachers hold about their professional practices and to support the integration of theoretical and practical knowledge in teachers' discourses whilst they investigate and make meaning of the telling cases embedded in culturally diverse classrooms (Beck, King, & Marshall; 2002; Dolk et al., 2003; Toom, 2006).

Although digital video is currently a state of the art technology and clearly has something new and powerful to offer for inquiry-oriented teacher education, the conceptualization of this 21st-century artefact requires further theorizing and empirical research. It is important that the application of such technology be located and examined within the situated contexts of teacher education. The potential role of video cases in supporting future teachers' agency work and professional identity formation also requires further research.

THE STUDY

In this chapter, we report our findings on the nature of student teachers' agency work in the context of a teacher education course that purposefully employed video cases from a European data corpus on the teaching and learning of mathematics for student teachers' collaborative inquiry and reflection. The course focused on learning and teaching mathematics in classroom across Europe. The empirical analyses of our study focus on the students' reflective essays composed as part of the course. The theoretical and methodological approaches that guide our study are grounded in the sociocultural, situated and sociolinguistic theories of language and learning (Bloome & Egan-Robertson, 1993; Gumperz & Hymes, 1972; Fairclough, 1992; Ivanic, 1998; Santa Barbara Classroom Discourse Group, 1992).

Video case material

The video case material used in the teacher education course, MILE International, is a digital representation of mathematics teaching and learning practices in various European classrooms, namely in Dutch, British and Finnish schools. The video material in the environment covers altogether six mathematics lessons, two from each country. Each lesson is taught by a different teacher and participated in by a unique group of students as a part of their authentic, everyday school practices. The age of the student groups varies from five to twelve, depending on the country and the lesson topic. The topics of the lessons deal with early number sense or percentage. In addition to digitalized video material of classroom lessons, the learning environment includes videotaped interviews with teachers as well as materials and assignments produced by the classroom communities as a part of the lessons.

Each classroom lesson and teacher-interview session of the MILE International digital school has been transcribed and translated into English, Dutch and Finnish. The transcribed texts appear directly below the actual video, highlighting the author of each turn of interaction. In addition to direct transcription of the interactions, the full video material has been content-analyzed at an episodic level. The analysis of the episodes, defined as narrative clips (Dolk, 2000), is based on educational, psychological and subject-matter literature. The narrative clips of the video material appear in the environment in the form of descriptive abstracts and key words. Examples of narrative clips found in the video material are "Scaffolding a student", "Active engagement", "Exploratory interaction" and "Collaborative construction of mathematical understanding". Consequently, in addition to investigating transcribed video material in its full complexity, the learning environment allows users to investigate the video material at an episodic level, facilitating the searching, viewing and re-viewing of specific narratives and their sequential construction in the flow of the lessons. The search tool provides users with additional support in locating specific video clips that fulfil certain criteria or address a certain question.

Course Description

The MILE International learning environment was used during a mathematics pedagogy course that focused on learning and teaching mathematics, i.e., how to plan, realize and evaluate mathematics education in European classrooms. The instructional methods used during the course included inquiry learning, collaborative investigations and reflections, as well as the construction of personal reflective essays. The course was built upon student participation in all the activities and was largely practical in nature, building upon their experiences in previous mathematics education courses and their time in schools. In total 37 students in a four-year International Master of Education Programme took part in the course, the mean age of the students being 24.

The students were asked to write two essays in which they described their experiences in learning and teaching mathematics. In the beginning of the course, the students wrote their first reflective essays where they considered their own learning experiences and orientation to mathematics. In addition, they were asked to articulate their goals and expectations for the course as a whole. After the course, the students wrote their second reflective essay, where they reflected upon their experiences in learning and teaching mathematics as a result of the course. In the second essay, the students were also asked to describe their collaborative working processes during the course and the meaning of the course for their professional learning as whole. The students were given some guiding questions to help them construct their essays. The guiding questions for the essays were:

Personal experiences and attitudes
How would you describe yourself as a learner of mathematics? Provide examples.
Which role does mathematical thinking play your life?
Which role does mathematical thinking play in today's life?

Professional identity
Which examples have you got on teaching mathematics? Describe them via examples.
How would you describe yourself as a teacher of mathematics?
Which are your strengths as a teacher?
How would you like to develop yourself as a teacher of mathematics?

173

Learning and teaching mathematics
How do you see the role of student in a mathematics classroom?
Which kind of knowledge does an expert teacher of mathematics need in order to provide their students with optimum opportunities?

DATA ANALYSIS

In this study, we focus on the analysis of altogether 74 reflective essays, written by 37 student teachers at the beginning and end of the course. The essays are examined in a chronologic manner in order to understand the evolving nature of students' reflection processes over the course. All the students enrolled in the course took part in the study and in the essay writing at the beginning and at the end of the course.

Ivanic's ethnographic approach to discourse has guided our analyses of the ssays (Ivanic, 1998). Ivanic (1998) emphasizes a discoursal approach to identity construction and views writing as an act of identity. Ivanic emphasizes that there is no such thing as impersonal writing; writers negotiate 'a discoursal self', an impression of themselves, through the discoursal choices they make when writing. In order to avoid creating the impression of social identity as coherent and unified, Ivanic (1998) employs the term 'positioning', stressing the multi-faceted realization of identities in social action. A person can move among different positions, while identifying with a certain group of people. Positioning is often implied by the use of pronouns (i.e. words such as 'I','you','me','us') and determiners ('a', 'the', 'his') (see also Hermans, 1996, 2001).

Our data analysis proceeded as a series of cycles during which we tried to identify critical moments, or telling cases, in the students' reflective essays, moments evidencing the nature of the students' agency work as mediating their identity formation. Our analytical approach is not linear. Central to the analysis is a multi-step, multi-phase recursive analysis process.

We started the analysis process by taking a rough overview of all the essays in order to conduct a preliminary content analysis of the most commonly occurring themes. We also paid close attention to the students' positioning of themselves in the themes they were describing. We read the essays several times to identify episodes in which agency was made visible in the students' writing. We extracted these critical episodes, or 'telling cases', (Mitchell, 1984) for further interpretation. The dominating themes and the students' positioning are presented in Table 1.

Table 1. The dominating themes and the students' positioning (in grey) in their reflective essays.

Discoursal element / Dominating theme	Self	Student/ learner	Student teacher	Future teacher	Profess. teacher	I – me	they,those s/he, you	We –us	Passive
Pedagogical knowledge of teaching math			grey		grey	grey			grey
Being a mathematics teacher			grey		grey				grey
Experiences as a learner of math	grey	grey				grey			
Experiences as a teacher		grey				grey			
Challenges to the teaching profession			grey		grey	grey			
Methods and materials for the course		grey						grey	
Emotions and personal feelings about math	grey	grey	grey						grey
Criticism of educational technology	grey	grey				grey		grey	grey

RESULTS

In this section, we shall describe the emerging and dominant themes in the students' reflective essays and the ways in which the student teachers positioned and identified themselves within these themes. We shall consider the relevance of these discourses for the student teachers' agency work and professional identity formation.

Pedagogical Knowledge of Teaching Mathematics

The most dominant theme in the student teachers' reflective essays dealt with issues of pedagogical knowledge in teaching mathematics. Here, the students reflected on their views regarding the principles of mathematics teaching as well as describing the meaning of pedagogical content knowledge for teachers' professional practice. When discussing this theme, the students often used a distancing mode or wrote about professional teachers.

The most important thing of all is that the teacher could provide a variety of ways to teach children maths, so that all the students would be at least a little bit motivated and able tO learn and succeed in mathematics. (Paula)

Occasionally, the students reflected on some recent notions of pedagogical knowledge by approaching it from the perspective of being a student teacher.

My experiences have made me think of two things that I would like to do differently when teaching math. The first one is to teach it in a more creative way, and the second is tO take more effectively into consideration the weak students, those who learn a bit slower. (Sally)

Being a Mathematics Teacher

The second dominant theme in the students' essays, being a mathematics teacher, differs from the first in the sense that it specifically describes the students' ideas about what it is to be a mathematics teacher: what characteristics are required, what problems teachers face and how they conceptualize the essence of being a teacher. It is interesting to note that while describing the characteristics of the mathematics teacher, the students adopted a distancing position although these ideas are often based on personal experiences. For instance, in the following extracts Helen and Sara do not position themselves in the description of their pedagogical knowledge, but use the expression "the teacher":

Nowadays teachers are facing many challenges; students have different kinds of problems with learning, class sizes are bigger etc. Teachers need to be on top of everything and keep up with new methods that are being created all the time. (Helen)

The expert teacher of mathematics needs pedagogical knowledge. Theoretical knowledg of children's learning of mathematical skills is the basis for planning activitieshe teacher's own mathematical skills naturally have to be sufficient, but more than that, the general attitude towards mathematics counts: is mathematic important in life? (Sara)

Experiences as a Learner of Mathematics

With the third theme, experience as a learner, the students reflected upon their learning experiences as students of mathematics. The students positioned themselves in their own histories of mathematics learning and in their earlier experiences constructed in teacher education. Those experiences were often based on emotions and personal attitudes towards the subject matter.

Mathematics has never really been difficult for me. I am sure that my own thoughts about me as a maths learner have had an effect on my motivation to study maths. (Helen)

As a child I was very insecure in mathematics and managed to avoid the subject as much as possible. The main reason for my insecurity was my first and second grade teachers. They made me fear maths classes more than anything. (Susan)

Experiences as a teacher

Within the fourth theme, experience as a teacher, the students described their earlier teaching experiences:

One of my strengths as a teacher must be my ability to "read people". I think that I am able to sense some things from people. (Liz)

I think that I can also be good at simplifying things and in explaining things in a way that everybody understands. (Hannah)

Challenges to the teaching profession

With the fifth theme, challenges to the teaching profession, the students reflected upon questions that a teacher might face in everyday classroom teaching situations. The students considered various complicated and problematic situations that teachers might face in their daily life at school. They presented these challenges both in the *first person* position and in the *third person* position, suggesting that the students were preparing themselves for their future teaching profession.

If I had to describe myself as a teacher of mathematics, I believe that the same generalization goes for other subjects as well. I am patient, understanding and good in explaining things. I am creative and quite practical so I am certain, that when teaching math I would try to find the most interactive and creative ways to teach it. (Helen)

I generally feel that I have no tools with which to start. I honestly don't know how I should teach for example the second graders. (Lara)

What I find extremely challenging is that it is not enough to know mathematics, but hoW to transfer your knowledge into practice. (Maria)

Methods and Materials for the Course

The sixth theme emerging from the essays is 'methods and material for the course', i.e. course arrangements, case methods, case materials and other materials received from their tutors. Group work and peer collaboration evoked the most reflections within this theme. The students also described their investigation practices of the video cases and elaborated on the meaning of the case material for their professional learning. Moreover, the students focused on reflecting what they had learned from the course and what their thoughts were about the course as a whole. In all, the students appeared to value the role of video case material in supporting their professional development. For example,

> *To observe other teachers teach has been a wonderful help for me in creating my own teacher image. Watching different teachers "in action", their cultural differences and differences in teaching styles, I have also learnt to see the benefits and positive effects of ways of teaching that I never would have used myself. (Lauren)*

> *Also this was a good way to get a glimpse of teaching mathematics in other countries. Master of Education students have the problem that quite often we learn the Finnish teaching model, but it is very important to get other viewpoints as well, especially if someone is planning to teach outside Finland. (Agatha)*

The students considered the discussions evoked by the video cases as convenient way to analyse teaching systematically. DVD tools enabled "breaking down" the elements of teachers' practice in video cases by providing the students with possibilities to return to the teachers' expressions, phrases, gestures and, especially, to pedagogical decisions and solutions as many times as necessary.

> *For us as teachers the MILE environment made it possible to analyze, to examine and to break down into parts different mathematics lessons from many places in the world with a variety of teaching methods and approaches to maths lessons. I could not think of a better way to become a brilliant teacher than to learn from others. (Katie)*

> *It was interesting to share thoughts about the different teaching styles of the teachers with others. It is amazing how many different reactions and opinions can rise from one video clip. (Jane)*

Video cases also inspired the reflection on cultural elements of teaching. It was evident in the essays that the students were interested in the multicultural nature of video case environment; most writers emphasized the cultural differences between teachers' classroom practices.

> *While working with MILE I observed many different aspects into teaching. Not only did I look for good and bad things in different teachers' lessons but*

178

I also tried to differ some cultural differences showing in the clips. I also paid attention to such things as starting the lesson and ending it, taking individuals pupils into consideration, supporting children,giving immediate feedback and so on. I noticed that lesson in Finland are slower than in Britain or the Netherlands. In Finland the pupils were also often gathered on the floor or in chairs around the teacher – near him/her, and not in their desks such as in other countries. In the Netherlands the teacher used more book and written materials such as different worksheets. In Britain the tempo of the lesson was fastest. They also had most playing and mathematical games. (Joanna)

Comparing to field practice observation, video case investigations provide with possibilities of dynamic reflective practise. The following quote illustrates the dynamicity in video case investigations.

Process proceeded nicely in a group, because we could discuss about our observations immediately. (Nelly)

Emotions and Personal Feelings about Mathematics Teaching and Learning

When discussing 'emotions and personal feelings about mathematics' the students elaborated on their attitudes and experiences about learning and teaching mathematics.

My tutor gave me lots of space to teach maths and I did spend many nights preparing the classes. I felt I grew more secure in maths, I learnt many useful rules in many sections of the course and I enjoyed it. (Liz)

It was also interesting to note that at times the students had a tendency to use the *first-person plural* position and distancing modes when describing some embarrassing or puzzling situations during the mathematics course. For many students, it was more secure to reflect upon sensitive themes in an impersonal manner.

The multicultural approach made the course very interesting to follow. The atmosphere of the course was collaborative due to the student-centred and discourse-oriented approach. Discussion always makes one think and also see other views. (Mary)

Criticism of Educational Technology

The eighth theme emerging from the essays is 'criticism of educational technology'. There were students who did not appreciate the role of information and communication technology in teacher learning. Some students held negative attitudes towards technological tools as part of their learning and were opposed to using them.

Somehow the course drowned in technology when it could have sailed briskly with the win of good ideas. I think that the next course like this should concentrate more on the contact between lecturers and the students. Now there was a huge gap in communication and a huge number of zeros and ones in between. I cannot work that way. We are working with our personalities, not by hiding ourselves behind facades of technology. (Matt)

In my opinion, a better method for achieving my aims would have been to have such tasks as "how would you teach multiplication in your math class?" The other thing that I did not quite understand in our course, was all the electronic equipment. I began to wonder for what and for whom this course had been organized. (Liz)

Concluding Reflections: Engaging and Viewing Mathematics Teaching and Learning from Multiple Positions

Overall the analysis reveals that there were certain positions and identities that particularly featured in the students' reflective essay writing. The students appeared to find it easy to approach their reflections from a *first-person position*. They reflected themes mostly in a first-person, using the pronouns 'I', 'me', 'my'. That is, the students examined and argued about their experiences, linking their emerging ideas about the course to their prior knowledge and experiences. Indeed, the students typically adopted this position in their written reflections. This finding gives evidence of the students' agency work and efforts to learn for themselves. The students were firmly and personally engaged in the issues they reflected, assuming personal authority for their own professional learning and development.

The student teachers also saw themselves as part of a learning community and reflected in *the first-person plural*. This indicates that they had started to adopt a collective stance towards their meaning-making and collective problemsolving in teaching and learning mathematics. For example:

*Investigating teachers and learners in different countries through MILE was fruitful especially because **we** could observe and discuss in small groups. Everyone in the group noticed not only same aspects but also brought up different views. **We** also saw some aspects of teaching in a different light. Some of **us** liked calm teachers when others thought they were boring. (Mary)*

The data analysis also reveals that occasionally the students distanced themselves from certain themes by using *third person and second person* positions. This was particularly visible in reflections describing the qualities and requirements of a professional teacher. The student teachers appeared to hold many ideas and ideals about being a professional teacher:

A good maths teacher does not do what the book says, she uses her imagination. A good maths teacher never compares the children's knowledge and skills. (Helen)

Patience is the most important characteristic a teacher should have when interacting with children with learning difficulties. If a student senses that the teacher is not concentrating on his/her problems or shows impatience while explaining the rules, the student is probably going to stop trying. (Evelyn)

The data also reveal that the student teachers were not especially eager to view mathematics teaching and learning from the viewpoint of the future teacher. This observation suggests that the students felt comfortable having the present dominate their daily lives, whereas visions of the future were not so acute or clear to them at the time. Yet, they showed that they had become conscious of their professional learning needs. For example:

My tutor gave me lots of space to teach maths and I did spend many nights preparing for the classes. I felt I grew more secure in maths, I learnt many useful rules in many sections and I enjoyed it. It was rewarding to see a smile on one girl's face when she grasped the idea and managed to do her homework easier. (Evelyn)

I believe that the same generalization goes for other subjects as well. I am understanding, patient and good in explaining things. I am creative and quite practical, so I am sure that when teaching maths I would try to find the most interactive and creative ways to teach it. (Helen)

In addition, the students approached many issues in their writings from their earlier experiences as learners and students of mathematics. This gives evidence that the students drew upon their earlier experiences as school students and harnessed this personal knowledge in their meaning-making of the video cases. The students' experiences as learners provided a fertile ground for exploration and reflection.

For me, primary school taught that girls are worse in mathematics than boys. (Lara)

The role of a student in a classroom is very essential: she/he should be encouraged to be active at all times. (Helen)

The data illuminate the multidimensional nature of the student teachers' positioning in their reflective essays. The students explored issues of teaching and learning mathematics both as members of the student teachers' community and as future teachers. They also reflected upon their experiences as mathematics learners. In sum, these results demonstrate the ways in which student teachers' reflections are imbued with their drawing upon their histories and experiences as they interact with and learn from the discursive resources made available by the collaborative investigation of video cases. The following example illustrates the role of video investigations in not only strenghtening the students' collaborative inquiry skills but also in supporting teacher identity work by enhancing the students' reflection on themselves as teachers.

Teacher has to be capable to hear others perspectives and also share his/her own and maybe even change them. – I raised one aspect during the course to be one of the most important things in teaching and that is to be your self. This I learned already when observing MILE but also during the field practise. One should not try to be something else than s/he is but build the teaching on one's own personality. Because we are all different there is not one and only way to be a teacher. (Mary)

Teacher identity work is a long-term process continuing in teachers' working practice. Still, it is teacher education that should launch and support intensively the identity work by offering the discursive resources. In the context of the students' reflective essays, the video cases appeared to have become potential texts to be read for reflection, identity work and professional learning.

DISCUSSION

The results of this study highlight two major affordances digital video cases can potentially have in teacher education: supporting student teachers' agency work and creating social spaces and possibilities for future teachers to participate in a 'community of inquirers and reflective practitioners' (see Fisher et al., 2006; Shulman & Shulman, 2004). MILE environment enabled the reflective investigation of the teachers' classroom practice by the possibilities of DVD tools. In other words, MILE tools provided with collaborative dynamicity that cannot often be reached in field practice: with video cases the students could discuss reflectively during the observation and return instantly to the moments of classroom practice that evoked reflection. The study also suggests that teachers' understanding of their work is a complex system that is constructed and situated across their professional lives (see also Clandinin & Connelly, 1995). Our study illustrates the dynamics of student teachers' identity formation processes, which appear to have as many different realisations as there are students. Nevertheless, there are many congruent elements in the students' essays that highlight certain unified characteristics of those processes pre-service teachers typically experience in their professional learning trajectories.

We can draw three conclusions about the educational significance of our study. Firstly, the collaborative investigation of video cases as part of the teacher education course created pedagogical spaces for the student teachers' agency work and identity formation. This included taking both self-related and collegial positions towards teaching and learning mathematics in local and global classrooms. Secondly, the students elaborated on significant elements of the teaching profession in their essays: they problematised everyday practices, identified limitations and perceived critical notions, both of themselves and of colleagues. Thirdly, the results demonstrate the power of video case materials in facilitating student reflection. The themes reflected upon in the students' essays characterize the richness of the students' experiences of the course, as well as of their agency work and identity formation processes. Most of the students implied in their writings that the group was an essential element in their personal learning. On the other hand, most of the essays began with the students' memories and personal experiences as learners of mathematics. This implies that the students considered their own experiences as mathematics learners to be very significant for their learning and identity formation processes towards professionalism. Altogether, the students discussed many themes and approached them from diverse positions. The themes discussed indicate the potential of video cases in supporting pre-service teachers' inquiry and reflection as elements of their agency work and identity formation.

Some of the student teachers' essays also signalled negative orientations to collaborative working modes and to educational technology. Negative orientation and weak learning experiences (based on the students' own reflections) go hand-in-hand in the essays. These features of the data call attention to the need for scaffolding in the educational use of video technology. Resistance is generally a verified element in courses where educational technology is utilized (e.g. Brophy, 2004). Nevertheless, this is not an impossible challenge. On the contrary, by systematically familiarizing student teachers with video cases and with the educational goals and practices of the course, educators can motivate students to work successfully with educational technology as a community of learners.

All in all, our study gives promising results about the ways in which student teachers' reflective practices and professional identity formation processes can be enhanced via the use of digital video cases and reflective essay writing. Most of the students in the study went through significant changes in the ways they positioned themselves and how they thematized their essays. They reflected, argued and, most importantly, elaborated on their professional selves.

Investigating authentic classroom practices as part of an inquiry-oriented teacher education course appears to have the potential to reveal teachers' tacit notions about their conceptions of learning and teaching as well as about their social and cultural contexts. The nature of the students' participation and social positioning of themselves and others, evidences a cultural world in which the student teachers are seen by themselves and by others as knowledgeable and committed participants whose identities are variable, multivocal, and interactive (Holland, Lachicotte, Skinner, & Cain, 1998).

CONCLUSIONS

Ongoing discussions on the work of teachers emphasize agency as a pivotal professional capacity (Edwards, 2005; Edwards & D'Arcy, 2004; Engle & Faux, 2006; Reeves, 2009; Roth et al., 2004). Teacher professional agency is needed in the creation of meaningful and engaging learning environments that extend beyond traditional contexts and practices, in the development and implementation of innovative teaching methods, in integrating recent theoretical knowledge into classroom practice and school development as well as in multiprofessional work. Agency is also a highly significant resource for teachers in mediating their professional learning paths and career trajectories (Biesta & Tedder, 2007; Billett, 2006; Billett & Pavlova, 2005; Hammerness, 2006; Vähäsantanen & Billett, 2008).

In this chapter, we have discussed the nature of student teachers' agency work and identity formation processes in a teacher education programme embedded in the collaborative investigation of video cases. On the basis of our study, we suggest that the collective exploration of video cases illuminating authentic classroom practices gives student teachers opportunities for agency work and identity formation processes (Edwards & D'Arcy, 2004; Engle & Faux, 2006). Here, students are encouraged to problematize teaching and learning practices, ask questions and contribute to collective meaning-making and the advancement of ideas. In the interactional spaces of these learning communities, students have opportunities to express various forms of agency and take both self-related and collegial positions. As pointed out by Edwards (2005, 2007), when students have these kinds of experiences during their teacher training, they are likely to have the competency and will to support their students' agency work in real classroom situations and beyond.

Our study demonstrates that when student teachers are given opportunities for collaborative investigation and reflection within the social context of video case material, they are able to exercise transformative agency. That is, they are able to take initiatives, adopt different positions and change the course of activities (Virkkunen, 2006). Transformative agency is not often possible in very traditional instruction where students are positioned more like passive receivers of knowledge (Lipponen & Kumpulainen, 2011).

The needs to link theory with practice meaningfully and provide possibilities to learn from practice are unquestionably among the main challenges to teacher education. Also the 'discipline of noticing' (Mason, 2002) is highly important for teacher education and professional learning. This has to do with developing teachers' sensitivity and awareness to notice pedagogically powerful moments in the flow of situated practice. Every teacher should be alert to the possibilities of investigating and reflecting on situated teaching and learning practices. All these needs create expectations for the development of new methods and learning tools for teacher education. Video cases embedded in reflective and collaborative working modes can be seen as potential meditational tools or as 'rich texts' to be read in efforts to support the agency work of future teachers.

REFERENCES

Bandura, A. (1989). Perceived self-efficacy in the exercise of personal agency. *The Psychologist: Bulletin of the British Psychological Society, 2*, 411-424.

Beck, R.J., King, A., & Marshall, S.K. (2002). Effects of videocase construction on preservice teachers' observations of teaching. *The Journal of Experimental Education, 70*(4), 345-361.

Beijaard, D., Meijer, P.C., & Verloop, N. (2004). Reconsidering research on teachers' professional identity. *Teaching and Teacher Education, 20*, 107-128.

Biesta, G., & Tedder, M. (2007). Agency and learning in the lifecourse: Towards an ecological perspective. *Studies in the Education of Adults, 39*(2), 132-149.

Billett, S. (2006). Relational interdependence between social and individual agency in work and working life. *Mind, Culture and Activity, 13*(1), 53-69.

Billet, S. & Pavlova, M. (2005). Learning through working life: Self and individuals' agentic action. *International Journal of Lifelong Education, 24*(3), 195-211.

Bloome, D., & Egan-Robertson, A. (1993). The social construction of intertextuality in classroom reading and writing lessons. *Reading Research Quarterly, 28*(4), 304–334.

Boaler, J., & Greeno, L. (2000). Identity, agency and knowing in mathematics worlds. In J. Boaler (Ed.), *Multiple perspectives on mathematics teaching and learning* (pp. 171-200). Westport, CT: Ablex Publishing.

Brophy, J. (2004). Introduction. In J. Brophy (Ed.), *Using video in teacher education. Advances in research on teaching* (vol. 10). New York: Elsevier Science.

Brown, J.S., Collins, A., & Duguid, P. (1989). Situated cognition and the culture of learning. *Educational Researcher, 18*(1), 32–41.

Brown, R., & Renshaw, P. (2006). Positioning students as actors and authors: A choronotopic analysis of collaborative learning activities. *Mind, Culture, and Activity, 13*, 247-259.

Clandinin, D.J., & Connelly, F.M. (1995). *Teachers' professional knowledge landscapes.* New York: Teachers College Press.

Day, C., & Gu, Q. (2007). Variations in the conditions for teachers' professional learning and development: sustaining commitment and effectiveness over a career. *Oxford Review of Education, 33*(4), 423-443.

Davydov, V.V., Slobodchikov, V.I., & Tsukerman, G.A. (2003). The elementary school student as an agent of learning activity. *Journal of Russian and East European Psychology, 41*, 63-76.

Dolk, M. (2000). Crossing the borders: Investigating mathematics education in an international version of MILE. In K. Kumpulainen (Ed.), *In search of powerful learning environments for teacher education in the 21st century* (pp. 173-187). Oulu: Acta Univeristy Series, University of Oulu.

Dolk, M., den Hertog, J., & Gravemeijer, K. (2003). Using multimedia cases for educating the primary school mathematics teacher educator: A design study. *International Journal of Educational Research, 37*(2), 161-178.

Edwards, A. (2005). Relational agency: Learning to be a resourceful practitioner. *International Journal of Educational Research, 43*, 168-182.

Edwards, A. (2007). Relational agency in professional practice: A CHAT Analysis. *Actio: An International Journal of Human Activity Theory, 1*, 1-17.

Edwards, A., & D'Arcy, C. (2004). Relational agency and disposition in sociocultural accounts of learning to teach. *Educational Review, 56*, 147-155.

Edwards, A., & Protheroe, L. (2003). Learning to see in classrooms: What are student teachers learning about teaching and learning while learning to teach in schools? *British Educational Research Journal, 29*(2), 227-242.

Emirbayer, M., & Mische, A. (1998). What is agency? *American Journal of Sociology, 103*, 962-1023.

Engeström, Y. (2005). *Development, movement and agency: Breaking away into mycorrhizae activities.* Paper presented at the International Symposium 'Artefacts and Collectives: Situated Action and Activity Theory' (ARTCO), Lyon, 2005.

Engle, R.A., & Faux, R.B. (2006). Towards productive disciplinary engagement of prospective teachers in educational psychology: Comparing two methods of case-based instruction and teaching. *Educational Psychology, 1*, 1-22.

Fairclough, N. (1992). *Discourse and social change.* Cambridge: Polity Press.

Fisher, T., Higgins, C., & Loveless, A. (2006). *Teachers learning with digital technologies: A review of research and projects.* Bristol: Futurelab. Retrieved June 19, 2007, from http://www.futurelab.org.uk/resources/documents/lit_reviews/Teachers_Review.pdf

Giddens, A. (1991). *Modernity and self-identity: Self and society in late modern age.* Cornwall: Polity Press.

Greeno, J.G. (1997). On claims that answer the wrong questions. *Educational Researcher, 26*(1), 5-17.

Greeno, J.G. (2006). Authoritative, accountable positioning and connected, general knowing: progressive themes in understanding transfer. *The Journal of the Learning Sciences, 15*, 537-547.

Gudmundsdottir, S. (1995). The narrative nature of pedagogical content knowledge. In H. McEwan, & K. Egan (Eds.), *Narrative in teaching, learning and research* (pp. 24-38). New York: Teachers College Press.

Gumperz, J.J., & Hymes, D. (Eds.). (1972). *Directions in sociolinguistics: The ethnography of communication.* New York: Holt, Rinehart & Winston.

Hammerness, K.M. (2006). *Seeing through teachers' eyes: Professional ideals and classroom practices.* New York: Teachers College Press.

Hermans, H. (1996). Voicing the self: From information processing to dialogical interchange. *Psychological Bulletin, 119*, 31-50.

Hermans, H. (2001). The dialogical self: Toward a theory of personal and cultural positioning. *Culture & Psychology, 7*(3), 243-281.

Holland, D., Lachicotte, W., Skinner, D., & Cain, C. (1998). *Identity and agency in cultural worlds.* Cambridge, MA: Harvard University Press.

Ivanic, R. (1998). *Writing and identity. The discoursal construction of identity in academic writing.* Amsterdam: Benjamins.

Korthagen, F. (2001). A broader view of reflection. In F. Korthagen, J. Kessels, B. Koster, B. Lagrwerf, & T. Wubbels (Eds.), *Linking practice and theory: The pedagogy of realistic teacher education* (pp. 231-238). Mahwah, NJ: Lawrence Erlbaum Associates.

Kumpulainen, K. (2004). Helping teachers to frame constructivism as practice: The possibilities of case-based learning with digital media. In N. Hall, & D. Springate (Eds.), *Occasional papers of the European Teacher Education Network (ETEN)* (pp. 71-85). Greenwich: University of Greenwich Press.

Lampert, M., & Ball, D.L. (1998). *Teaching, multimedia, and mathematics. Investigations of real practice.* New York: Teachers College Press.

Lave, J., & Wenger, E. (1991). *Situated learning: Legitimate peripheral participation.* Cambridge: Cambridge University Press.

Lipponen, L. & Kumpulainen, K. (2011). Acting as accountable authors: Framing agency across teacher-student boundaries.

Mason, J. (2002). *Researching your own practice: The discipline of noticing.* London: Routledge-Falmer.

Merseth, K.K. (1996). Cases and case methods in teacher education. In J. Sikula (Ed.), *Handbook of research on teacher education* (2nd ed.) (pp. 722-744). New York: Macmillan.

Mitchell, C.J. (1984). Typicality and the case study. In R.F. Ellens (Ed.), *Ethnographic research: A guide to general conduct,* New York: Academic Press.

Moran, S., & John-Steiner, V. (2003). Creativity in the making. Vygotsky's contemporary contribution to the dialectic of creativity and development. In K. R. Sawyer, V. John-Steiner, S. Moran, R. J. Sternberg, D. H. Feldman, H. Gardner, J. Nakamura, & M. Csikszentmihalyi (Eds.), *Creativity and development* (pp. 61-90). Oxford, New York: Oxford University Press.

Opettajankoulutus 2020. (2007). [Teacher Education Report 2020]. Opetusministeriön työryhmämuistioita ja selvityksiä 2007:44. Opetusministeriö, koulutus- ja tiedepolitiikan osasto.

Packer, M. & Goicoechea, J. (2000) Sociocultural and constructivist theories of learning: Ontology, not just epistemology. *Educational Psychologist, 35*, 227-241.

Putnam, R.T., & Borko, H. (2000). What do new views of knowledge and thinking have to say about research on teacher learning? *Educational Researcher, 29*(1), 4-17.

Reeves, J. (2009). Teacher investment in learner identity. *Teaching and Teacher Education, 25*, 34-41.

Roth, W.-M., Tobin, K. Elmesky, R., Carambo, C., McNight, Y.-M., & Beers, J. (2004). Re/Making identities in the praxis of urban schooling: A cultural historical perspective. *Mind, Culture, and Activity, 11*, 48-69.

Santa Barbara Classroom Discourse Group (1992). Constructing literacy in classrooms: Literate action as social accomplishment. In H. Marshall (Ed.), *Redefining student learning: Roots of educational change* (pp. 119-150). Norwood, NJ: Ablex.

Schwartz, D. & Okita, S. (2009). *The productive agency in learning to learning by teaching.* http://aaalab.stanford.edu/papersProductive_Agency_in_Learning_by_Teaching.pdf. Retrieved 30 April 2009.

Shulman, L., & Shulman, J.H. (2004). How and what teachers learn: A shifting perspective. *Journal of Curriculum Studies, 36*(2), 257-271.

Toom, A. (2006). *Tacit pedagogical knowing: At the core of teacher's professionality.* Research Reports 276. University of Helsinki: Department of Applied Sciences of Education.

Virkkunen, J. (2006). Dilemmas in building shared transformative agency. *Activités, 3,* 19–42.

Vähäsantanen, K., & Billett, S. (2008). Negotiating professional identity: Vocational teachers' personal strategies in a reform context. In S. Billett, C. Harteis, & A. Eteläpelto (Eds.), *Emerging perspectives of workplace learning* (pp. 35-50). Rotterdam: Sense Publishers.

Wenger, E. (1998). *Communities of practice: Learning, meaning and identity.* Cambridge: Cambridge University Press.

Wertsch, J. (1991). *Voices of the mind: A sociocultural approach to mediated action.* Cambridge, MA: Harvard University Press.

Zeichner, K. (1996). Teachers as reflective practitioners and the democratization of school reform. In. K. Zeichner, S. Melnick, & M.L. Gomez (Eds.), *Currents of reform in preservice teacher education* (pp. 199-214). New York: Teachers College Press.

Zuckerman, G. (2007). On supporting children's initiatives. *Journal of Russian and East European Psychology, 45,* 9-42.

Kristiina Kumpulainen
Finnish National Board of Education
Finland

Auli Toom
University of Helsinki
Finland

Merja Saalasti
University of Oulu
Finland

ANNEMIEKE ENSING, GEERDINA VAN DER AALSVOORT AND
PAUL VAN GEERT

13. HOW DYNAMIC PATTERNS OF TEACHER-CHILD INTERACTION CAN PROVIDE INSIGHT IN THE LEARNING POTENTIAL OF FIVE YEAR OLDS

INTRODUCTION

This chapter deals with the meaning of the patterns that emerge during instruction for understanding a child's learning potential. For a long time the potential to learn was assessed by means of dynamic assessment (DA). This procedure has now been available as a diagnostic procedure for well over thirty years, with ideas related to its development ranging back to the beginning of the twentieth century (Van der Aalsvoort & Lidz, 2007). DA is a generic term for procedures that embed intervention within the ongoing assessment, and that usually include a pretest-training-posttest format that directly links assessment to intervention. As the child engages in the assessment task, the assessor can observe the child's strengths and weaknesses. By looking at the learning processes during the course of problem-solving, the examiner can discover how the child learns and how the child can best be instructed. Thus, both the child's current levels of functioning as well as responsiveness to intervention are tapped. The processes, however, that are responsible for responsiveness are still unclear. With responsiveness we refer to questions such as: Is it verbal instruction that evokes a child's response or are non-verbal behaviors responsible for his reaction to instruction? The current study tries to answer these questions by means of a naturalistic observation of the interaction between two pupils and their teacher.

Since our investigation was carried out with two young Dutch students we will first describe the Dutch primary education system. Next, we will explain how competence level of young students is determined, and what the meaning is of dynamic assessment of learning potential. In addition, we will present learning potential as a dynamic system that allows insight in the actual emergence of learning processes. The findings of two students are then described in full detail to illustrate how dynamic patterns emerging during instruction are probably supposedly responsible for learning processes to take place.

E. Hjörne et al. (eds.), Learning, Social Interaction and Diversity – Exploring Identities in School Practices, 189–202.

SHORT HISTORY OF PRIMARY EDUCATION IN THE NETHERLANDS

In the last two decades there has been an increase in attention for preschool education for Dutch children. Before 1985 four and five year old children went to Kindergarten for two years and changed schools when they were six years old to start the first year of primary school. This change did not always go smoothly; some children had problems with the transition from informal learning to formal instruction and had a hard time living up to the expectations of the first year of primary education. Therefore, there was not always an uninterrupted course of learning. In 1985 a new Act on primary education was passed and an integration of Kindergarten and formal education was realized. This resulted in continuous education from Grade 1 to Grade 8. Children may start primary school at the age of 4 but it is obligatory only at the age of 5. Children leave primary school at the age of 12. The Act states that education is tuned to the developmental potential of the child and will be adapted in such a way that each child will be able to develop uninterruptedly. According to Van der Aalsvoort and Ruijsenaars (2002) primary education strives to offer the young child a coherent educational system by means of early detection and systematic and continuous guidance of the child.

Nowadays 90 percent of all children in The Netherlands enter primary school at the age of 4. Grade 1 and 2 can be characterized as Kindergarten and formal education on reading, writing and arithmetic starts in Grade 3. The students are then six years old. There is no national curriculum in Kindergarten and primary school, although general educational goals are defined and evaluated on a regular basis by the School Inspection Board for both regular and special education. Kindergarten and primary school education is financed by the Ministry of Education, Culture, and Science. As the Dutch educational system became more and more differentiated, special education in particular, two new Acts have forced changes of the educational system. For this chapter we will describe the first Act which came into force in 1998 as the *Act on Primary Education (APE)*. This act includes a movement called 'Going to school together again'. The Act refers to a change in organization of schools. One main school-board includes the boards of several regular primary schools within a specific region and the board of one school for special primary education for students with behavioral and or learning problems. The board follows the regulations with respect to identifying children with special educational needs. Access to special education is the result of a referral procedure by a committee that is part of the school-board. The procedure includes collection of information from an educational psychologist, a medical doctor, a social worker, and a school report with respect to academic progress of the child. The information is exchanged and discussed in the committee, and a decision is made about either referral to the special school or keeping the child in regular education while being offered help from the special school. Teachers can thus profit from expertise that is offered through consultation by their colleagues from the special school. Although the APE aims at decreasing the number of students referred to special schools, it does not explicitly require inclusion policy (Van der Aalsvoort, 2007).

Right from their entrance into the Dutch school system, mostly at the age of 4, it becomes clear that some children have difficulties in learning. These are not referred to as 'learning impairments', as this term is related to the formal learning tasks which are offered from Grade 3. These children do not seem to profit from their new environment and they are experiencing difficulties with the activities which prepare them for a formal school career. We define this group of at-risk students in line with Elliott and Hall's definition:

> children who manifest some or all of the following behavioral characteristics: difficulty in using language fluently and effectively in a range of situations, inability to attend to and persevere with tasks and activities, lack of purposefulness, imagination and variety in play, lack of initiative; lack of "normal" social and emotional maturity. (Elliott & Hall, 1997, p. 198)

In young children various developmental domains (e.g. language, cognition, play etcetera) are closely intertwined. Stagnation in one domain, can therefore have an immediate effect on another domain (Van der Aalsvoort, 2006). Since these problems can have an ongoing negative effect on further development, they need to be recognized as soon as possible. The reason for the difficulties these children experience, can be found in their relatively poor ability to profit from instruction, they are showing what is called a low *learning potential*. In the next session we will discuss how learning potential can be assessed.

THE NEED TO REVEAL LEARNING POTENTIAL

A common way for assessing the competence or skills of young children is by the use of static tests, for instance intelligence tests for establishing a child's level of intelligence. Static tests tend to get a lot of criticism. Resing (2006) lists the following: Static tests only measure what a child has learned up to the moment of testing. Moreover, the knowledge level of a five-year old is very dependent on the environment in which he grows up, such as socio-economic background, type of parenting etcetera. This may cause problems with children from ethnic minorities: Their language development is more complicated as they learn a mother tongue that is different from the language in school. They often end up with a lower score on language tests than they would have when they had grown up in different circumstances. Moreover, static test scores do not indicate what went wrong during learning processes. The scores do not allow process analysis, whereas in the case of learning difficulties it is of great importance to know exactly how and where in the process the problems arise and continue. A further problem with static testing is that especially in young children intra-individual variability in task behavior is common even within one test. The results of the study of Tunteler, Pronk and Resing (2008) for example show considerable inter-and intra-individual variability in the use of analogical strategies in geometric tasks by 6-8 year olds.

As a consequence of this intra-variability a child tested at one point in time, may achieve a different score when tested at another moment. Findings like these make it unconvincing that test scores achieved this way are reliable and have predictive validity for individual children. More valuable than information about what a child has learned up to a certain moment, is information about what a child *can* learn, i.e. information about the child's learning potential. The construct of learning potential is often based on the socio-cultural theory of higher mental functions (Vygotsky, 1978). The zone of proximal development, one of the major concepts in this theory, is the distance between a child's developmental level as determined by independent problem solving, and the level of potential development as determined through problem solving under adult guidance or in collaboration with more capable peers. This distance corresponds with the child's learning potential.

The zone of proximal development is a social construct. It only appears in social interaction, as a product of that interaction. It becomes visible in the form of a process in which the knowledge construction moves from the interpersonal into the intrapersonal plane within the child as learner. This process is the process of internalization, which is the core process of learning in which the transition from proximal development to actual development takes place (Verhofstadt-Denève, Van Geert & Vyt, 2003). The question is how to evoke and measure a child's learning potential. Resing (1990) defines learning potential as the way in which an individual is able to profit from instruction. Dynamic testing is a way to reveal learning potential.

Dynamic assessment (DA) has now been available as a diagnostic procedure for well over thirty years, but its development ranges back as early as the beginning of the twentieth century. Applications of this assessment model with very young children are more scarce than those developed for older learners, and development of procedures for this population is a continuing area of need. DA is a generic term for procedures that embed intervention within the ongoing assessment, and that usually include a pretest-training-posttest format that directly links assessment to intervention. As the child engages in the assessment task, the assessor can observe the child's strengths and weaknesses. By looking at the learning processes during the course of problem-solving, the examiner can discover how the child learns and how the child can best be instructed. Thus, both the child's current levels of functioning as well as responsiveness to intervention are tapped.

Dynamic assessment (DA) refers to the *format*, and not to the content of the testing procedure. Static, combined with dynamic learning assessments, are better predictors of the abilities of individual children than either one of these measures alone, reflecting what Vygotsky (1978) referred to as the zones of actual and proximal development that are both required to have a full and complex understanding of the child's functioning.

DA is most appropriately used when the assessment questions concern responsiveness of the learner, the nature of processes that characterize the learner, and generation of ideas for potentially useful interventions. Other assessment approaches fail to consider the nature of the relationship between the assessor and the child or to use this relationship to generate instruction-relevant insights or strategies. Insights into the behaviors of the assessor that relate to responsiveness of the learner are important for providing linkages between the assessment and the classroom (Van der Aalsvoort & Lidz, 2007).

However, the dynamics of learning processes are not into consideration during DA. Many questions remain about the way the zone of proximal development emerges as a reciprocal process between assessor and assessed individual. Moreover, these dynamics are the main source of information with regard to its consequences for classroom instruction.

Evoking Learning Potential as Part of a Dynamic System

As described before, instruction is a highly dynamic process. In this process the teacher cannot be seen as the independent variable, with the child and its competences as dependent variable. Both, teacher and child influence each other mutually and continuously, with processes in the form of iterations with non-linear effects and self organization as a consequence. This implies that the ability to profit from instruction is not a static property or variable along which children can be compared. Instruction is dynamic process between teacher and child and therefore different for every child and teacher dyad. The dynamic nature of the process poses a methodological problem in that the standardization of instruction conditions is required for measurement. Trying to overcome this methodological problem by standardizing instruction conditions, results in complete ignorance of the influence the child normally exerts on the instruction it receives and thereby on the expression of the learning potential one wishes to measure.

Viewing instruction as a highly dynamic process, implies that the definition of learning potential as the way in which an individual is able to profit from instruction needs elaboration. The fact that both the child and the instructor play a great part in the dynamics of instruction and thereby in evoking the learning potential of the child, needs to be expressed in the new definition: *learning potential is the way in which a child is able to profit from instruction as it arises within the dynamics between teacher and child.*

This dynamic definition, transforms learning potential into a contextual concept. Therefore, we state that in order to know more about the learning potential of a child, the focus has to be on what happens during the dynamic process of instruction. Four main factors are expected to be of importance within this dynamics of instruction and thereby in evoking learning potential. The first one is the way the child is able to elicit scaffolding behavior from the teacher. Which child behavior reveals to the teacher that the child needs help? Some children for example may simply ask for help, whereas others start talking about completely irrelevant subjects. Therefore another important factor is the way in which the teacher is able to recognize this scaffolding eliciting behavior. Is the teacher able to interpret the behavior of the child as asking for help? The next factor in the dynamics of instruction is the way in which the teacher is able to adapt the instruction to the child's needs in such a way that the child will profit to the maximum. The last important factor is the way in which the child is able to deal with different kinds of support; does the child need a very specific kind of instruction, or is it able to profit from different sorts of help? Figure 1 shows the four factors and the way they influence each other.

The model in Figure 1 functions as a framework for the analyses of theoretically meaningful patterns with regard to learning potential as a dynamic system. This framework allows insight in the actual emergence of learning processes. In order to learn more about the dynamic process between teacher and child during instruction, we have to focus on the principles and patterns of behavior that occur during this process and how they relate to the factors as described above.

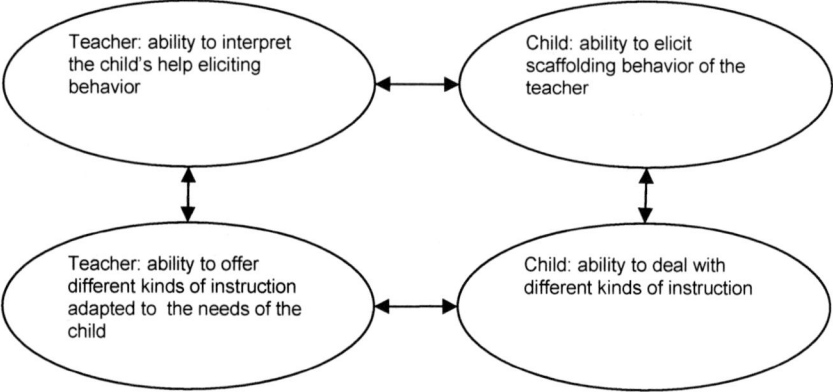

Figure 1. The four main factors in the dynamics of instruction

In this pilot study, we will show how sequences of behavior that occur during the teacher-child interaction can be analyzed. We wish to reveal whether specific behavior of the teacher is followed by specific behavior of the child and vice versa. The specific teaching behavior we shall focus on is the teachers dividing a problem-solving strategy into smaller parts in order to make the task easier for the child. The question we pose is: *What is the probability that the dividing strategy of the teacher leads to a correct answer from the child?* The second question is whether the likelihood that this teaching strategy occurs depends on the teacher child dyads in question: *Does the teacher use dividing a problem-solving strategy into smaller parts more often in instructing one child than in instructing another child?*

In order to look for patterns within the dynamics of instruction, we need a coding system which allows us to specify separate units of behavior in interaction during instruction. Such units can then be analyzed in terms of frequency and succession and provide insight in the dynamics of instruction.

METHOD

Design

Two video-tapes of instruction during a curriculum related task were observed and scored by means of a categorical system. The first tape showed the interaction of a teacher and a five year old boy (12.07 min), the second tape showed the interaction between the same teacher and a five year old girl (13.32 min). The nature of the study is merely qualitative and exploratory, but also includes description and hypothesis testing.

Procedure

The teacher volunteered to participate in this study after being approached by the researcher. After the parents' consent for the children's participation, the teacher was asked to select two children for participation in this study. According to the teacher one child was perceived as a weak student and the other one as a strong student. The task that was used allowed instruction to take place and the instruction was recorded when the teacher worked with each child in an empty classroom. A coding system was developed and tested in terms of reliability. The video tapes were transcribed and scored with the coding system. The scores were collected in the program Mediacoder 2008 (Bos & Steenbeek, 2008). Analyses were done in Excel.

Participants

The teacher was an approximately 50 year old female with many years of teaching experience. She worked full time with the class which contained 25 students. Lena was a five year old girl, who was perceived by the teacher as a fairly weak student. Leo was a five year old boy, who was perceived by the teacher as a fairly strong student. Both children visited primary school since they were four years old. The teacher knew the children since Grade 2. At the time of the study the children had almost completed Grade 2. The socioeconomic background of the students was similar. Both children had parents from a low socioeconomic background as most of the students from this school.

Materials

Curriculum related task
The task that each child had to perform with the teacher was a board game. This task represented a common assignment for children in Grade 2 according to the

teacher. The task includes a board that is divided into sixteen equal empty squares. In addition there are sixteen small cardboard pictures with figures to put on the empty squares. On the upper side of the board is a row with four figures and on the left side of the board is a row with four figures. The child has to combine the figures above and beside the board and then decide which picture suits the combination of information and is to put this picture on the empty square. Each child received instructions about the strategy required to complete the task.

Video recordings
The recordings were carried out by using one camera on a stand.

Coding system
Since there was no fitting coding system available, a coding system was developed in order to classify separate behaviors that occurred within the interaction between child and teacher. Three researchers looked at an instruction video separately in order to distinguish as many behavioral units as possible. Afterwards they compared and discussed their findings to reach a consensus about the categories. For both teacher and child three main categories were defined: Verbal behavior, Non-verbal behavior, and Visual behavior. The first two categories were chosen since all behaviors can be classified as either verbal or non-verbal. Visual behavior, i.e. looking towards or scanning a particular visual target, is a form of non-verbal behavior. It occurs frequently in combination with other non-verbal behaviors. Therefore, it was decided to score it as a separate category in order to avoid scoring problems (Veldmans, 2008).

The coding system distinguishes originators of the behavior (teacher and child); form aspects of the behavior and functional aspects of the behavior. The form aspects refer to expressive behaviors, which can be either verbal or non-verbal, and visual behavior, such as visual checking. The functional aspects refer to functions of the behaviors. Main functions of the teacher's behavior are to inform and present the task to the child, to help the child by structuring, by dividing into subtasks, by reinforcing the child, by checking the child's problem solving etcetera. These functions can be fulfilled by actions in various forms (verbal, non-verbal and visual). The main functions of the child's behavior are to solve the task, to ask for help and for additional information, to perform required actions and so forth, which can take a verbal, non-verbal and visual form.

Mediacoder
Mediacoder is a computer program, which allows the researcher to watch and analyze video material (Bos & Steenbeek, 2008). While watching, the observed behaviors can be scored as characters (letters). Thus, a file of codes becomes available and the program exports the codes directly into an Excel file. The format of an Excel file enables further analyses of the data.

Analyses

Based on the two pilot recordings a coding system was developed. The two pilot recordings were then scored with the developed coding system by two different people. Based on these scores the inter observer reliability was computed. The inter observer reliability for the six behavior groups in the coding system was as following: Teacher verbal 0.80, Teacher non-verbal 0.91, Teacher visual 0.64, Child verbal 0.89, Child non-verbal 0.83 and Child visual 0.91. Reliability was defined in terms of percentage of simple (dis)agreement among coders. The likelihood that the observed agreement could result from chance was calculated by means of a random permutation test, which is a widely used form of Monte Carlo analysis. All agreement scores were highly reliable, i.e. it is very unlikely that they are based on similarity due to chance.

Statistical Procedure

Data exported by the Mediacoder consist of columns specifying lists of behavioral codes and the times at which the behavior occurred. In order to prepare these data for visual inspection followed by statistical processing of the time series, the data columns are transformed into time series. For instance, an observation lasting 800 seconds is transformed into a series of 800 steps of one-second, each second specifying a particular behavioral code (or none, if no such code occurred).

It is common for teachers to divide a strategy into smaller parts in order to make the task easier for the child. To investigate *if dividing a strategy into parts is followed by a correct answer from the child in most of the time*, it was observed whether category 'D' (dividing the strategy) was followed by category 'a' (correct answer by the child) within a time-frame of 10 seconds.

To answer the question whether the teacher makes more use of dividing a strategy into smaller parts in instructing one child than in instructing another child, it was counted how many episodes of category D, for division, appeared in both tapes. Subsequently statistical testing was carried out by means of a Monte Carlo analysis, based on the null-hypothesis that the observed differences were accidental.

RESULTS

Figure 2 shows that in instructing the boy, the teacher made use of dividing the strategy into parts seven times whereas in instructing the girl she made us of this category 23 times. This difference is significant with a p-value of .001. This means that the teacher made more often use of dividing the strategy into parts to make the task easier in teaching the girl than she did in teaching the boy. Figure 2 also shows that for the boy dividing the strategy into parts was followed by a correct answer five times out of seven (71 %) whereas for the girl this category was only followed by a correct answer eleven times out of 23 (48%).

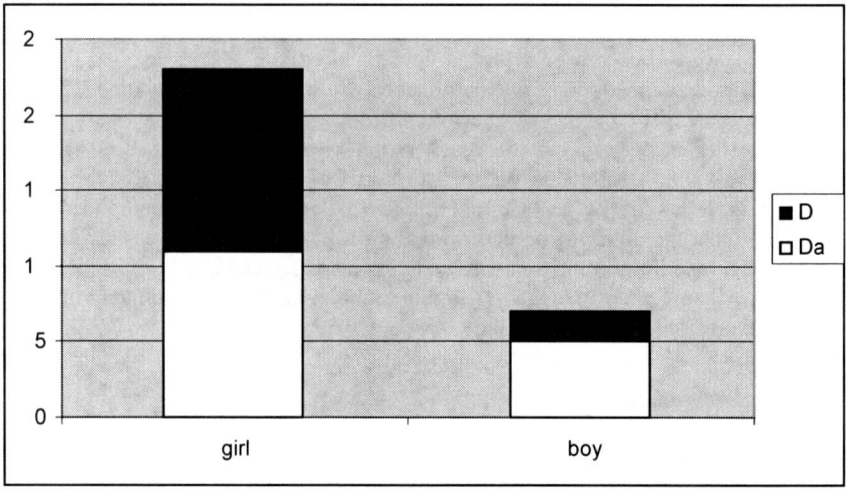

Figure 2. Prevalence of dividing the strategy followed by a right answer (Da) and dividing the strategy not followed by a right answer (D) for the boy and the girl

Figure 3 shows the prevalence of dividing the strategy by the teacher followed by a correct answer of the boy (line 3), the prevalence of a correct answer not preceded by dividing the strategy into parts (line 2), and the prevalence of dividing strategy into parts not followed by a correct answer (line 1) for the boy over time.

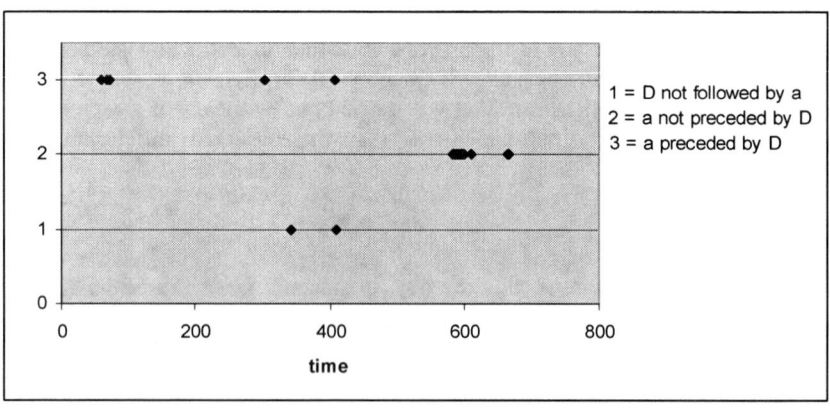

Figure 3. The prevalence of patterns D-not a; a-not D and D-a for the boy over time the course of 800 seconds

Figure 4 shows the prevalence of dividing the strategy by the teacher followed by a correct answer of the girl (line 3), the prevalence of a correct answer not preceded by dividing the strategy into parts (line 2), and the prevalence of dividing strategy into parts not followed by a correct answer (line 1) for the girl over time.

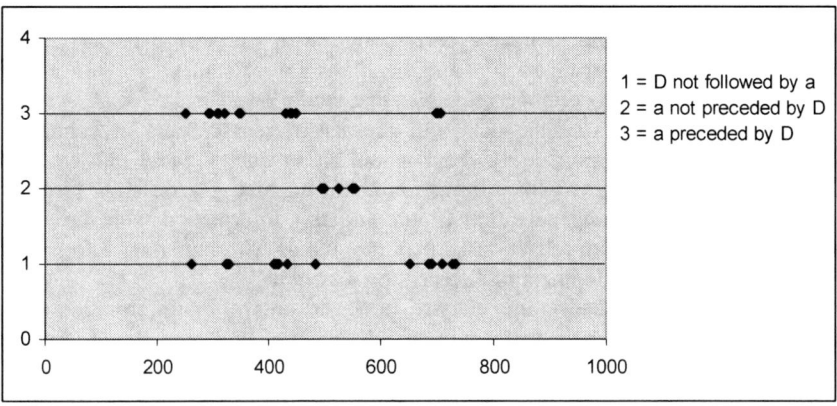

Figure 4. The prevalence of patterns D-not a; a-not D and D-a for the girl over the course of 800 seconds. The prevalence of category D (dividing the strategy by the teacher) followed by category 'a' (correct answer) for the girl over time

CONCLUSIONS AND DISCUSSION

The two case studies presented before illustrate that it is possible to analyze and compare sequences of behavior as they occur within teacher-child interaction during instruction of a curriculum related task. A significant difference was observed in the use of dividing the strategy into parts in order to make the task easier by the teacher in instructing the boy and the girl. The teacher made much more use of this category in teaching the girl, who was considered a weak student, than in teaching the boy, the strong student. Also it was shown that in case of the boy, using the category led to a correct answer in 71% of the time whereas for the girl this was the case in 48% of the time only. Findings like these show in a reliable way how differently instruction situations can develop for two teacher-child dyads who are working on the same task. The fact that the teacher as well as the children in this study are typical and representative of their kind, suggests that analyzing similar data will further support the discovery of different patterns of behavior in teacher-child interactions.

Nevertheless, we expect that within the individual diversity of these behavioral sequences there will be common principles for most dyads. Figure 2 shows such a common principle of instruction, described before as scaffolding (Van Geert &

Steenbeek, 2005). First, the teacher offers help by dividing the strategy into parts which is followed by a correct answer from the boy most of the time. Over time this helping behavior declines and the boy gives the right answers by himself. The patterns shown by the girl are more diverse. She is offered more helping behavior by dividing the strategy but only half of the time this is followed by a correct answer from the girl. Moreover, the helping behavior does not decrease over time. Apparently the teacher is deciding along the way that the girl needs more help than the boy. Moreover, this behavior corresponds with the fact that the teacher perceives the boy as a strong student and the girl as a weak student.

Apart from potential common principles that would occur in almost all dyads, it could be that analyses of the data will reveal different clusters of behavioral sequences and that almost every dyad would fit in one of these clusters. The clusters might provide us with information about qualitatively different forms of the dynamics of learning potential. Combining this information with the actual results on the curriculum related tasks may provide us with important information with regard to the development of intervention programs.

The example described in this chapter, however, only offers information about two elements of a complicated chain of interactions. We have shown that the teacher behaves differently on one aspect: dividing the strategy for the task into parts in teaching the boy and the girl. We also showed that the two children respond differently to the instructing behavior of the teacher. At the same time the teacher responds differently to the children. When we apply these observed behavioral chains to our theoretical model we see that we have gained some information about the complicated process of interaction but that there still remain a lot of questions. We know that the teacher has interpreted certain behaviors of the children as help eliciting behavior, since she decided to adapt the instruction to what she perceived to be the needs of the child. She did this by means of dividing the strategy into smaller parts in order to make it easier. We do not know yet which child behavior preceded this instructional behavior and if there is intra-individual and inter-individual variability in this help eliciting behavior. Also it is unclear if all help eliciting behavior of the child is perceived as such by the teacher. In order to answer these questions, we have to start by theoretically defining what kind of behavior can be classified as help eliciting behavior. We expect that different, passive and active forms of help eliciting behavior will be revealed, which have to be interpreted by the teacher correctly in order to allow optimal learning potential to be revealed. What the current data analysis show is that the offered help was in most cases well adjusted to the needs of the boy, whereas in case of the girl it did not lead to the expected result. It would be interesting to investigate whether the teacher has also offered different kinds of help besides dividing the strategy, and whether other types of help have indeed led to a correct answer.

In other words, the study enabled the development of interesting tools to examine the interactions, but in order to gain real insight in the dynamics between teacher and child during instruction, it has to be further investigated which behaviours in the coding system are relevant in terms of the model as described in

Figure 1. When combined with information about if and how there is a relation between these dynamics and the student's actual level of achievement, these tools will hopefully provide us with valuable knowledge about how teachers perceive a child's potential to learn.

REFERENCES

Bos, J., & Steenbeek, H.W. (2008). Media Coder 2008. A simple application for coding behavior within media files. Dutch Manual. Groningen: Groningen University, Faculty of Developmental Psychology.

Elliott, A., & Hall, N. (1997). The impact of self-regulatory teaching strategies on "At-Risk" preschoolers' mathematical learning in a computer-mediated environment. *Journal of Computing in Childhood Education, 8*, 187-198.

Resing, W.C.M. (1990). *Intelligentie en leerpotentieel. Een onderzoek naar het leerpotentieel van jonge leerlingen uit het basis- en speciaal onderwijs* [Intelligence and learning potential. A study about the learning potential of young students from regular and special primary education]. Amsterdam/Lisse: Swets & Zeitlinger.

Resing, W.C.M. (2006). *Het potentieel van dynamisch testen* [The potential of dynamic testing]. Oratie. Leiden: Universiteitsdrukkerij.

Tunteler, E., Pronk, C.M.E., & Resing, W.C.M. (2008). Inter- and intra-individual variability in the process of change in the use of analogical strategies to solve geometric tasks in children: A Microgenetic analysis. *Learning and Individual Differences, 18*, 44-60.

Van der Aalsvoort, G.M. (2006). *Jonge leerlingen met een risicovolle ontwikkeling. Achtergronden, diagnose en behandeling* [Young students developing at-risk: Backgrounds, diagnostic decision-making, and treatment]. Leuven: Acco.

Van der Aalsvoort, G.M. (2007). Moving forward? Addressing the needs of young at-risk-students in the Dutch educational system. *Early Childhood Education, 84*(1), 20-24.

Van der Aalsvoort, G.M., & Lidz, C.S. (2007). A cross-cultural validation study of the Application of Cognitive Functions Scales, a dynamic assessment procedure, with Dutch first grade students from regular primary schools. *Journal of Applied School Psychology, 24*, 91-108.

Van der Aalsvoort, G.M., & Ruijsenaars, A.J.J.M. (Eds.) (2002). *Jonge risicokinderen bij de start van het onderwijs. Een succesvolle aanpak door integratie?* [Young children developing at-risk. A successful approach by integration?]. Leuven: Acco.

Van Geert, P., & Steenbeek, H.W. (2005). The dynamics of scaffolding. *New ideas in Psychology, 23*, 115-128.

Veldmans, H.E.R. (2008). The connection between eye contact and confirmations and compliments. Master thesis, internal publication. Groningen: Department of Developmental Psychology.

Verhofstadt-Denève, L., Van Geert, P., & Vyt, A. (2003). *Handboek ontwikkelingspsychologie. Grondslagen en theorieën* [Handbook on developmental psychology. Foundations and theories]. Houten: Bohn Stafleu Van Loghum.

Vygotsky, L.S. (1978). *Mind in society. The development of higher psychological processes*. Cambridge, MA: Harvard University Press.

Annemieke Ensing
Department of Developmental Psychology
Groningen University

ANNEMIEKE ENSING, GEERDINA VAN DER AALSVOORT AND PAUL VAN DER GEERT

Geerdina M. van der Aalsvoort
School of Education
Saxion University of Applied Science Deventer

Paul van Geert
Department of Developmental Psychology
Groningen University

MARCELA COSTANZI, NÚRIA GORGORIÓ AND
MONTSERRAT PRAT

14. PRE-SERVICE TEACHERS' REPRESENTATIONS OF SCHOOL MATHEMATICS AND IMMIGRANT CHILDREN[1]

WHY STUDY TEACHERS' REPRESENTATIONS?

Contextualizing the Study

Catalonia (capital city Barcelona), located in the north-eastern part of the Iberian Peninsula, is one of the 17 autonomous communities into which the Spanish state is organized. It has two official languages, Catalan and Castilian (Spanish). Because language is one of the defining features of Catalan culture and identity, it is the official language of instruction, even though Spanish is often used as well.

In Spain education is compulsory and free from age 6 to age 16. Primary school corresponds to ages 6-12, and compulsory secondary school to ages 12-16. Students who complete their compulsory secondary education successfully receive a graduation diploma and may continue their secondary education for another two years. Those whose grades are insufficient to obtain the diploma receive a school-leaving certificate, and may go on to the first level of vocational training. Post-compulsory secondary education consists of two tracks: Mid-level vocational and technical training and the baccalaureate, which prepares students for university or for high-level technical training. The legal age for starting work in Spain is 16 years, but the chances of getting a job, or a good one, are strongly connected with gaining school certificates.

In the context of our research work, we use the word 'immigrant' with a restrictive meaning consciously retrieved from a common social representation. Thus, by immigrant we do not refer to any foreign person that comes to live permanently in our country, but one that does so in particular conditions. When we refer to immigrant students, we are not speaking of the children of highly skilled professionals who come to work at the high end of the occupational hierarchy and are commonly named "foreigners". These children do not normally attend

[1] The research reported in this chapter is supported by the Dirección General de Investigación, Ministerio de Ciencia e Innovación (SEJ2007-60111/EDUC), and the Agència de Gestió d'Ajuts Universitaris i de Recerca, Generalitat de Catalunya (2007ARAFI1 00022).

E. Hjörne et al. (eds.), Learning, Social Interaction and Diversity – Exploring Identities in School Practices, 203–221.

public schools. In our work, we use the words "immigrant students" to refer to the children of those who come to Spain for the purposes of seeking employment at the lower end of the scale where native workers shun jobs that are difficult or demanding or carry little prestige. Thus, in fact we are referring among others to Morocan, Ecuadorian, Romanian, Colombian or Chinese children and not to Japanese, German or British.

Many immigrant schoolchildren, even those who have learned to speak Catalan well and have been partially educated in Catalan primary schools, experience difficulty later in compulsory secondary school. Moreover, at the baccalaureate level, and to an even greater extent at university, immigrant students, or students born in Catalonia to immigrant families, are rare. That is especially true when their academic path includes mathematics.

Earlier studies by members of the EMiCS[2] research group (Burgos, 2008; Burgos, Gorgorió, Prat & Santesteban, 2009; Gorgorió & Abreu, 2009; Gorgorió & Prat, 2009; Santesteban, 2006) uncovered numerous examples of how mathematics teachers' social representations may lead them to 1) ignore the contributions of some students; 2) distribute opportunities for students to participate in classroom activity in an unequal way; 3) offer some students the possibility of participating in classroom activities at very different levels of mathematical complexity; and 4) attribute mathematical identities to students in an *a priori* fashion.

Ronnie's Story

In what follows, the case of Ronnie will serve to illustrate how teachers' social representations mediate practices in the mathematics classroom, conditioning the possibilities of student participation, legitimating certain ways of learning, and favouring the development of certain mathematical identities.

Ronnie came to Barcelona at the age of 9 from Ecuador,[3] where he was born and attended school regularly. We met him when he was 16, since he is one of the participants in an ongoing study aimed at understanding the transition processes of immigrant students learning mathematics in Catalan schools. To date we have

---

[2] The EMiCS group – Educació Matemàtica i Context Sociocultural (Mathematics Education and its Sociocultural Context) – is recognized by the Direcció General de Recerca of the Generalitat de Catalunya (the research office of the Catalan autonomous government) as a Consolidated Research Group (2005SGR-00211 and 2009SGR-00590). Its aim is to develop and explore the explanatory potential of theories that enable a better understanding of the experience of immigrant schoolchildren in the mathematics classroom.

[3] Ecuadorians represent the second largest immigrant population in Catalonia. 3.93% of children attending Catalan public schools are of Ecuadorian origin. As with most students of Latin American origin in Catalan schools, the Ecuadorians have a variant of Spanish as their home language. At primary education, they represent 4.55% of the total number of students and 1.7% of the total number of foreign students; at compulsory secondary education they are 5.44%, of the total school population and 2.7% of the total number of foreign students, while at the baccalaureate they represent 2.96% and 1.2% of the foreign students. Unfortunately, we have found no data of how many of them are successful in the university entrance examinations. Retrieved from http://www.gencat.cat/dasc/publica/butlletiIMMI/xifres4/educacio-4.htm on 27th April 2010.

interviewed 33 Ecuadorian students in compulsory secondary school. In one of these schools, we have worked with 15 boys and girls, Ronnie among them, and their mathematics teachers.

In the interviews we conducted, Marta, Ronnie's mathematics teacher, told us repeatedly that she did not consider her students' place of origin to be relevant information. However, although she said that all students are equal, in response to our questions, she described Ecuadorian students as "not hard workers, unmotivated, like other students their age. They're not up to grade level, but they're good kids." Marta has a variety of strategies for "helping her students", and among these are extra points for doing their homework on time, taking notes in class, or keeping their notebook in order. She says that she will explain "tricks" for getting the right answer to the exercises as many times as necessary and that she makes them repeat tests until they pass. She told us that in her mathematics class "there's no room for activities that are challenging, mathematically speaking. They're too weak; we can only do exercises if our goal is to get the students to pass. We can't do problems." Her students confirm what Marta has told us. As observers of this situation, we ask ourselves what has happened to the higher-level classroom activities that are necessary to guarantee not only equal access to education, but equal access to quality education.

At age 16, Ronnie is now in the third year of the four years of compulsory secondary education, one year behind where he should be. He told us that "when I got here I couldn't talk" – by which he means speaking Catalan – and that "since I was not up to grade level in mathematics because I came from Ecuador", he was placed in a class a year behind where he should have been according to his age. He speaks Catalan well and says he wants to go to university, although he understands that it will require hard work. Despite this, although he still has three more years to complete, he also believes that "since I'm not good enough in math, I won't be able to pass the entrance exam to go to university."

Ronnie is an adolescent like many of his contemporaries who were born in Barcelona. Despite having spent eight years in the Catalan public school system, however, he is still described as working below grade level in mathematics because he is of Ecuadorian origin. He accepts this at its face value and doubts his ability to get into university. Where is the gap in the educational system into which he has fallen? Why is it that after so many years Ronnie is still lagging behind in mathematics? Is Ronnie truly incapable of learning real mathematics, not just doing routine exercises? What happened to the higher-level mathematical activities the schools should have made available to him, and to all students? Could the answer be that, from the very beginning, Ronnie was assigned an identity of "low mathematical ability"? Are we dealing with a representation that operates as a self-fulfilling prophecy? Are we all lost in representations?

Representations, Transitions, and Identities

Ronnie's trajectory as a mathematics student can be explained from several perspectives. In this section we will explain how the reigning social representations

205

in the context of school mathematics shape the possibilities and limitations of the immigrant students learning process understood as a transition process.

Social representations constitute an interpretive framework (Moscovici, 1984; Zittoun, Duveen, Gillespie, Ivinson, & Psaltis, 2003) that allows us to impose meaning on and organize reality, both social and physical, and to relate to other persons and groups. They arise out of interpersonal communication and regulate interactions within groups and between groups, and mediate the processes through which we interpret what is happening around us and act in our surroundings.

Social representations theory offers a way of understanding the social construction of reality that takes into account both the cognitive and the social dimensions of this construction (Ibañez, 1988). Identifying the representations surrounding social phenomena is an approach that allows us to understand how persons both construct and are constructed by social reality through processes of communication and interaction. Social representations theory is particularly useful for understanding phenomena related to the teaching and learning of mathematics in classrooms in which immigrant pupils are present (Abreu & Elbers, 2005; Gorgorió & Abreu, 2009).

Among the functions of social representations Abric (1994) includes the following: 1) knowledge of reality through pre-coding and integration of information into a common frame of reference that is consistent in the values, social norms and practices of the group; 2) definition of identity and group belonging, and identification and positioning in relation to other groups; 3) guidance for forms of action and social practices through definition of the purpose of a given situation, production of expectations and anticipations, and definition of what is normative and counter-normative; and 4) justification of opinions and actions in regard to people and objects and, on a more general level, the maintenance of social differentiation.

We understand Ronnie's schooling in Catalonia as a transition process. Transitions originate in changing contexts of social practice, changes in persons, or changes in the relations between persons and objects (Zittoun, 2007). Transitions require processes of adjustment to new life circumstances and involve multiple changes in frames of reference and meanings. Changes require people to modify routines and interpretations, explore new possibilities, and develop new ways of acting and interacting. Social representations, as a means of constructing reality, have a special impact on the transition processes of immigrant students, in particular on their processes of learning mathematics and the construction of mathematical identities.

In this chapter, we approach the processes of mathematics learning by immigrant students as transition processes. These involve new contexts of mathematical practice, different relationships with both persons and knowledge, and different ways of understanding actions and interactions in the classroom. Transition processes involve the reconstruction of identities, construction of knowledge, and negotiation of meanings between persons and across contexts (Zittoun, 2006, 2007). In school transitions, students' difficulties are often related to processes of attribution of meaning to the learning situation, and to processes of identity reconstruction.

Transitions do not depend solely on the individual experiencing them, since they are shaped by social, representations, valorisations, and expectations surrounding the role, success and skills of each of the persons involved. In the context of school mathematics practice, transition processes are co-constructed. Together, the various classroom participants reconstruct the meanings attributed to different persons, situations and mathematical objects (Gorgorió, Planas & Vilella, 2002). Besides the students themselves, in the processes of reconstruction of identities, construction of knowledge, and creation of meaning, other significant persons are involved, among whom the teacher is possibly the most important.

In the particular case of mathematics education in diverse classrooms, Zevenbergen (2008) argues that the knowledge teachers have about their students and their cultural background is a determining factor in school success among minority students. Mulat and Arcavi (2009) analyze the successful school trajectories of 5 Israeli students of Ethiopian origin in order to identify the elements the students interpreted as facilitating their academic trajectories. Among other elements, the students pointed to those linked to their immediate academic surroundings, in particular the teacher. Similarly, Tangen (2009) argues that the way in which teachers regard each student has a significant impact on the quality of the children's lives at school and on their motivation to study.

As Howarth (2006) writes, social representations are not 'a quiet thing' without consequences in people's lives. The 'unreflective use' (Zittoun et al., 2003) of existing dominant social representations related to what immigrant students are like and what mathematical knowledge consists of in a school context gives rise to an attempt to assimilate the immigrant student into 'normality' that is often expressed in terms of reducing obstacles to learning by improving language competence and explaining learning difficulties as student deficits (special needs, cognitive problems, or lack of motivation).

Teachers' social representations play an important role in how immigrant students construct their learning experiences and in how they view themselves as learners. As in Ronnie's mathematics classroom, social representations condition students' opportunities for participation in mathematical activities in the classroom and the complexity of the activities in which they are asked to participate. In this way social representations influence not only what the students may learn in terms of content, or the quality of their mathematics education, but also the identities they develop as mathematics learners.

Inclusion, Social Representations and Teacher Education

In countries such as Ireland, Spain and Italy, the percentage of students born in other countries has increased threefold since the year 2000 (European Commission, 2008; de Heus & Dronkers, 2009). If access to education continues to be an important milestone of progress, concern for educational quality and completeness is also a priority. In the education of immigrant students we cannot disconnect the effort to ensure access to learning opportunities for all from the effort to ensure knowledge acquisition and the development of skills. Issues of access and quality in the education of immigrant children must be addressed together.

Miles and Singal (2010) point out that equal educational opportunity and quality education for all will require changes in the values, principles and ideas of educators. In particular, inclusive education requires a systemic shift in values, practices and forms of understanding. The values and representations we hold are reflected in the educational systems we construct, from national-level educational policy down to what happens in individual classrooms. "Inclusion" is not a "mechanism" that allows immigrant students to be placed in ordinary schools. According to Laluvein (2010), inclusive education requires schools to participate in the construction of meaning through processes of negotiation that involve students, teachers, and parents.

The mathematics classroom in particular has the potential for becoming a space of either inclusion or exclusion through the orchestration of mathematical participation. By mathematical participation, we mean the contributions students make to mathematical conversations that attempt to establish the meaning of a particular concept or procedure when discussing, or resolving a question or problem collectively (Gorgorió & Prat, 2009). The responsibility for orchestrating participation is essentially the teacher's. If we want to achieve an inclusive mathematics classroom, the contributions of all involved in the negotiation of social and mathematical meanings must be valued equally. It is not enough, however, to invite everyone to participate in the discussion; it is also necessary to provide students with real challenges, mathematically speaking; activities that go beyond the repetition of routine exercises.

Social representations are at the root not only of the establishment of the norms that regulate participation, but also of the management of participation by the teacher (Gorgorió & Planas, 2005). The teacher's daily work environment often presents problems that are ambiguous, and hard to identify and define. In situations in which the classroom dynamics require an immediate response, strategies that involve processing pedagogic or didactic knowledge are of little use in deciding, at any given moment, what information to use, what actions to take, and how to organise participation. In these situations of immediacy teachers tend to fall back on social representations.

We were drawn to the study of the social representations of mathematics teachers because of their implications for an inclusive model of education. Earlier studies by the EMiCS research group (Burgos, 2008; Burgos et al., 2009; Gorgorió & Abreu, 2009; Gorgorió & Prat, 2009; Gorgorió et al., 2006; Santesteban, 2006) identified the representations of secondary-school mathematics teachers, and also teachers and other adults working in transitional classrooms. Given the current social composition of primary-school classrooms, we believe it is also important to study primary-school teachers because, today, as a consequence of immigration policies that make family reunification possible, most of the immigrant students in Catalan public secondary schools have spent part of their school lives in Catalan primary schools.

Prior to starting secondary school, Ronnie had spent 5 years in a Catalan elementary school. Assuming that upon arrival someone had "verified" that he was working "below grade level," could the school not have taken steps to remedy this situation? Could someone have specified what "working below grade level" consisted of, assuming that this was in fact the problem? Could something have been done to bring his work up to "standard" by the time he reached secondary school?

Unfortunately, cases like Ronnie's are all too frequent among immigrant students, whatever their country of origin. Moreover, in Catalan schools there are more and more schoolchildren born in Catalonia to parents who immigrated from Ecuador and other countries. For these children, the argument that they do not work at grade level because they are from elsewhere makes no sense. Moreover, we would like to see such perceptions disappear from the dominant social representations of teachers.

The preparation of teachers for working with diverse school populations is a key issue facing teacher educators (Guo, Arthur & Lund, 2009). As researchers we have tried to make the results of our work available through publication and recommendations to those in charge of implementing educational policy concerning the training of secondary-school mathematics teachers. We are aware that, regrettably, our influence on secondary education cannot go far beyond making recommendations. As educators of primary-school teachers, however, we are both responsible for making a positive impact and are well positioned to do so. Pre-service teachers' own school experience, along with knowledge of the subject matter and pedagogical knowledge acquired in their teacher training, influence primary-school teachers' development of representations concerning processes of learning and teaching. It is our job to provide future primary-school teachers with tools for reflecting on their representations. For these reasons we embarked on a study of future primary-school teachers' social representations and possible strategies for making them consciously aware of them.

APPROACHING STUDENT TEACHERS' SOCIAL REPRESENTATIONS

Even before their first contact with university teacher education programs, the students who enroll in them already have their own representations of the curriculum and content they will one day teach. They also have images of what classroom interaction among students, the teacher, and particular subjects are like, as well as representations of processes of teaching and learning, of learners, and of institutional frameworks and expectations. These representations are the result of their own experiences in relation to education, but they are the experiences of learners, not of teachers.

Social representations are linked to specific social groups and positions, and related to past experience. The students enrolled in our School of Education have probably experienced similar learning trajectories and have had similar relationships to mathematical knowledge. The majority of them have probably had little contact with people from other socio-cultural contexts or individuals with different educational trajectories.

The persistence of certain dominant social representations may be an obstacle to change. As teacher training professionals, we would like our students to become agents of change, and it is this concern that leads us to attempt to identify their social representations in relation to processes of teaching and learning mathematics that involve pupils from other social and cultural backgrounds. We feel impelled to engage our students in this way because, as Moscovici (1984) points out, the less thought we give to these representations, the greater their influence.

The purpose of the research described here was to compare what student teachers say when asked about the teaching and learning of mathematics in general with what they say when asked about the teaching and learning mathematics in classrooms with immigrant students, in order to identify future teachers' representations of immigrant schoolchildren as mathematics students. The results were used to design strategies to help student teachers become aware of their representations of immigrant schoolchildren as mathematics learners. The aim of the larger project of which this study is a part is to determine whether our student teachers have reservations about their future responsibilities when teaching mathematics to culturally diverse students, whether they experience any tension between their personal values and their future task as teachers, and whether they feel anxious or intimidated by the prospect of teaching immigrant schoolchildren.

Study Design

This is an exploratory case study of an interpretive type. The data was collected from two groups of first-year students enrolled in the primary education teacher training program of the School of Education at the Universitat Autònoma de Barcelona during the academic year 2007-2008. We collected two kinds of data: responses to two questionnaires using open-ended questions; and the interactions during two discussion sessions with the same students after a series of lectures on different ways of doing mathematics developed in other parts of the world. These lectures formed part of their regular coursework and were delivered by a faculty member who was not part of the research team.

We chose first-year students for two reasons. First, in order to be able to frame their responses as social representations we needed to be sure that they were not linked to their training as teachers. Second, if the results of the study indicated the presence of representations likely to make the inclusion of immigrant schoolchildren difficult, then we would still have three more years of teacher training in which to work on addressing this.

We were looking for social representations of the teaching and learning of mathematics, school mathematical knowledge, and the nature of the social responsibility of teachers in relation to mathematics education. Following Araya (2002), we decided to use questionnaires with open-ended questions as opposed to classroom observation and/or interviews. The goal of the research was to compare what student teachers said about the teaching and learning of mathematics in general with what they said when the teaching of mathematics takes place in the multicultural classroom. The fact that we wanted to compare their responses to two separate but related issues led us to use two complementary questionnaires, administered on different days: one of a general nature, and the other specifically in reference to immigrant schoolchildren.

Once the research aims were established and the respondent population identified, the two questionnaires, A and B, were formulated and were validated in similar empirical contexts and also with the help of experts. The items used in both were structured in parallel form (see examples below). Each questionnaire begins with an introduction and a series of questions about the respondents' characteristics (age, sex, place of birth and prior educational and professional experience).

The questionnaire items refer to students' difficulties in learning mathematics (1A and 1B), changes needed in the way mathematics is taught (2A and 2B) and limitations in the teaching of mathematics (3A and 4B); diversity in the mathematics classroom (4A and 5B); the possible benefits or disadvantages of cooperative work (5A and 6B); textbook use (6A and 7B); equal opportunity (7A and 3B); personal memories of mathematics learning (8A) and a hypothetical classroom situation requiring a projective response (8B). We present below some of the items relevant to the results discussed in this chapter.

About students' difficulties in learning mathematics:

1A – It is often said that students have more difficulty with mathematics than with other subjects. If you agree with this statement, explain the most important reasons why you think this is the case. If you disagree, explain why.

1B – It is often said that immigrant schoolchildren find it harder to learn mathematics than native-born students. If you agree with this statement, explain the most important reasons why you think this is the case. If you disagree, explain why.

About changes needed in the way mathematics is taught:

2A – It may be necessary to change the way mathematics is taught in schools. What do you think these changes might be?

2B – It may be necessary to change the way mathematics is taught in multicultural classrooms. What do you think these changes might be?

About limitations in the teaching of mathematics:

3A – What is the source of the limitations on what is taught in mathematics classes?

4B – What is the source of the limitations on what is taught in multicultural mathematics classes?

About a hypothetical classroom situation:

> 8B – In a meeting with her son's teacher, the Latin American mother of a second-grade student explains how subtraction is done in their country of origin. She asks the teacher to let her son subtract in his own way, and the teacher replies, "He can do it however he wants, but the first time he gets a wrong answer, he'll have to start subtracting the way we do it here." Do you agree with the teacher's response? Explain why, or why not.

We decided to administer the questionnaires as close as possible to the beginning of the academic year in order to minimize distortion of the responses as a result of students' exposure to their university coursework. Because of the delay involved in obtaining the respondents' consent to participate in the study, questionnaire A was administered one month into the academic year, and questionnaire B two weeks later. This two-week time difference was necessary in order to minimize the risk of obtaining undifferentiated responses to the questions.

We administered questionnaires A and B to two groups of students, one enrolled in the morning session and one enrolled in the afternoon session. The total number of responses was 162. Since our intention was to compare responses, we analyzed only the responses of the 68 students who responded to both questionnaires, and as a result our data are drawn from the responses to 136 questionnaires.

Analysis

Analysis of the results began with the indexing, simplification and classification of the data in order to facilitate a process of interpretation that would allow us to draw conclusions (Flick, 2007). Thus, we first grouped and coded the questionnaires, assigning each a number.

The responses were then transcribed in order to be exported and analyzed using a software to assist qualitative data analysis, MAXqda. This software permits the importation and display of rich text, coding of text fragments, construction of code lists and hierarchies, recovery of coded texts, viewing of texts in the context of the original document, and writing of notes that can be linked to codes and documents. Relationships can be established between codes and represented in a variety of ways. MAXqda is possibly the simplest software of its type to use, and with the most user-friendly interface (Gibbs, 2007).

The first type of information we derived from coding of the data concerns the characteristics of the study population. Of the 68 students who responded to the questionnaire, 57 were women, 8 were men, and 3 did not identify themselves by sex. At least 7 out of every 10 were between the ages of 19 and 23, one in every 10 was between the ages of 24 and 28, and the rest were at least 29 years old. There were no non-Spanish citizens, and 9 out of every 10 were born in the province of Barcelona. Nearly half had no teaching experience, and of those who had teaching experience, in the majority of cases this was peer tutoring. Only 6 had worked in pre-school children day care centres.

From the transcribed questionnaire responses we developed a thematic analysis of the material (Flick, 2006) based on thematic coding and recurrent comparison in order to construct concepts and establish relationships between them. The software we used facilitates the processes of coding the data, generating themes, and comparing and identifying relationships among themes and concepts. Thus, we identified and reported emergent patterns and themes, selecting aspects of the responses that were relevant to the research questions (Braun & Clarke, 2006). The identification of themes is a constructive and flexible process, and can involve many steps, as identified or emerging themes can be grouped, systematically checked and reviewed in an iterative process of going backwards and forwards between data, research questions and theories.

Proceeding item by item, we analyzed the responses to our questions focusing on phrases that appeared to be related to our research aims, identifying them as units of meaning. In a process that is simultaneously inductive and deductive, we organized the units of meaning into referents. We observed that the students selectively constructed their answers using the information at their disposal, selecting and then using images to make sense of their interpretations. The term 'referents' was used to designate the images the students used in describing their understanding of the processes of teaching and learning mathematics and, in particular, those that involve immigrant students. As the analysis proceeded, new groupings and sub groupings emerged.

To ensure triangulation of the analysis the assignment of units of meaning to referents was reviewed three times and, when necessary, referents were reorganised. Integrating the units of meaning identified in the two questionnaires, involved another stage of reorganisation and creation of new referents. The final step in the process was the establishment of relations among the referents that emerged from pairing the items in the two questionnaires.

What the Student Teachers Say

Next, we report the most significant results from the analysis of the answers obtained in response to items 1A-1B, 2A-2B, 3A-4B and 8B, indicating the various referents that appear in them and emphasizing the differences observed in the responses to the two questionnaires. What we want to show is how words such as "immigrant" and "multicultural" as part of the question engage ideas that otherwise would not emerge in the responses.

Difficulties in Learning Mathematics

All the respondents agreed that mathematics is one of the most difficult subjects for schoolchildren to learn. They explained the difficulties in learning mathematics mostly as linked to individual characteristics, but also to issues related to the

213

teaching of mathematics and to the intrinsically demanding nature of mathematical knowledge.

When the question focused on the multicultural classroom, nearly half of the students stated that an immigrant schoolchild does not necessarily experience more difficulty in learning mathematics than a native-born classmate. Some respondents said that aptitude for learning mathematics is independent of schoolchildren's countries of origin. Others even suggested that in some cases immigrant schoolchildren may have better grounding in mathematics than their native-born classmates.

In the responses of those who agreed that immigrant schoolchildren have more trouble with mathematics, we located a referent – the pupil's sociocultural context – that does not appear when they speak about schoolchildren in general: "Feeling isolated, problems at home or problems of the family fitting into a different culture, cultural baggage, not knowing enough beforehand to be able to grasp new concepts." We find it significant that this referent only appears in response to the question, which explicitly refers to immigrant schoolchildren.

When learning difficulties are attributed to schoolchildren's personal characteristics as individuals, the responses diverge according to whether they refer to all children or to immigrant children. When speaking about schoolchildren in general, the respondents related learning difficulties to attitudinal and emotional issues such as tastes, preferences or fears, and to cognitive issues such as skills, abilities and previously acquired knowledge. However when the question is formulated in terms of difficulties experienced by immigrant schoolchildren, the respondents only frame their explanations in terms of lack of knowledge or ignorance of the language of instruction.

The answers that related difficulties in learning mathematics to concrete aspects of teaching, when referring to schoolchildren in general, state that problems might have to do with a style of teaching inappropriate for the pupil's needs, unexciting, de-contextualized, excessively mechanical or authoritarian. In contrast, they attribute immigrant schoolchildren's difficulties to having been exposed to different teaching methods, having had a deficient school experience, or a lack of resources in general.

Again, when respondents explained schoolchildren's learning difficulties in terms of the intrinsic nature of mathematical knowledge, the responses differ. For children in general, respondents associate learning difficulties with mathematical knowledge being abstract, complex, exact, cumulative and based on understanding. When the respondents talk about the difficulties immigrant children have with mathematical knowledge, they retain from their earlier responses only the arguments based on the idea of complexity, and a new idea appears, namely the universality of mathematical knowledge: "Precisely, mathematics is universal and can be understood everywhere because its language is based on numbers and symbols". This idea reinforces the notion that the problem lies in the educational deficits of immigrant schoolchildren.

Changes in the Way Mathematics Is Taught

When talking about teaching mathematics in general, all the responses mention possible changes. More than half the units of meaning we identified have to do with changes in classroom management – the majority related to teaching methods – while the rest make reference to concrete aspects of how the material is taught. We found only one unit of meaning that refers explicitly to the need for change in how teachers are trained.

When talking about teaching mathematics to immigrant students, the number of units of meaning that have to do with changes in classroom management rose up to two thirds, and more shades appeared in the responses. Nearly half of the units of meaning propose changes in teaching methods. Among them a considerable proportion point to the need for taking the language factor into consideration: "Maybe the problem is the language used, it would be easier for the immigrants if their native language was used." Ability grouping is also a frequent suggestion: "I'd group them according to ability; I know that sounds discriminatory, but I think it would be the best way since the whole class would be at the same level and they'd progress faster."

Although in a smaller proportion than when referring to changes needed in general, and with different distribution, the remaining units of meaning make reference to particular aspects of how the material is taught. Some of them explicitly say that the teaching of mathematics to immigrant children needs to be contextualized. Others propose various ways to adapt the teaching of mathematics to the pupil's ability level. It is noteworthy that this idea emerges only when we refer to the multicultural mathematics classroom in the question. Surprisingly, we identified four units of meaning that explicitly reject any need for change in the way mathematics is taught in multicultural classrooms "Personally, I don't think mathematics should be taught differently in multicultural classrooms. Being an immigrant doesn't mean not being able to learn in a different way."

Limitations in the Teaching of Mathematics

Once again, when we asked about the origin of limitations in the teaching of mathematics in general and in the case of multicultural classrooms, we observed differences. The number of units of meaning that in the first situation attribute limitations to the educational system – from policy and planning to their curricular outcomes – is significantly higher than in the responses when the question is framed in the multicultural classroom. Insufficient time as a limitation appears only in response to questions about the mathematics classroom in general.

The language of instruction, classroom diversity, classroom management, teacher preparation for a variety of classroom eventualities, teachers' knowledge of educational realities in other societies and in some cases their unwillingness to teach in a multicultural classroom appear only when the question has to do with multicultural classrooms. It is significant that we identified eight units of meaning in which the respondents said they were at a loss to know what caused these limitations since they were unfamiliar with multicultural classrooms.

The Use of Different Algorithms

Next, we would like to comment on the responses to the question referring to the Latin American pupil who learned to subtract their own way. Nearly 1 in every 10 units of meaning we identified was in agreement with the teacher, and the respondents based their answer on the need for the students to share common ways of doing mathematics.

However, the majority of units of meaning expressed disagreement with the teacher, in some cases only because of the tone of his response to the boy's mother. Those that went further in their arguments against the teacher's position fall into two groups: those addressing acceptance of different ways of performing mathematical operations, and those expressing ideas related to the notion of error.

The first group represents half of the total units of meaning identified for this question, and is divided into three subgroups. Firstly, there are those based solely on the need to accept other ways of doing mathematics: "I think we should be tolerant of different ways to solve math problems". Secondly, those that argue for acceptance of different ways of doing math provided the student understands the difference: "I think kids should be taught to subtract the way we do it here, and understand that there's more than one way to do it. But beyond this point, kids should have the right to do subtraction in whatever way is easiest for them." Finally, we find those that support acceptance of different ways of doing math as long as they are correct: "As long as they do it correctly, pupils should be allowed to do it the way that's easiest for them and they understand best."

Student Teachers' Social Representations of Immigrant Schoolchildren as Mathematics Learners

In what follows, we synthesize the results of our study, discussing how certain social representations emerge, are reinforced, or disappear when the question under consideration is situated in the context of the multicultural classroom.

As in previous studies (Burgos, 2008; Burgos et al., 2009; Gorgorió & Abreu, 2009; Santesteban, 2006), we observed an interpretation of the learning process from a psychological perspective focused on the individual, with less attention to the fact that learning is a social and cultural process. This is evident in student teachers' identification of the most significant sources of learning difficulty for schoolchildren in general as individual and cognitive. It also underlies responses that frame the reduction of obstacles to mathematics learning by immigrant students in terms of improving their language competence, or adapting content to their ability level. Moreover, the socio-cultural context appeared only in discussion of immigrant schoolchildren, as if it did not significantly influence any learning process regardless of the pupils' place of birth or prior school experience. Student teachers refer to the richness of diversity, but at the same time point to the need to have all pupils in a given classroom working at the same level. These arguments are consistent with responses justifying the need to adapt mathematical content to the child's ability level as a way of ensuring equal opportunity for all pupils.

Interestingly, we noted two clearly opposed positions with respect to the question of whether immigrant schoolchildren experience more difficulty than their native-born counterparts in learning mathematics. The representations supporting these positions, however, are the same in both cases. The respondents who said that both groups of schoolchildren experience the same difficulties supported their argument by drawing on the social representation of mathematics as a universal form of knowledge. Some of them, however, added that any difficulties were attributable to the language of instruction. By contrast, the respondents who said that immigrant schoolchildren had more difficulty learning mathematics justified their opinion by linking this difficulty either to the pupil's inability to work at grade level, or to ignorance of the language of instruction. These arguments, again, rest on the representation that school mathematics knowledge is universal. As in the abovementioned studies, we found that the representation of school mathematical knowledge as universal is associated with the representation that once the immigrant schoolchild has learned Catalan, there are no further obstacles to learning mathematics.

Although the most frequent representation is the idea that school mathematical knowledge is universal, it is less dominant among student teachers than among secondary-school teachers and those in charge of transitional classrooms who participated in our previous studies. We believe this difference is attributable to the fact that our student teachers have not yet been socialized into the community of mathematics teachers. In addition to the internalization of norms and practices, the socialization of teachers also involves learning to identify with the social representations shared by the professional community.

Despite this, among student teachers the representation of mathematical knowledge as universal is clearly acquired prior to their professional experience, and is linked to the fact that they do not distinguish between mathematical knowledge in general and school mathematical knowledge. The coercive nature of this representation makes it difficult for student teachers to question it, despite evidence to the contrary, and locate alternative meanings. Thus, we observed that the students only refer to the universality of school mathematical knowledge in the context of the multicultural classroom. It is precisely in situations in which this universality may be called into question that they invoke it, not just once but repeatedly.

It seems clear that if we do not challenge our students to pay attention to their social representations and their possible implications, these representations may become fossilized, justifying inequitable pedagogical practices.

DISCUSSION: WAYS FORWARD

To conclude this chapter we present some general considerations that emerged from our research and propose strategies intended to lay the groundwork for a new way of teaching mathematics that is both respectful of diversity and ensures a quality education for all.

We observed a repeating pattern in our students' responses. The idea of "us" vs. "others" emerged in a variety of ways, suggesting that both problems and solutions in the teaching of mathematics have to do with those "others". These understandings promote rather than disrupt practices that sustain socially widespread perceptions of immigrants.

Although the responses to the questionnaires were more coherent in some cases than in others, the ideas expressed by the student teachers as a group reflect a confused and sometimes contradictory image of the possibilities and limitations involved in teaching and learning mathematics in multicultural classrooms. What they told us corresponds clearly to ideas that originate neither in their training at the School of Education, which they have only just begun, nor in their own experience in multicultural classrooms, whether as students themselves or in some cases as teachers. In addition, only a very small minority said that they lacked information about what we were asking. It seems clear, then, that the responses we collected belong in the domain of representations.

As we argued at the end of the first section of this chapter, when faced with the complexity of the multicultural classroom, when classroom dynamics demand a particular immediate action, reaction, or response, teachers fall back on representations. From our standpoint, whether or not the student teachers' representations correspond to statistically verifiable facts is less important than the potential influence of incomplete images that are the outcome neither of reflection on teaching practice nor of an explicit process of knowledge construction. Without a conscious process of reflection on their own social representations, teachers may, however unintentionally, help to create situations in which immigrant pupils are not afforded the same opportunities to participate in classroom activities as their native-born counterparts.

Although we may use representations unconsciously, the fact that we can reflect on the possible implications of our actions opens up possibilities for change. Unless those of us responsible for training future generations of teachers actively promote reflection on dominant representations, their non-reflexive use will continue to create obstacles to providing a quality mathematics education for all schoolchildren. We must challenge our student teachers to examine their own representations, helping them to develop a critical awareness of the pedagogical implications they may have and to construct alternative representations that make an inclusive quality education possible.

We propose the development of training activities in which student teachers are confronted with situations that have a variety of possible outcomes. One good training strategy is the study of teaching cases (Llinares & Krainer, 2006), in which students must analyze real and complex classroom situations, reflect on critical incidents, and search for information to resolve them. The use of critical incidents may help student teachers to examine learning processes linked to transitions between contexts with which they are unfamiliar.

Teacher training programs must go beyond informing students about the cultural backgrounds of immigrant students and must help student teachers to examine critically the cultural and social backgrounds that have influenced their own representations and practices. The study of critical incidents may help student teachers to explore and reflect on their own identities, representations, and the privileges that accompany them, and to value diversity as a source of potential. The complex intersection of the pupils' and the teacher's cultural, linguistic, ethnic, gender and class identities, and the ways in which the teacher's identities affect the decisions he or she makes in the classroom, should also be discussed.

Mathematics teachers have roles and responsibilities as agents in the integration of immigrant children. As educators of future teachers, we need to communicate to our students that institutionalization of racism is a risk for any educational system, when representations support and justify structures, practices and attitudes favouring dominant social groups over members of minority groups. It is our responsibility to help pre-service teachers learn to question and challenge school curricula, materials, activities or discussions that may perpetuate social inequity, and to instil in them a commitment to educational equality, inclusion, and quality. Teacher education programs must prepare future teachers for the task of translating concepts into practical and inclusive approaches to teaching that respect diversity. For these reasons, it is also our responsibility to engage in reflexive practices concerning our own cultural identity.

REFERENCES

Abreu, G. de, & Elbers, E. (2005). Introduction: The social mediation of learning in multiethnic classrooms. *European Journal of Psychology of Education, XX*(1), 3-11.

Abric, J.C. (1994). *Pratiques sociales et réprésentations* (Social practices and representations). Paris: PUF.

Araya, S. (2002). *Las representaciones sociales: Ejes teóricos para su discusión* (Social representations: Theoretical axes for its discussion). Colección Cuadernos de Ciencias Sociales. Costa Rica: FLACSO.

Braun, V., & Clarke, V. (2006). Using thematic analysis in psychology. *Qualitative Research in Psychology, 3*, 77-101.

Burgos, S. (2007). *Matemáticas y aula de acogida: Aproximaciones a las representaciones sociales subyacentes* (Mathematics and reception classes: Approaching its social representations). Doctorado en Didáctica de las Ciencias y de las Matemática. Barcelona: UAB, Master Thesis.

Burgos, S., Gorgorió, N., Prat, M., & Santesteban, M. (2009). De què parlen els professors de matemàtiques quan els preguntem pels alumnes immigrats? (What do mathematics teachers say when we ask them about immigrant children). *Collecció "ciutadania i immigració", 2*, 85-101. Barcelona: Secretaria per a la Immigració.

European Commission (2008): *Migration & mobility: Challenges and opportunities for EU education systems.* Green Paper. Brussels, 3.7.2008. COM(2008) 423 final. Retrieved from http://eur-lex.europa.eu/LexUriServ/LexUriServ.do?uri= COM:2008:0423:FIN:EN:PDF.

de Heus, M., & Dronkers, J. (2009). Immigrants' children scientific performance in a double comparative design: The influence of origin, destination, and community. *Mobility and inequality: Intergenerational and life course perspectives,* Meeting of the ISA RC 28. Yale University, New Haven, Connecticut, August 3-6, 2009.

Flick, U. (2006). *An introduction to qualitative research*. London: SAGE Publications.

Flick, U. (2007). *Designing qualitative research*. London: Sage Publications.

Gibbs, G.R. (2007). *Analyzing qualitative data*. London: Sage Publications.

Gorgorió, N. (2009). Multicultural mathematics classrooms: When the difference challenges well established ideas. In F. Spagnolo, & B. Di Paola (Eds.), *Changes in society: A challenge for mathematics education. Proceedings of CIEAEM 58* (pp. 168-182). Palermo: GRIM.

Gorgorió, N., & Abreu, G. de (2009). Social representations as mediators of practice in mathematics classrooms with immigrant students. *Educational Studies in Mathematics, 72*(1), 61-76.

Gorgorió, N., & Planas, N. (2005). Cultural distance and identities-in-construction within the multicultural mathematics classroom. *Zentralblatt für Didaktik Der Mathematik, 37*(2), 64-71.

Gorgorió, N., Planas, N., & Vilella, X. (2002). Immigrant children learning mathematics in mainstream schools. In G. de Abreu, A. Bishop & N. Presmeg (Eds.), *Transitions between contexts for mathematics learning* (pp. 23-52). Dordrecht, the Netherlands: Kluwer.

Gorgorió, N., & Prat, M. (2009). Jeopardizing learning opportunities in multicultural mathematics classrooms. In M. César, & K. Kumpulainen (Eds.), *Social interactions in multicultural setting* (pp. 145-170). Rotterdam: Sense Publishers.

Gorgorió, N., Prat, M., & Santesteban, M. (2006). El aula de matemáticas multicultural: Distancia cultural, normas y negociación (The multicultural mathematics classroom: Cultural distance, norms and negotiation). In J.M. Goñi (Ed.), *Matemáticas e interculturalidad* (pp. 7-24). Barcelona: Graó.

Guo, Y., Arthur, N., & Lund, D. (2009). Intercultural inquiry with pre-service teachers. *Intercultural Education, 20*(6), 565-577.

Howarth, C. (2006). A social representation is not a quiet thing: Exploring the critical potential of social representations. *British Journal of Social Psychology, 245*, 65-86.

Ibáñez, T. (Ed.). (1988). *Ideologías de la vida cotidiana* (Ideologies of everyday life). Barcelona: Sendai.

Laluvein, J. (2010). School inclusion and the «community of practice. *International Journal of Inclusive Education, 14*(1), 35-48.

Llinares, S., & Krainer, K. (2006). Mathematics (student) teachers and teacher educators as learners. *Handbook of research on the psychology of mathematics education: Past, present and future* (pp. 429-459). Rotterdam: Sense Publishers.

Miles, S., & Singal, N. (2010). The education for all and inclusive education debate: Conflict, contradiction or opportunity? *International Journal of Inclusive Education, 14*(1), 1-15.

Moscovici, S. (1984). *The phenomenon of social representations. Social representations*. Cambridge: Cambridge University Press.

Mulat, T., & Arcavi, A. (2009). Success in mathematics within a challenged minority: The case of students of Ethiopian origin in Israel (SEO). *Educational Studies in Mathematics, 72*, 77-92.

Santesteban, M. (2006). *Representaciones sociales del profesor de matemáticas acerca de los alumnos inmigrantes: Un primer anàlisis* (Mathematics teachers' social representations about immigrant students: a first análisis). Doctorado en Didáctica de las Ciencias y de las Matemática. Barcelona: UAB, Master Thesis.

Tangen, R. (2009). Conceptualising quality of school life from pupils' perspectives: A four-dimensional model. *International Journal of Inclusive Education, 13*(8), 829-844.

Zevenbergen, R. (2008). *Tensions, contentions and connections in learning mathematics for students from significantly diverse backgrounds*. Rome: Paper presented at the Symposium on the Occasion of the 100th Anniversary of ICMI, Working group 3, Mathematics Education and Society.

Zittoun, T. (2006). *Transitions. development through symbolic resources* (Series on Advances in cultural psychology: Constructing development). Greenwich (CT): InfoAge.

Zittoun, T. (2007). Symbolic resources and responsibility in transitions. *Young, 15*(2), 193-211.

Zittoun, T., Duveen, G., Ilespie, A., Ivinson, G., & Psaltis, C. (2003). The use of symbolic resources in developmental transitions. *Culture & Psychology, 9*(4), 415-448.

Marcela Costanzi
Facultat de Psicologia, Ciències de l'Educació i l'Esport
Universitat Ramon Llull

Núria Gorgorió
Facultat de Ciències de l'Educació
Universitat Autònoma de Barcelona

Montserrat Prat
Facultat de Ciències de l'Educació
Universitat Autònoma de Barcelona

GEERDINA VAN DER AALSVOORT AND EVA HJÖRNE

15. LEARNING, SOCIAL INTERACTION AND DIVERSITY – FUTURE CHALLENGES

The book presents results of empirical research from classroom and settings related to learning, diversity and identity. It includes findings from regular classrooms and from special classes organised for children and young people described as having socio-emotional problems, learning disabilities or having reading and writing difficulties. It also includes research in classrooms outside of mainstream provision, such as minority ethnic groups language and culture schools.

Thus, the content of the book allowed an opportunity to read on narratives about diversity and social interactions in multicultural settings, and to discuss the role they play in the construction of school achievement from a sociocultural perspective. It is a book on multiculturality as well as a multicultural book that includes chapters from authors representing 11 countries, and many more cultures. The journey of reading through the contributions brings different settings, situations and scenarios to the fore. The vivid descriptions allow readers to enjoy an authentic taste of them. Diverse approaches to investigate classroom practice are presented and discussed. Main themes are encompassing different timescales and emphasis on learning as a process that develops over time. Two elements are found in each chapter. The first one is an explicit conception of the meaning of interaction for learning and instruction. The second one is that all the authors address polysemy of language: They try to meet the issue that meaning is context-related and that this requires specific solutions for analysis at the same time wishing to keep meaning as a whole. Finally, the contributions require that classroom interaction is approached from a transdisciplinary perspective.

In this book we stress the importance of social interaction in learning and instruction in all types of classrooms. We take into consideration practices in regular classrooms, multicultural classrooms and practices in special classrooms organised for children who require special educational opportunities to elicit learning, for example for children described as having socio-emotional problems, reading and writing difficulties, learning disabilities et cetera, and issues of diversity. All of those contribute to the development of socio-cultural theory in aspects that are crucial to develop the potential to learn. For instance, the studies shed light on what is a "resource" for the learner, and what are the "resources" for key social actors, such as parents, to make sense of their child's learning in school.

E. Hjörne et al. (eds.), Learning, Social Interaction and Diversity – Exploring Identities in School Practices, 223–229.

The authors elaborate on cultural diversity, but not only. In addition, we also present analysis of gender in relation to learning and instruction in regular classes and classes for students with special educational needs.

Thus, with this book we address readers to broaden empirical, theoretical and methodological perspectives on how to understand learning and diversity and the role of social interaction in diverse school settings. The empirical perspective of the contributions is broad as it includes studies on social interactions, that are contextualised in the wider socio-cultural context. For instance, it includes studies on the relationship between home and school, and on the relationship between being a student in a mainstream school and being a student in one's home minority community school. The theoretical perspective is also expanded in comparison to the former EARLI books about social interaction in learning and instruction. Both practices in regular classrooms, practices in special classrooms as well as issues of diversity contributing to the development of socio-cultural theory in aspects that are crucial to develop learning potential are included. Many facets of diversity are reported to allow insights into aspects of schooling practices that promote or hinder inclusion.

The following paragraphs intend to discuss distinctive aspects of the studies to allow researchers to become inspired once more and challenge themselves to improve future studies.

METHODOLOGICAL CONSIDERATIONS

The meaning of discourse for the construction of knowledge was the main theme in the first EARLI book on contributions about studies on social interactions on learning and instruction. In this book one chapter is devoted to methodological approaches. Van der Aalsvoort and Harinck (2000) describe the empirical tradition, the ethno-methodological paradigm, the linguistic approach and a multi method pluralism approach as four major paradigms to study the complicated process of social interaction in learning and instruction. Moreover, they recognize the methods to allow theoretical progress of the contributors on the theme, systematic observation including sequential analysis, rating scales, ethnographic approach and discourse analysis in the contributions of the book, but stress a multi method approach as the most appropriate one for studying the process of knowledge construction.

The two volumes of investigating classroom interaction by Kumpulainen, Hmelo-Silver and César (2009) and César and Kumpulainen (2009) allow another view on the progress of interpreting classroom reality. Mercer, Littleton and Wegerif (2009) add to increasing knowledge about methods to study the process of interaction by pointing at improved computer software facilities to address the problems of analyzing on-going interactions. Grossen (2009) describes methodological challenges when she discusses the contributions to the book. She mentions that the main choice of the authors is a mix of methods, which encounters problems, such as adding a quantitative to a qualitative approach is not sufficient in itself. The dynamics of interaction over time to reveal emergent collaboration for instance or the connection between collective and individual activities require a theoretical understanding, a 'certain conception of language' as Grossen states (2009, p. 270). At this point the value of Césars and Kumpulainens (2009) volume on studies with regard to multicultural settings comes forward. Especially Perret-Clermont (2009) stresses that language is a major mediation tool for learning and therefore requires that a main role in the methodology is contributed to the way language and its value for learning is analyzed.

The messages of the former editors of volumes about social interaction in instruction and learning were added to discuss the contributions for this volume. In that sense we hope to supplement to the ongoing debate of EARLI researchers who have enriched our understanding of processes of instruction and learning through thorough investigations and reflections upon theoretical issues related to social interaction in multicultural educational settings.

A first remark concerning methodology in this volume is that it makes a difference whether the authors use sociocultural theory as a means to frame their study, or as a way to focus upon the meaning of interaction for instruction and learning through excerpts of transcripts that were part of the dataset. Wen and Irvinson chose for the first option whereas the main number of authors of the book present a sociocultural theoretical framework of the meaning of interaction in classrooms followed by presenting excerpts of interactions that are part of the dataset. The examples are used to interpret the excerpts in line with the theory. Examples of this procedure are the following. Zittoun and Grossen describe the theme of boundary crossing events and use the transcripts of three different types of lessons in high school to show the types of boundary crossing events they detected. Wuttke describes types of questions during classroom talk between teacher and students in high schools, and presents her findings after analyzing the transcripts of the observations to reveal which types of questions were posed by the teachers. Crafter enlightens the way homework needs to be understood as a cultural phenomenon by offering excerpts of interviews with parents about their child's attitude towards homework. She thus underlines how cultural models are the base of parents' conceptions about their role towards their child's homework. Kumpulainen, Toom and Saalasti frame their study on teacher identity formation as sociocultural practices and present the results on teacher identity by asking student teachers to reflect upon their practice in short essays before and after a mathematic course. The excerpts they offer illustrate the most dominant themes that came forward in these essays. Costanzi, Gorgorgió and Prat used lists of statements about immigrant students as mathematics learners to reveal how students who are taught to become teachers have social representations of the students in their classes. Hjörne and Larsson explain the strategies of corrections as a means to 'socialize' children from a historical perspective on special education. They illustrate this point of view by using excerpts of transcripts that reveal how corrections enhance institutionalizing children with behavioural problems. Evaldsson and Karlsson demonstrate how a more permanent (and deviant) identity as 'boys with behavioural, social and emotional difficulties' is talked into being during a remedial activity organized in a special educational needs unit.

Although the main approach to understand social interaction in classrooms seems to be a sociocultural perspective alternative theoretical frameworks are possible. A dynamic systems approach also elicits interest in teaching and learning processes. Ensing, Van der Aalsvoort and Van Geert present their findings from this point of view and describe a predictive model that is used to reveal patterns in social interaction during teaching and learning. From yet another theoretical perspective Prokopiou, Cline and de Abreu show that dialogical self theory allows understanding of social interaction with regard to community schooling by analyzing episodic interviews.

In line with the former discussion about methodologies with regard to social interaction studies we maintain that the topic of generalizability is still poorly documented in the contributions of this volume. It could be said that the data are theoretically well framed as the interpretation of the data is closely connected to the dataset at hand. Questions about generalizability, however, are not posed or discussed. This leaves it to the reader of the chapter whether he feels inspired to use the suggested system of categories, to try out the way of processing the data, or to grasp classroom reality on the merits that he takes from the study, just to name some of the opportunities after reading the contributions. We are not sure that this procedure improves the theoretical framework of the meaning of social interactions in classroom settings. What it does is that the presented studies offer a Zeitgeist of the type of research that was carried out. We stress, however, that framing a theoretical perspective requires an explicit discussion of methodology for future purposes in order to improve the value of the studies that are carried out. Discussing the methodology when the findings of a study are described is even more urgent when we try to grasp the meaning of the results for teacher education. We would prefer to add to understanding classroom reality from a researcher perspective instead of increasing the gap between learning to become an excellent teacher and understanding classroom reality from an outside perspective. The next paragraphs describe themes that may be helpful to reflect upon ways to embrace research findings about classroom practice for teacher-practitioners who apply research to enhance teacher quality.

MOVING THROUGH CULTURES BY ALLOWING DIALOGICAL SELVES

Hermans and Dimaggio (2007, p. 37) state that individuals and groups are 'increasingly living on the interfaces of cultures'. The contributions of this volume are examples of how teachers address this interconnectness in everyday classroom reality. They are coping with issues of choice of artefacts, in the way they decide about subject content et cetera. Interconnectedness is not an issue solely related to teacher orientation or instruction and feedback issues, it concerns students too. The interface of cultures is shared both between teacher and student as well as within them. A so-called multiplicity of cultural positions or voices is represented in the self of each teacher and each student, the so-called dialogical self, the self "that is always simultaneously participating in different discourse communities" (Gerge, 1994 in Akkerman & Meijer, 2011, p. 309). We discuss the value of the concept of the dialogical self by presenting the main issues of this dialogical approach to teacher identity based upon Akkerman and Meijer's (2011) excellent elaboration of the theory of the dialogical self and illustrating this by examples that can be found in this volume. First of all the self is composed of multiple I-positions. An I-position can be considered as a 'voiced' position with a specific viewpoint and story, and driven by its own intentions. The various positions can conflict, such as misunderstanding, question, agree et cetera. In that sense identity is both unitary and multiple, the self is a negotiated space. The chapter of Prokopiou, Cline and de Abreu is an example of this characteristic when they show how students can talk about their position in school as being: An I as ethnic minority student in their Pakistani or Greek community school; an I as an ethnic minority student in the mainstream school, and an I as being of a Pakistani/Greek background in the United Kingdom.

Thus, identity changes according to the type of situation one finds itself in. This implies that the child will be given a specific identity in for example the school context as a 'special' pupil. Children will be treated by the people they meet (the staff, classmates and others) on the basis of the identity ascribed to them. Thus, from this perspective identity should not be understood as the passive adoption of a particular personal character. Rather, identities are shaped by people in interactional settings, and people actively contribute to establishing and maintaining a certain identity for themselves and for others (Antaki & Widdicombe, 1998).

The chapter of Costanzi, Gorgorió and Montserrat illustrates how student teachers express an unwillingness to teach in a multicultural classroom whilst being prepared to become teachers in classroom settings that will most certainly contain several ethnic groups. The consequence of this attitude with regard to teacher identity is discussed by Costanzi et al. when they suggest that teacher training programs should go beyond informing students about the cultural backgrounds of the pupils in their classes, and assist the students to examine the cultural and social backgrounds that have influenced their own representations and practices. The dialogical self is also both social and individual: "The dialogical self is social in the sense that other people occupy positions in a multi-voiced self" (Hermans & Hermans-Jansen, 2001, in Akkerman & Meijers, 2011). Teaching college communities can inform and play an important role in the development of I. This is illustrated by Kumpulainen, Toom and Saalasti's contribution about the way student ultural diversity, by acting this diversity in each and every interaction with students, in their teachers adopted a collective attitude towards their meaning-making and collective problem-solving in teaching and learning mathematics.

Accepting teacher identity as a dialogical self has consequences for studying teacher identity and teacher development. The main message to elaborate on the topic in the discussion of this volume is exactly the same. We wish to draw attention to social interaction research in special needs settings as well as multicultural settings by pointing at a fruitful way to frame to results of the investigations in this volume on a higher level of awareness of the many voices that speak up in the examples in each chapter both from a theoretical perspective as well as for the consequences of grasping the voices from a methodological point of view. Boundary crossing, as presented by the contribution of Grossen, Zittoun and Ros may be a nice example of a way forward to understand the dialogical self through tensions in the dynamics of teaching and learning. A thorough meta-analysis on the subject of boundary crossing has recently been published by Akkerman and Bakker (2011).

MESSAGE TO TEACHERS

So what does the volume mean for teacher education? Desimone suggests that "we do not have sufficient evidence to indicate which features of professional development are effective for eliciting improvements in student learning" (Desimone, 2009, p. 183). The core conceptual framework that she describes based upon elaborate literature analysis contains four elements. The first element represents the core features of professional development, content focus, active learning, coherence, duration and collective participation, which should enhance the second element which includes teacher knowledge and skill, change in attitudes and beliefs, leading to the third element, change in instruction, which supposedly leads to improved student learning as the fourth element. Her model allows interconnectedness of the elements. Although the model seems one step back in relationship to the claims of the dialogical self Desimone points at the opportunities to use research findings with regard to teachers' professional development. The contributions in this volume allow several ways to enrich teacher education with regard to professional development that can be derived directly from several of the chapters such as Wuttkes description of students' participation in classroom talk, or Bagga-Gupta's explanation of the roles of visual manual signs in bilingualism. A final issue that we wish to focus upon in this paragraph is the meaning of the contributions: "What teachers actually do is most relevant to student learning" (Kennedy's, 2010, p. 591). She suggests that teacher accountability is overestimated. The volume contains many rich and thick descriptions of classroom reality. Through in-dept analysis of classroom interactions we can bring to the fore that the romantic idea of teachers who can meet every challenge in the classroom is a harsh contrast to the actual complexity of classroom reality, but nevertheless a future challenge for the next generation of teachers.

The implications of successful schooling of children and young people with a multicultural background and children categorized as having learning disabilities are profound for their well-being and future career in school and in life.

REFERENCES

Akkerman, S. F., & Meijer, P. M. (2011). A dialogical approach to conceptualizing teacher identity. *Teaching and Teacher Education, 27*, 308-319.
Antaki, C. & Widdicombe, S. (1998). *Identities in talk*. London: Sage.
César, M., & Kumpulainen, K. (Eds.) (2009). *Social interactions in multicultural settings*. Rotterdam: Sense.

Cowie, H., & van der Aalsvoort, G. (Eds.) (2000). *Social interaction in learning and instruction.* Amsterdam: Pergamon Press.

Desimone, L.M. (2009). Improving impact studies of teachers' professional development: Toward better conceptualizations and measures. *Educational Researcher, 38*(3), 181-199.

Grossen, M. (2009). Commentary. In K. Kumpulainen, C. Hmelo-Silver, & M. César (Eds.), *Investigating classroom interaction* (pp. 263-277). Rotterdam: Sense.

Hermans, H.J.M., & Dimaggio, G. (2007). Self, identity, and globalization in times of uncertainty: A dialogical analysis. *Review of General Psychology, 11*(10), 31-61.

Kennedy, M.M. (2010). Attribution error and the quest for teacher quality. *Educational Researcher, 39*(8), 591-598.

Kumpulainen, K., Hmelo-Silver, C., & César, M. (Eds.) (2009). *Investigating classroom interaction.* Rotterdam: Sense.

Mercer, N., Littleton, K., & Wegerif, R. (2009). Methods for studying the processes of interaction and collaborative activity in computer-based educational activities. In K. Kumpulainen, C. Hmelo-Silver, & M. César (Eds.), *Investigating classroom interaction* (pp 27-43). Rotterdam: Sense.

Perret-Clermont, A-N. (2009). Introduction. In M. César, & K. Kumpulainen (Eds.), *Social interactions in multicultural settings* (pp. 1-12). Rotterdam: Sense.

Van der Aalsvoort, G., & Harinck, F.J.H. (2000). Studying social interaction in instruction and learning: Methodological approaches and problems. In H. Cowie, & G. van der Aalsvoort (Eds.), *Social interaction in learning and instruction* (pp. 5-20). Amsterdam: Pergamon Press.

Geerdina van der Aalsvoort
School of Education
Saxion University of Applied Science Deventer

Eva Hjörne
Department of Education and Special Education
University of Gothenburg

Lightning Source UK Ltd.
Milton Keynes UK
UKOW030751150612

194479UK00002B/2/P

9 789460 918018